From Text t

From Text to Performance

Narrative and Performance
Criticisms in Dialogue
and Debate

Edited by
Kelly R. Iverson

Ⓛ

The Lutterworth Press

The Lutterworth Press
P.O. Box 60
Cambridge
CB1 2NT
United Kingdom

www.lutterworth.com
publishing@lutterworth.com

ISBN: 978 0 7188 9398 9

British Library Cataloguing in Publication Data
A record is available from the British Library

First published by The Lutterworth Press, 2015

Copyright © Wipf and Stock Publishers, 2014

Published by arrangement
with Cascade Books

To my Mom,

The strongest and hardest working person
I have ever known . . .

Whose love and sacrifice have made it possible
for me to perform at my best.

CONTENTS

Preface · *ix*
Abbreviations · *xi*
Contributors · *xiii*

1   Performance Criticism: A Paradigm Shift in
    New Testament Studies · 1
        David Rhoads and Joanna Dewey

2   Those Sitting around Jesus: Situating the Storyteller
    within Mark's Gospel · 27
        Philip Ruge-Jones

3   Characters in Text and Performance:
    The Gospel of John · 53
        Holly E. Hearon

4   Audience Asides and the Audiences of Mark:
    The Difference Performance Makes · 80
        Thomas E. Boomershine

5   Sound and Structure in the Gospel of Matthew · 97
        Margaret E. Lee

6   The Present Tense of Performance: Immediacy
    and Transformative Power in Luke's Passion · 131
        Kelly R. Iverson

7   From Performance to Text to Performance:
    The New Testament's Use of the Hebrew Bible
    in a Rhetorical Culture   ·   158
        Kathy Maxwell

8   "This Is My . . . ": Toward a Thick Performance of
    the Gospel of Mark   ·   182
        Richard W. Swanson

    Bibliography   ·   211
    Author Index   ·   221

PREFACE

IN THE WORLD OF BIBLICAL STUDIES, PERFORMANCE CRITI-
cism is a proverbial new kid on the block. This is not to suggest that performance criticism developed *ex nihilo*. Performance criticism is indebted to
various hermeneutical trajectories spawned over the last two hundred years.
But performance criticism is an emerging discipline in that it attempts to
account for the dynamics of the biblical texts within an oral/aural environment.[1] Since the inception of critical scholarship, biblical interpretation has
been governed by literary methodologies that have largely ignored and/or
neglected the oral milieu in which the biblical texts arose, and it is only recently that scholars have begun to explore the media context that shaped the
composition, transmission, performance, and reception of the biblical texts.
Although performance critics are concerned to understand how the biblical texts were received in an environment where illiteracy was high and
orality the norm, such an endeavor is neither clear-cut nor simple. Prob-
ing beyond the literary artifacts is a daunting task, particularly when the
codified texts are all that remain. Yet, despite the challenges, performance
critics are concerned to situate the biblical texts within their ancient context. To neglect the social and communicative media is to ignore a crucial
component of the interpretive process. If "the medium is the message,"[2]
then appreciating the impact of orality deserves more focused attention
in biblical studies.

Like all new endeavors and methodologies, the task facing performance critics is not only to articulate *what* is performance criticism, but
why it makes an interpretive difference. This collection of essays, by leading
scholars in the field of performance criticism, seeks to advance the conversation while addressing both questions. More specifically, the volume engages

1. On performance criticism as an emerging discipline, see Rhoads, "Performance
Criticism: An Emerging Methodology in Second Temple Studies—Part I," 118–33;
Rhoads, "Performance Criticism: An Emerging Methodology in Second Temple
Studies—Part II," 164–84.

2. This famous aphorism was coined by McLuhan (*Understanding Media*).

in dialogue with narrative criticism—one of the main literary approaches employed by biblical scholars over the last thirty years. The engagement is not to intended to diminish or express a lack of appreciation for the various narrative-critical studies that have provided insight into ancient storytelling practices (indeed many performance critics began their work as narrative critics!). Rather by exploring selected features of biblical narratives, both at the theoretical and exegetical levels, it is hoped that a more discernible picture will begin to emerge as to how performance criticism illuminates the biblical texts. Collectively, these essays reflect upon the hermeneutical shift taking place in the field of biblical studies and provide detailed examples from the Gospels in order to demonstrate how performance critics are attempting to navigate these uncharted waters.

Of course, a volume of this nature could never have been completed without a host of contributors, whose expertise and insight were matched only by their commitment to the project. Their enthusiasm throughout the process was a constant encouragement, and their perseverance along the way ensured the timely publication of the volume. As well, special thanks goes to Mike Whitenton and Jeremiah Bailey, doctoral students at Baylor University, who graciously assisted in the copyediting of the volume. Collectively, their careful review was of invaluable assistance during the final stages of the project. To these, and certainly many more along the way, I owe a debt of gratitude.

—Kelly R. Iverson

ABBREVIATIONS

AB	Anchor Bible
ABR	*Australian Biblical Review*
ABRL	Anchor Bible Reference Library
BDAG	W. Bauer, F. W. Danker, W. F. Arndt, and F. W. Gingrich, *Greek-English Lexicon of the New Testament and Other Early Christian Literature*. 3rd ed. Chicago, 1999
BETL	Bibliotheca Ephemeridum theologicarum Lovaniensium
Bib	*Biblica*
BPCS	Biblical Performance Criticism Series
BTB	*Biblical Theology Bulletin*
BZNW	Beihefte zur Zeitschrift für die neutestamentliche Wissenschaft
CBC	Cambridge Bible Commentary
CBQ	*Catholic Biblical Quarterly*
GBS	Guides to Biblical Scholarship
HTR	*Harvard Theological Review*
ICC	International Critical Commentary
Inst.	*Institutes of Oratory* (Quintilian). Translated by Donald A. Russell. 5 vols. LCL. Cambridge: Harvard University Press, 2002
Int	*Interpretation*
JBL	*Journal of Biblical Literature*
JSNTSup	Journal for the Study of the New Testament: Supplement Series
J.W.	*Jewish Wars* (Josephus)
LCL	Loeb Classical Library
Life	*The Life* (Josephus)
LNTS	Library of New Testament Studies
NICNT	New International Commentary on the New Testament
NTS	*New Testament Studies*
SBLDS	Society of Biblical Literature Dissertation Series
SBLRBS	Society of Biblical Literature Resources for Biblical Study
SBLSP	Society of Biblical Literature Seminar Papers

SemSt	Semeia Studies
SNTSMS	Society for New Testament Studies Monograph Series
SP	Sacra pagina
STDJ	Studies on the Texts of the Desert of Judah
SubBi	Subsidia biblica
TSAJ	Texts and Studies in Ancient Judaism
VT	*Vetus Testamentum*
WUNT	Wissenschaftliche Untersuchungen zum Neuen Testament

CONTRIBUTORS

THOMAS E. BOOMERSHINE is Professor Emeritus of New Testament (1979–2000) and Christianity and Communications (2004–2006) at United Theological Seminary in Dayton, Ohio. He holds the PhD in New Testament from Union Theological Seminary in New York (1974). Dr. Boomershine is the founder (1982) and past chair (1982–1989) of the Bible in Ancient and Modern Media group. He founded the Network of Biblical Storytellers (NBS) in 1977 and has lectured and led biblical storytelling workshops around the world. In 2004 he organized the NBS Seminar, a group of biblical scholars and biblical storytellers that is exploring the intersection of the performance of biblical stories and biblical scholarship. He has published *Story Journey: An Invitation to the Gospel as Storytelling* (Abingdon, 1988) and a number of scholarly and popular articles on the Gospels as performance literature. In addition, Tom served as Chief Consultant for Multimedia Translations for the American Bible Society (1989–1993). He was an Executive Producer for the award-winning American Bible Society video/multimedia program *Out of the Tombs*, an audiovisual translation of Mark's story of the Gerasene demoniac.

JOANNA DEWEY is the Harvey H. Guthrie, Jr., Professor Emerita of Biblical Studies at the Episcopal Divinity School in Cambridge, Massachusetts. Her PhD is from the Graduate Theological Union in Berkeley, California. Her recent publications include *Mark as Story: An Introduction to the Narrative of a Gospel* (Fortress, 2012, 3rd edition with David Rhoads and Donald Michie) and *The Oral Ethos of the Early Church: Speaking, Writing, and the Gospel of Mark* (Cascade Books, 2013).

HOLLY E. HEARON earned her PhD from the Graduate Theological Union (Berkeley) and is T. J. and Virginia Liggett Professor Emeritus of Christian Traditions and New Testament at Christian Theological Seminary. She writes on the uses of media in the construction of meaning. Among her articles are "Storytelling in Oral and Written Media Contexts of the Ancient

Mediterranean World," in *Jesus, the Voice, and the Text* (Baylor University Press, 2008); "Music as a Medium of Oral Transmission in Jesus Communities," *Biblical Theology Bulletin* 43 (2013) 180–90; and "Uses of the 'Technical' Language of Tradition for Constructing Memory and Identity in Early Christian Communities," *Journal of Early Christian History* 1/2 (2011) 55–70.

KELLY R. IVERSON received his PhD from the Catholic University of America (Washington DC) and is Associate Professor of New Testament at Baylor University. He is the author of *Gentiles in the Gospel of Mark: "Even the Dogs under the Table Eat the Children's Crumbs"* (T. & T. Clark, 2007), and the coeditor of *Mark as Story: Retrospect and Prospect* (Society of Biblical Literature, 2011) and *Unity and Diversity in the Gospels and Paul* (Society of Biblical Literature, 2012).

MARGARET E. LEE holds a ThD from the Melbourne College of Divinity, Melbourne Australia. She is Dean of Developmental Education at Tulsa Community College in Tulsa, Oklahoma, and teaches Introduction to the New Testament part time. Her initial exploration of the spoken dynamics of Hellenistic Greek compositions, "The Grammar of Sound in Greek Texts: Toward a Method of Mapping the Echoes of Speech in Writing," is published under her former name, Margaret Dean. Her dissertation, "A Method for Sound Analysis in Hellenistic Greek: The Sermon on the Mount as a Test Case," sets forth a process for analyzing Hellenistic Greek compositions as speech. She coauthored *Sound Mapping the New Testament* (Polebridge, 2009) with Bernard Brandon Scott. Her most recent illustration of sound mapping is "Melody in Manuscript: The Birth Narrative in the Gospel of Matthew," in *Testimony, Witness, Authority: The Politics and Poetics of Experience* (Cambridge Scholars, 2013).

KATHY MAXWELL received her PhD in Religion from Baylor University in 2007. Her research interests include New Testament studies, especially literary and rhetorical methodologies; biblical interpretation; and performance criticism, particularly how the memorization/internalization, delivery, and hearing of the biblical text transforms both the speaker and the hearer. Her dissertation project, "Hearing Between the Lines," explores the audience's active role in receiving—and telling—the story of Luke–Acts, and was published by T. & T. Clark in the Library of New Testament Studies series in 2010. She currently serves as Associate Professor of Biblical and Theological Studies at Palm Beach Atlantic University in West Palm Beach, Florida.

DAVID RHOADS is Emeritus Professor of New Testament at the Lutheran School of Theology at Chicago. After receiving his PhD from Duke University in 1973, he taught for fifteen years at Carthage College. He is the author of *Mark as Story: An Introduction to the Narrative of a Gospel* (Fortress, 2012, 3rd ed., with Joanna Dewey and Donald Michie); *Reading Mark, Engaging the Gospel* (Fortress, 2004); and "Performance Criticism: An Emerging Discipline in Second Testament Studies" (Parts 1 and 2) *Biblical Theology Bulletin* (2006). He is also the editor of *From Every People and Nation: The Book of Revelation in Intercultural Perspective* (Fortress, 2005). He does performances of selected New Testament writings. Rhoads is director of Lutherans Restoring Creation and two websites that provide environmental resources for faith communities. He edited *Earth and Word: Classic Sermons on Saving the Planet* (Continuum, 2007) and coedited *The Season of Creation: A Preaching Commentary* (Fortress, 2011).

PHILIP RUGE-JONES received his PhD from the Lutheran School of Theology at Chicago. He is currently Professor of Theology at Texas Lutheran University. He is a coeditor with Holly Hearon of the volume *The Bible in Ancient and Modern Media* (Cascade Books, 2009) and the storyteller for *The Beginning of the Good News*, a DVD of a live performance of the Gospel of Mark (Select Learning, 2009). Ruge-Jones convenes an annual summer seminar featuring interaction between trained storytellers and biblical scholars called the NBS Seminar in coordination with the Network of Biblical Storytellers.

RICHARD W. SWANSON earned his PhD at Luther Seminary in St. Paul, Minnesota. He is Professor of Religion/Philosophy/Classics at Augustana College in Sioux Falls, South Dakota and is the Director of the Provoking the Gospel Storytelling Project, a group of actors and interpreters who create performances of biblical narratives. Working with composer Christopher Stanichar and poet Patrick Hicks, he created the *St. Mark Passion*, a performance for actors, choir, and instrumentalists. He is currently working with composer John Pennington on *The Book of Job: A Man, a Simple Man*. He has written a commentary series on the four canonical gospels using the performance-critical approach he developed with the Provoking the Gospel Storytelling Project.

PERFORMANCE CRITICISM

A Paradigm Shift in New Testament Studies

David Rhoads and Joanna Dewey

BIBLICAL PERFORMANCE CRITICISM IS THE STUDY OF THE BIB-
lical writings as oral performances told from memory or sometimes as
prepared readings in performance events before communal audiences in
a predominantly oral culture. It is our conviction that this way of thinking
about biblical writings represents a paradigm shift in biblical studies. Our
focus here is on the significance of performance criticism for study of the
New Testament writings in the first and early second centuries.

The paradigm shift comes as a result of our recognition of the first-
century biblical worlds as cultures in which orality and memory predominated over writing. Performance criticism as a method is one way to focus
the dynamics of orality, memory, and writing so that this paradigm shift is
clear and explicit. Performance criticism represents a foundational change
in communication media from print to speech, a shift from treating biblical
writings as modern printed texts toward treating them as scripts and *aides
memoires* for oral performance in antiquity. This shift refocuses the object of
study toward the orality of early Christianity, toward memory as the primary
repository of tradition, toward writing as ancillary to orality and memory,

and toward performance events of New Testament texts. This shift challenges us to reframe our image of early Christianity and to recast and expand the methodological tools we scholars use in New Testament studies.

Orality criticism in New Testament studies began in the early 1980s with the work of two scholars, Werner Kelber and Thomas Boomershine. Of course, there were studies related to the oral nature of early Christianity before that time, most viewing orality as a temporary stage leading to the written texts. These two scholars, however, made oral dynamics central to early Christianity and the New Testament writings; and both understood that they were advocating for a profound media shift for the study of the New Testament. Kelber came to this shift through theory and orality studies, along with fresh exegesis of selected early Christian texts. Boomershine came to it through narrative exegesis and storytelling performances. Around the same time, Boomershine was instrumental in the formation of the Bible in Ancient and Modern Media section of the Society of Biblical Literature, and Kelber was an influential early contributor to the group. As these and other scholars grappled with the media world of ancient Christianity, we have come to recognize the importance of memory as the primary bearer of tradition, such that writing did not replace memory; writing supported memory. Performance criticism builds on these studies of orality and memory, adding a focus on performance events. In a predominately oral culture, performance involves a performer performing orally to a particular communal audience in a particular cultural ethos and a concrete historical context at some specific point in time.

Paradigms Shifts in Science

To understand the nature of paradigm shifts more clearly, we have turned to the classic study by Thomas Kuhn, *The Structure of Scientific Revolutions*.[1] We do not, of course, think of biblical studies as a scientific discipline. However, understanding the way science has developed provides a useful analogy to illuminate methodological developments in the history of biblical studies. Kuhn argues that major changes in scientific methodology have come about less through linear development of one new discovery or methodology added to what preceded and more by paradigm shifts, the old paradigm being inadequate to account for new developments or discoveries.[2] Kuhn cites as examples the work of Copernicus, Newton, Darwin, and Einstein. Such developments involved the abandonment of one paradigm

---

1. Kuhn, *Structure of Scientific Revolutions*.
2. Ibid., 2, 6, 138, 140.

and the adoption of a new one with a new set of perceptions, a new set of commitments, and, generally, a new set of methods. They are "revolutions."

What Kuhn calls "normal science" involves applying accepted para-digms and current methods to confirm expected outcomes and to solve puzzles without looking for the novel or the unexpected.[3] It is not oriented toward innovative developments. Many advances in normal science do indeed come through an accumulation of discoveries as brick by brick a scientific house is built. In such cases, the basic paradigm is adjusted to accommodate the new developments.

By contrast, the first step in a scientific revolution involving a paradigm shift may be the awareness by one or more scientists of an anomaly, a factor that current methods cannot account for.[4] Examples are the use of x-rays or the identification of oxygen, which came about through the occurrence of anomalies.[5] Such anomalies resulted in a new perception of things—not an expansion or adjustment of current paradigms, but a fresh way of look-ing at things. Therefore, the revolutionary shift involves the eventual loss or abandonment of the old paradigm and the embrace of another.[6] Sometimes, the old and new paradigms continue to be used alongside each other. Some-times, the old paradigm is radically revised to incorporate the new paradigm. In other cases, the old may be incorporated into the new more encompassing paradigm. Most commonly the new paradigm replaces the old one.

The process of transition to a new paradigm takes time.[7] There is a period needed to rethink and retool.[8] The initial efforts to formulate a new paradigm may be problematic and need further refinement.[9] Resistance is often strong because the new paradigm usually stands in opposition to deeply held commitments and expectations.[10] Nevertheless, gradually, more and more scientists come to embrace the new paradigm as more adequate and eventually abandon the old paradigm.[11] As time passes, most of the scientific field comes to see the new paradigm as the new normal.

One crucial aspect of a paradigm shift is a change in perception. People look at the same phenomena and see them radically differently.

3. Ibid., 109, 175, 34–35, 52.

4. Ibid., 52, 96.

5. Ibid., 92.

6. Ibid., 66, 77, 98.

7. Ibid., 86, 144.

8. Ibid., 76.

9. Ibid., 156.

10. Ibid., 59, 62–65, 149.

11. Ibid., 152, 158.

Pre-Copernican scientists looked at Earth as immovable, with the sun and moon as planets rotating around Earth. Copernican scientists saw Earth moving around the sun, and the moon as a satellite of Earth.[12] The change in perception is tantamount to a fundamental change in worldview. Similarly, the shift from Newton's way of seeing the world to Einstein's way of seeing the world resulted in a radical shift in perspective. The same could be said in biology of Darwin's theory of evolution. Kuhn speaks of these shifts in perception as "conversions of perspective,"[13] "transformations in vision,"[14] and "gestalt switches."[15] Since we do not see the world piecemeal, these fundamental shifts become a "new world."[16]

The model for scientific revolutions put forth by Kuhn is a generic model meant to enable us to see the nature of such events more clearly. The actual situation may be more complex than the model suggests, but as a heuristic device offering a dynamic explanation, the model is quite illuminating and helpful. It can also shed light on transformations in biblical studies.

Paradigm Shifts in Biblical Studies

We can use Kuhn's model to look at points in biblical studies that may be considered paradigm shifts involving revolutions in perception and method. Surely the onset of the historical-critical method in the eighteenth and nineteenth centuries would qualify: generally speaking, the shift was from uncritical acceptance of the historicity of the Gospel materials to radical questioning of them. Instead of conflating all four Gospels into one supposedly historical whole, scholars used the critical methods of the Enlightenment to ask how the Gospels related to each other and how that knowledge could help to trace back to what really happened in the life of Jesus. The consequent development of source criticism and the attendant flourishing of lives of Jesus in the nineteenth century represented a revolution in the approach to the Bible as compared to what went before. This shift involved a fundamental change in perspective about the nature and status of the texts themselves.

Problems became apparent in the application of this new historical-critical paradigm. At the beginning of the twentieth century, Albert Schweitzer's *Quest of the Historical Jesus* exposed the fact that biographers of

---

12. Ibid., 114–15.
13. Ibid., 113.
14. Ibid., 111.
15. Ibid., 117.
16. Ibid., 6, 128, 150.

Jesus had failed to carry out the mandate, that their portraits were anachronistic, and that efforts to write biographies of Jesus were not defensible
because they reflected the nineteenth century as much as or more than the
first century.[17] Schweitzer's elevation of apocalyptic as a prominent (and, to
the nineteenth century, anomalous) dimension of Jesus' life and teaching,
which made Jesus a strange and irrelevant figure, put the quest for the historical Jesus on hold for almost half a century while New Testament scholars
developed new methodological tools for better historical reconstruction.

The advent of form criticism in the first half of the twentieth century
followed by redaction criticism in midcentury did not constitute a paradigm
shift in biblical method but rather important additive developments. Form
criticism and redaction criticism developed the same basic source-critical
paradigm of analyzing layers of the Gospel traditions in search of history.
Both form and redaction criticism were designed to reconstruct history—
the historical Jesus, the history of the earliest church, and the history of the
evangelists' communities. In other words, New Testament scholars sought
to address the historical problems exposed by Schweitzer by refining and
expanding the existing paradigm of the historical-critical method with new
methodological tools, still with the aim of historical reconstruction.

In the late 1970s, however, the onset of narrative criticism set in motion
a revolutionary paradigm shift in the perception of the status and purpose of
the texts themselves. Instead of dissecting a Gospel text into layers of tradition and redaction in order to reconstruct history, a group of scholars began
to look at the text as a story and saw the final product as a relatively holistic
narrative designed to have a powerful impact upon readers. Narrative criticism was quickly expanded to include reader-response criticism and other
forms of literary criticism. Historical-critical scholars looked at a Gospel, the
Gospel of Mark for example, and saw layers by means of which they could
view the historical Jesus, the early church, and the community of the evangelist. By contrast, narrative-critical scholars looked at Mark and saw it as
a story best understood by studying the settings, characters, and events of
an imaginative "narrative world." This was a shift from looking behind the
text for its origins to looking at the text for what impact it might have on
recipients and how it might be received: a shift from viewing the text as win-
dow to the history behind it to viewing the text as portrait to be viewed and
interpreted in front of it. A parallel development took place in the analysis of
New Testament letters—a shift from the focus on how they were composed
to a focus on the rhetorical impact of a letter on a community.

17. Schweitzer, *Quest of the Historical Jesus.*

It took a while for scholars to adjust to this new paradigm. Nevertheless, in the last several decades, narrative criticism has achieved normative status as a New Testament discipline. The historical-critical paradigm, however, continues to be used alongside the new narrative paradigm. The two paradigms address different questions: the one on the prehistory of a document and the other on the impact of the writing as a whole upon an early Christian community. Some scholars find both approaches useful, particularly in writing commentaries. These two radically different perspectives on the status and purpose of New Testament texts both continue to be useful.

Additional methodological advances have occurred in the last decades. Historical criticism has been expanded, even transformed, through the use of models from cultural anthropology. These models have illuminated our understanding of gender roles, kinship, ancient economies, dynamics of purity and defilement, and much more. Also, instead of viewing Christianity in relation to Judaism alone and considering the early churches as politically innocuous in relation to the Roman Empire, a number of scholars now view many of the New Testament writings as standing in opposition to the ideology and organizational dynamics of the Roman Empire. Far from being politically quiescent, early Christianity presented counterimperial ideologies and organized countercultural communities as alternative life-worlds to the realities of the Roman Empire. These two shifts have greatly enriched New Testament studies, but they are not fundamental paradigm shifts. Rather, they expand and enrich the historical and literary paradigms, much as form and redaction criticism earlier expanded the work of source critics.

More foundational than these additional methodologies has been the challenge to scholars' fundamental assumptions of objectivity in the historical and literary enterprises of biblical studies. As long as New Testament scholarship was the domain of educated European and American white males, the illusion of scholarly objectivity could be maintained. The influx of women, minorities, Third World critics, and others into biblical studies—along with the development of theories of postmodernism—showed that scholarly neutral objectivity was indeed an illusion. This has been a paradigm shift that represents a change in perception about the nature and status of the texts—a shift from seeing the text as something that could be studied objectively (with many interpreters coming to the same conclusion) to realizing that the text has meaning only in relation to those who read it, and seeing that those who read the text come to it with very different perspectives and interests. Such a shift served to relativize the dominant interpretations and lift up the pluriformity of texts and interpretations. Postmodern approaches have dismantled our scholarly claims to objectivity and have affirmed the relative and situated nature of all interpretation. Fresh and insightful interpretations by feminists, womanists, other liberation exegetes of many kinds, and postcolonial critics have all shown how much the social location of readers shapes their interpretations and their appropriations of the biblical materials. There are no disinterested observers and no neutral interpretations; all interpreters are located and invested.

Furthermore, power dynamics exist between text and interpreter and between interpreters that should leave no one naïve about the potentially oppressive nature of interpretation *and* of the Bible itself. This revolutionary postmodern paradigm shift in New Testament studies is leading many interpreters to name their social location, to interpret self-consciously from their social location, to do so in dialogue with the interpretations of others from diverse social locations, and to illuminate or counter the ways in which the work of biblical scholars and/or the Bible itself can be oppressive.

This paradigm shift is not one that can exist alongside the earlier modernist paradigms, except insofar as the older paradigms are modified to encompass the new. Rather, the new paradigm replaces earlier hermeneutical claims to detached objectivity and to the notion of a single correct interpretation of a writing or to one correct historical reconstruction of persons and events.

Performance Criticism as a Paradigm Shift

We are convinced that New Testament studies (and biblical studies generally) is now facing another paradigm shift in the way we view early Christianity and in the methods we use to study the biblical texts. This is a shift from a focus on the New Testament *as writings* on the model of modern printed texts to a focus on orality and memory, a focus on texts as witnesses to *oral performances*. This paradigm shift represents a foundational change of medium (from written to oral and from writing to memory), a change that reorients our understanding of the purpose and status of the texts themselves. This new paradigm challenges the ways we view the New Testament writings and early Christianity with our print model mentality. The replacement will focus on the oral ethos, the predominance of memory, the generally subsidiary nature of scrolls—all coming together in performance events that reflect the collective memory of a community and that shape its social identity.

It is important to observe that we are not setting up an oral/written divide or a binary opposition but a model that encompasses interrelationships of speech, memory, and sometimes writing. We are advocating a major shift in gravity to a focus on orality, memory, and writing that are actualized in performances. When we perceive the same New Testament texts from a performance vantage point, everything changes. An historical or narrative critic may look at a New Testament work and imagine a fixed text written by an author and read by readers. A performance critic will look at the text and imagine how it may reflect oral performances done from memory before particular early Christian communities. Simply put, based on this new perspective, the writings we have that are preserved in the New Testament are examples of performance literature: that is, literature that was meant for performance and that may well have taken shape during many prior oral performances.

In 1974, Hans Frei lamented the "eclipse of biblical narrative," the loss of the power of biblical story in favor of a fragmentation of the text into sources for historical reconstruction or in favor of abstractions into doctrinal formulations and ethical lessons.[18] Through the new paradigm of narrative criticism, biblical scholarship has come a long way toward recovering the narrative dynamics and the rhetorical force of the biblical materials as standard New Testament practice. Therefore, much scholarly work now takes for granted the surface meaning and impact of the text as we have it, either as written narrative or as epistolary rhetoric.

Now we are addressing another threshold; we are becoming aware of the "eclipse of biblical performance"—the centuries-long loss of the immediacy and power of the Gospels and letters performed orally and in their entirety, as they were experienced in the early churches of the first centuries. Studies are now emerging to redress this loss. We are at the beginning of this process; yet already the various efforts seem to be coalescing into a discipline that may be called *performance criticism*.

The Old Paradigms Assumed the Print Model

Although we have long viewed the early church as part of a predominately oral culture and understood that traditions circulated orally, nevertheless, it has had little impact on our research or our methods. Biblical scholars have studied the literature of the New Testament for centuries without ever hearing them performed as stories or speeches or epistolary orations, without taking sound into account as an essential ingredient of interpretation, without trying to determine how they may have been performed in early Christian communities, and without constructing ancient performance scenarios as a basis for interpretation. It is difficult to imagine musicologists studying scores of music without ever hearing a performance. Nor can we imagine

---

18. Frei, *Eclipse of Biblical Narrative*.

theater scholars studying scripts of ancient drama without having seen contemporary performances of the plays and without trying to determine how they may have been performed and experienced in ancient times. Yet we biblical scholars have done precisely that with the performance literature that is the New Testament. Even when we have heard them read aloud as straight readings, such as in the context of worship, our experience has been of short passages and not of the work as a whole.

Traditionally, then, we have assumed that ancient manuscripts functioned as our own modern printed texts function. We have worked out of a model for print medium that is based on the way we experience the biblical writings in the modern world. In so doing, we have assumed a similar centrality and the authority of writings in antiquity. A print model might look like this:

Author ——— Written Text ——— Individual Silent Reader

Using the print model in our study of first-century writings, we have consistently spoken of the authors as writers and the recipients as readers. We have assumed that the author composed in the act of writing and produced a document that was meant to be fixed. We have treated the texts as fixed and stable (as one would expect to find in print), and we have sought to reconstruct this original text—what the author wrote—from extant variants considered to be corruptions of the original. We have viewed the texts as documents to be read silently without regard to their sound or to their embodiment by those who performed them, to be read at a time separate from and later than the act in which they were composed. Our scholarly interpretations reflect our modern experience of these texts as individual readers who study texts in silence and alone in private.

Given our assumptions based on our experience of print, we have considered the New Testament writings central to the life of the early church. True enough, we have traditionally acknowledged that a public reader would read a letter or Gospel aloud to a gathered audience. We have imagined, however, that such an oral presentation to an ancient community was a straightforward reading of what was written and therefore faithful to the text as silent text. We have assumed that writing was the dominant component while an oral presentation was peripheral and added little if anything to it. Therefore, the written text was all we needed. Based on these assumptions, we already know all that we need to know for interpreting the text. We do not need to imagine or to study performance events, for such study would make little difference to interpretation. The written text was what mattered.

The scholarship done in the last centuries using the assumptions of print media has given us many insights into the New Testament writings and the early church. Enlightenment scholarship in the historical-critical and narrative modes of analysis has been and continues to be significant and generative. We have no desire to discount earlier scholarship. Nevertheless, because it has treated the text in a medium different from its original medium, it has sometimes manifested limited and distorted perspectives that have entailed misconceptions, misinterpretations, and misappropriations. And it has missed the emotional and corporeal impact of performance. For example, with a print mentality, textual criticism has assumed an original, fixed text from which all subsequent manuscripts contain corruptions by inadvertent changes or by efforts at corrections happening in linear fashion from one manuscript to the next. By contrast, in an oral medium, compositions were made orally and were changed regularly to address different audiences and contexts, resulting in multiple originals. Scribes functioned like performers and, in interaction with oral performances, contributed in positive ways to the fluidity of the manuscript tradition. Source criticism, working on the same mistaken print model, has assumed that we could work back in linear fashion through written and oral traditions to the one original, fixed saying of Jesus, as if Jesus never said the same thing many times and in different ways.

The predominant print paradigm is in need of a serious replacement that embraces the oral nature of the texts and the oral dynamics of early Christianity. It is time to shift our perspective to performance. What follows is a description of orality, memory, writing, and performance as components of the first-century media world, a world that did not know print texts as they exist today. Embracing these factors constitutes a paradigm shift.

The New Paradigm Assumes the Fundamental Orality of the Text

The print scenario charted above is not what happened in the oral media cultures of the first centuries. In the print model, composition, text, and reception are three disparate phases separated in time and space. In the oral model of communication, all three occur together in particular performance events. The comparable oral model might look like this:

Oral Composer — Composing Orally from Memory — To a
Communal Audience

In this model, authors composed orally and may have been the first performers of the Gospel traditions—indeed of entire Gospels. Composing was not done with pen in hand in the act of writing. Rather, speeches and stories were composed in memory by ear for the sound of the composition (much like music) and were performed orally, often without recourse to anything written at all. For the Gospels, the traditions were composed and repeatedly recomposed, developed and refined in the course of many performances. For the letters, the performers would re-perform the letter from memory. It is likely that the early Christian tradition, even with lengthy compositions like Gospels and letters, often went from oral performance to oral performance. Gospels and letters were performed by people who often were not literate, were heard by other nonliterates, and were subsequently performed by them.

The contents of oral compositions (what we would call texts) were not fixed but fluid; each performer (including the composer who performed) would have done at least some recomposing in performance. Thus, each performance would be distinctive and in some sense an original. The composition-as-performance would manifest features typical of ancient oral arts as well as arts of performing. The receptor audience would be communal. The performer would interact with the audience during the performance. The performer would be focused not only on conveying to the audience the content of the composition but even more on persuasion, on arousing the emotional conviction of the audience to take action of some kind. In an oral culture, education, entertainment, and transformation are not separate activities.

Changing the model of communication from print to orality and memory has great significance for the methods we scholars employ to study the writings now in the New Testament and for the interpretations that result. Writing of course existed and will be discussed further below. It is because of writing that we have these texts today. It is hard for us today, however, to imagine how limited in importance writing and manuscripts were to the rise of Christianity in the first century. Our argument is that the recognition of this change of medium is nothing less than a fundamental paradigm shift in the field of biblical studies.

The New Model of Ancient Media

The new media model that replaces the print model has four interrelated components: oral ethos of communal identity, the predominance of memory, the functions of handwritten scrolls, and performance events. These are related to each other in diverse ways that need to be sorted out in specific cases. Here is a brief profile of each of these components.

The Oral Ethos of Early Christianity

The fundamental change in perspective from print to the first-century media world will embrace the predominantly oral nature of the first-century cultures and early Christianity. More than 95 percent of the population was nonliterate (or should we say *oralate* as distinct from *literate*). Literacy rates were higher (or less abysmal) among men than women, and in urban rather than rural settings, so perhaps a maximum of 15 percent of urban males were to some degree literate, mainly because of the high presence of elites there and those working for them.[19] Among the 2 percent of the population who were elites, literacy was common among the males, and frequent among women, but even here, reading and writing were considered labor and often handled by slaves who would read aloud or take down dictation. All, including literate elites, were steeped in oral culture.

Oral cultures were marked primarily by social interactions, with little individualism as we know it, and with limited privacy. Because virtually all communication was face-to-face in personal and communal interactions, the oral sharing of traditions—whether through informal conversation or by means of formal performances—was the primary means that formed a collective memory and shaped social identity.

In these predominantly oral cultures, manuscripts, including copies of Hebrew Scriptures, were expensive and few. For the most part, people learned about the Hebrew Scriptures, which were held in sacred esteem, as oral traditioning by storytellers and rabbis. Throughout the first century, most early Christian communities had no or few manuscripts, each of which might contain only a single writing.

Overwhelmingly, those in the first century who experienced the contents of the writings that came to be included centuries later in the New Testament experienced them as oral performances to gathered audiences. The direct experience of written scrolls was not unimportant, but it was limited and peripheral, especially in the first century. Storytelling of the Gospels would have been shared from memory or in lively public readings, most likely in their entirety at one time. The letters were also read aloud in a performative manner or performed orally from memory by the letter carrier and later performers. Here, what was important was not that Paul

---

19. Harris, *Ancient Literacy*, 267.

wrote a letter but that the performer of the letter conveyed what Paul was *saying* in his letter.

In such cultures, an oral/aural medium predominated. As Christianity developed in the late second and third centuries, scrolls and codices became increasingly important, at least among the literate few, and the manuscripts eventually began to show marks for dividing the texts for selective readings in worship. Nevertheless, the percentage of those who were not able to read remained substantially unchanged, even up to the time of the printing press.

Memory in Predominantly Oral Cultures

It is the role of memory in antiquity that makes possible an independence from writing. Among both literates and nonliterates alike, memory was more central than writing. Thus, the paradigm shift to performance is not only a shift in our perception from writing to speech but also a shift in perspective from written texts to memory as the dominant mode of creating and transmitting traditions. Therefore, it is not enough to speak of a shift from literacy to orality. Ancient Mediterranean cultures were memorial cultures, in which memory was more important than manuscripts as the repository of tradition; and writing—when present—served performance. Writing did not replace memory; it facilitated it. Speech and memory went together, and both could be served by writing.

In predominantly oral cultures, memory was highly valued. It was common in villages and communities for those with memorial gifts to stand out as storytellers and tradition bearers. People with gifts of memory and speech might regale communities for hours with stories and wisdom. Women and men alike engaged in performing traditions. Performances of the epics of Homer from memory were part of the Olympic Games. Lengthy stories spoken or sung were common at symposia meals. For the elites, memory was central to their education for public life. Memory as preparation for the delivery of an oration was one of the five key elements of the syllabus of rhetoric. Handbooks of rhetoric discussed techniques of memory. Ancients cultivated the natural memory and developed technologies of memory that enabled performers to recall lengthy stories and orations by associating portions of a story with the rooms of a house or images of animals or the backdrop of a stage. Stories about prodigious feats of memory by literates and nonliterates were common in antiquity.

Memory was the primary means by which a predominantly oral culture taught, reinforced, and retained its customs, values, history, and beliefs. This was the collective or social memory held in common by the people of a village, community, society, or by subgroups such as early Christian groups. Within the subgroup, memory was held in common because traditions were experienced together communally. The common memory about the past gave identity to the community or subgroup in the present. Traditions were formulated so as to make them memorable for both performers and audiences—through dramatic action and emotional appeal, with sayings, parables, wisdom pieces, stories, and orations, all of which made use of allit-eration, assonance, parallelism, chiastic ordering, sound patterns, and many more oral arts. Memory was the lifeblood of oral/aural cultures.

Memory was closely tied to performance. Memory was integral to the art of composing. Composers, familiar with the traditions, would compose in performance from memory. Performers of all kinds—storytellers, orators, rhetors, teachers, letter bearers, priests, and others—would use memory to hear and retain and re-perform. Compositions were structured and styled to facilitate the memory of the performer and the audience. There is some very limited evidence of verbatim memorization in antiquity, especially in relation to short poems, the epics of Homer, and some rabbinic traditions. However, for the most part, the memory was fluid, because performers would shape and recompose for particular audiences and would adapt tra-ditions to new situations.

In this kind of culture, memory provides a lens for the shift of para-digm. A traditional biblical critic looks at a text and sees a repository of tra-dition in print. By contrast, from a memorial perspective, the performance critic relates to a text more as a musical score, using all the memory arts in the composition to get the melody in the head and on the heart so that it can be heard as a performance. What are the rhythms and patterns? What does it sound like? What needs to be repeated in a variety of ways so that it does not get lost? Is it memorable for an audience? How do the patterns of structure and sound enable the performer to recall? How can the performer get the story into his or her body—through gestures, posture, movement, facial expressions—so as to make the story memorable? What emotions does the performer want to arouse in the audience so that they do not forget their experience? How does all of this come together to lead the community to change and act in certain ways? Hence, memory is a significant part of the paradigm shift.

Writing in Early Christianity

It is crucial but not enough simply to recognize the comparatively lim-ited role of writing; we must also rethink the nature of writing. We need, therefore, to reorient our perception of the function of scrolls in predominantly oral/memorial cultures so that we look at writing through the lenses of speech and memory.

As we noted earlier, only a very small minority could read or write, so it was not considered normative to be able to read and write. Reading and writing were thought of as crafts or trades that carried little status. Even among the few elites where literacy was common, it was often slaves who did the reading aloud or writing for them. Hence, within the populace, literacy was not a standard or common expectation from which nonliterates deviated.

Furthermore, scrolls were nothing like our modern printed books. The scrolls themselves were expensive and difficult to handle; frequent unrolling would wear away words. The function of the scrolls was to provide a record of sounds by means of lettering so that they could be recycled back into sound, similar to musical scores. Just as we hum the notes when we read music, so readers read aloud to make clear what sounds the scroll was triggering. The sounds were what mattered.

The writing on scrolls was not designed to facilitate public reading. The writing was made up of a continuous sequence of one uppercase letter after another without a break. The handwritten scrolls had no punctuation, no lowercase letters, no spaces between words, sentences, or paragraphs, and no chapter and verse designations. The primary unit was not the letter or the word; rather, the syllable was the primary unit of speech, combinations of which formed the words spoken for understanding. Given the lack of spaces between words and no punctuation to indicate the end of a clause or sentence, one had to sound out the syllables in order even to know what was to be said. For all intent and purpose, one needed to have studied the content and known it virtually by memory in order to enact a public reading with facility and in such a way as to make the content lively and meaningful. Sometimes a closed scroll may have been held in the left hand as a symbol of authenticity and authority, while the right hand was free for gestures. It is likely that the Gospels and letters were often performed without the presence of a scroll.

Thus, the markings on the scrolls were basically signs that recorded sounds to be retrieved as aids for those who needed to know the sounds for reading aloud or to remember them for performing. Oral dictation was the primary means to get something transcribed into writing; and virtually all reading was done aloud, as means to re-create the sounds. Hence, when writing occurred, it mostly served the needs of performance of prepared readings or oral performances from memory.

Therefore, the experience of the early church, even in relation to written scrolls, was overwhelmingly oral and memorial both for performers and for audiences. Biblical scholars have long acknowledged that short traditions such as parables and sayings and stories about Jesus circulated orally, but we have not acknowledged the fundamentally oral orientation of entire Gospels and letters as well. As transcriptions of performances or the result of dictations for performances, the scrolls are trace records of these performances. As we have said, they are examples of performance literature, similar to scores that denote musical sounds or to scripts to be enacted as drama. We need to redirect our focus onto the orality and memory of the early churches and to interpret the New Testament scrolls in terms of their relationship to orality and memory in performance.

Performances in Early Christianity

Performance criticism brings together the three foci of the ancient media complex in the study of performance—orality, memory, and (sometimes) writing. Performance was the main means in ancient society and early Christianity to carry traditions, establish and reinforce social memory, and secure communal identity. Performance criticism analyzes the traces of orality in the writings, seeks to imagine the dynamics of performances, and reconstructs possible performance events.

Performance criticism seeks to construct possible performance scenarios as a basis for understanding the nature of performances and their potential impact on specific communities. Elements of performance events include the social location and role of a performer, the composition being performed, the dynamics of its performance, the makeup of the audience and their participation in the performance event, the potential responses of the audience after the performance, the physical location of the performance, the cultural ethos and resonances of their traditions, the issues faced by the community, and the historical context.

The performer brings a story world to life and seeks to draw the communal audience into that world as a way of having a particular impact on them. It is critical to note that the composition not only depicts happenings in the story world but also at the same time gives what we might call cues and stage directions for performers. When a demon screams, or when Jesus lays hands on someone, or when Jesus begins a journey to Jerusalem or when Paul depicts receiving the right hand of fellowship from the pillars in Jerusalem, or when Paul graphically depicts the death of Jesus, these are triggers for the inflection or volume of the voice and for gestures and facial expressions by the performer who is portraying the characters and illustrating the actions. These represent the performance arts for the voice (inflection, volume, pace, voice characterizations), body language (gestures, movement, posture, location), facial expressions (scowl, winks, puzzlement, eye messages), and movement (re-creating in the performance space the changes of venue in the story world). Many other subtle things are designed to convey a message by the way a line is delivered, to indicate irony or suspense, to express and evoke emotion, to provoke laughter, to emphasize a point, and so on. These performance arts are critical for us to appreciate as we imagine the variety of ways a composition may have been performed, its diversity of meanings, and the potential impacts it may have had upon a community.

Performance may have differed in style depending on the size of the audience and the location of the performance. If done in a public square or marketplace, the performance may have needed to be loud and physically dramatic, even bombastic, at least by our standards. If done for a small group in a house church, the performance would have been more subdued. In either case, from what we know of descriptions in rhetorical handbooks, the performances were animated and emotional. And we know that audiences participated actively in the performance event. The composition itself suggests the identification of lines and phrases where audience responses were expected. The audience participated with intrusive comments, gestures of approval such as foot stomping or hand clapping, and emotional responses such as weeping and laughing. Of course, there may have been the equivalent of booing and walking out when there was resistance to a performance.

Furthermore, if the composition of a Gospel or letter admonishes a group or urges a community to persevere or to take certain actions, we may imagine how that played out in the communal audience after the performance, including conversation with the performer. How might the audience have dealt with the performance in relation to conflicts within the community or to echoes of events in their traditions or to stresses and persecutions from outside the community?

In addition to identifying the role that oral arts and memory arts played in any given performance, we also need to discern the ways in which resonances of common community traditions echoed in the performance. All these and more are relevant to our efforts to employ ancient media as means to understand the potential meanings and possible impacts of the writings in the New Testament that were once performed before early Christian communities.

Reorienting and Changing Our Methods

In light of the paradigm shift to performance, we need to put the spotlight on the methods we use to study the New Testament and to construct images of early Christianity in order to see in what ways our methodologies need to be revised, reoriented, replaced, or expanded so as to account for the oral and memorial nature of early Christianity in performance. Performance criticism has come to serve as an eclectic approach that seeks to bring together many perspectives and methods relevant to the paradigm shift. This is the case, both because so many disciplines are affected by the paradigm shift, and because the contributions of so many different disciplines are needed to understand and construct performance scenarios.

Some scholarly methods by which we study the New Testament may not be so much affected by performance criticism. For example, historical studies, archaeology, and cultural anthropology might not be much changed except to reframe their work in the context of a predominantly oral culture. Other areas of New Testament study, however, such as the synoptic problem, source criticism, and historical Jesus studies, may look quite different when approached with an oral paradigm that imagines multiple originals rather than with a print paradigm that assumes a single original. Textual criticism will need to change as we see the manuscript tradition not as a closed system of written documents but in interaction with an oral tradition that was fluid and creative. Form criticism and genre criticism may be changed significantly by considering how these texts worked as oral compositions performed from memory to ancient communal audiences. Likewise, narrative criticism and reader-response criticism would be reoriented to treat the Gospels as oral events by a performer to an early Christian community. Rhetorical criticism would be reconfigured to account for the emotional impact generated by performance. Discourse analysis would take the dynamics of sound into account. Ideological criticism might be reoriented to focus on the power dynamics involved in the face-to-face interactions during ancient performance events. The art of translation would be deeply affected as practitioners seek to go from the orality of the biblical texts to contemporary oral performances. Already substantive probes are being made to transform these disciplines for study of a predominantly oral world.

In addition, in order to develop the new paradigm fully, more recent methodologies might become central—methodologies such as cultural analysis of contemporary oral cultures, social-memory theory, performance studies in oral interpretation, theater studies, sound mapping, and speech-act theory. Already, some significant scholarly contributions have been made. And contemporary performances are being offered that reflect the revolutionary paradigm shift in the communication media of our studies.

The essays in this volume exemplify the kind of work that is being done to implement these changes: topics include the layers of oral tradition that resonate in an oral performance (Maxwell), the way narrative criticism needs to be transformed into a study of story in performance (Ruge-Jones, Hearon), the impact of a performance on communal audiences (Boomershine, Iverson), the careful analysis of oral and memorial arts in a composition (Lee), and the complexity involved in preparing a modern multimedia translation to convey an experience similar to that undergone by an ancient audience (Swanson).

Embracing the Paradigm Shift

Becoming performance critics requires major shifts in our ways of thinking. We need to move from a literary ethos to an oral one; from silence to sound; from writing to speech; from manuscript to memory; from one fixed, original text to multiple and fluid oral renditions; from individual reading to embodied performance. Performance is what brings this all together—sight, sounds, speech, memory, and emotion. Performance is embodied, public, and communal. Performance is an event with a performer, an audience, a setting, an ethos, and historical circumstances. The performance event places speech, memory and (sometimes) writing into a complex nexus of interrelationships.

Based on Thomas Kuhn's analysis of paradigm shifts in science, we can imagine several rather expected responses. A common response to this paradigm shift is to acknowledge it but not know what to do with it. It is difficult to see new possibilities clearly because our accustomed academic paradigms tend to predetermine what we see. Another reaction may be to think that we can just tack this method on as an added building block to be investigated but not as one that will challenge any of our time-honored methods or conclusions. However, it will not be adequate to keep everything the same and just assimilate the oral and memorial dimensions into existing paradigms. And even if we recognize the significance of the new paradigm, we may not be able easily to let go of methods in which we were trained and that we know so well. For those of us trained so exclusively in the analysis of texts, it may be difficult to let go of the idea of a fixed text we can work with. At the same time, young scholars are emerging who are being trained in the new disciplines. Gradually, however, new and more cogent methods will be developed. And, of course, there will be debates about the significance and extent of the shift. Nevertheless, gradually, many will come to see orality, memory, and performance as central dimensions in our field that will require significant revisions to traditional methods, thorough replacement for others, and the need for added tools of the trade. We are confident that the paradigm shift will eventually take place.

One significant resistance we scholars have to face is that most of us were trained in print analysis. We know how to analyze written texts. How do we shift to an analysis of performance and sound? Furthermore, what about our data? We do have the texts of the New Testament, but we do not have speech; nor, of course, do we have access to ancient performances. Speech is ephemeral and elusive. How could we know what an ancient performance of a letter was like? How could we imagine an ancient performance of a Gospel? There are so many unknowns and variables. Speech involves many cultural dynamics that we may have little way of knowing. How can we operate in the dark? Given all the uncertainties, will this endeavor help us to understand early Christianity and the New Testament texts any better than we do now?

Maybe all these questions are right on target; they certainly represent difficulties to be addressed. However, similar reservations have not stopped us in the past. There seems to be nothing as elusive as the historical Jesus; yet we continue to pursue one portrayal after another. And it is clear that the quest for Jesus has been worthwhile as each new study makes fresh contributions and raises new questions. At a minimum, can we not hope and expect that the same will be true here in this pursuit? We have long stressed the importance of historical context. Communication media are an essential part of that context. We cannot continue to ignore them.

Prospectus for Performance Criticism

While substantial beginnings have been made, the full implications of the paradigm shift continue to unfold. Much work has already been done; much more work is needed. Here we outline a prospectus: a list of areas for continuing study, research, and experimentation to move the process forward. The effort to be comprehensive results in overlap between areas.

1. Learning everything we can about the dynamics and ethos of the oral/aural cultures of the first century; making use of literature, rhetorical handbooks, ancient drama, archaeology, paintings, sculptures, manuscripts, papyri, and other artifacts. This effort includes information about proclaimers of all kinds, formal and informal storytelling and tradition sharing, venues, literacy rates, the nature and status of

manuscripts, how scribes and dictation functioned, what reading was, how performances took place, what audience responses could be, and the impact of performances on audiences.

2. Studying other predominantly oral societies. Oral cultures are collectivist societies in which social identity is shaped by the daily interpersonal relationships that take place among people. There is no individualism as we know in modernity and there is often little privacy or encouragement for introspection. In such a society, how does conversation and performance reflect, reinforce, shape, and change the collective memory and the social identity? Here analogies from studies of contemporary oral/aural cultures will be useful. How different are various oral societies from one another?

3. Attending to the differences between the elite culture and the popular cultures of the first century. This involves the roles that writing played in the power dynamics between the elites who used writing to dominate the populace, who in turn could use oral speech (and sometimes writing) to resist. And it involves understanding the evolution of ancient media taking place in the second century and later as the predominantly oral and memorial cultures of early Christianity became more and more influenced by—or controlled by—the presence of written manuscripts and literate institutional leaders.

4. Attending to differences between men's and women's oral cultures and what happens to women's traditions in the second century and following centuries as Christianity became more controlled by written texts and literate (generally male) leaders.

5. Giving attention to how traditions are passed on in predominantly oral cultures. What are the possible interrelationships between written traditions and oral tellings? How do traditions in oral media resonate with past associations and build new accretions? How do innovations take place? How are oral allusions different from intertextuality, and how do they convey layers of associations?

6. Focusing on the dynamics of memory in the predominantly oral cultures of the first centuries, on the different roles memory played in Greek and Hebrew cultures, on the common capacity to know traditions by heart, on the role of memory in storytelling and reading, and on its place in the rhetorical education among elites. Especially exploring the collective memory of an oral culture, how it shapes social identity, how it develops and changes, and the ways it interacts with manuscripts.

7. Reconsidering scribes and manuscripts, the practices of scribes, their role as shapers of the tradition, and the various uses of handwritten scrolls. How did the continuous script function? And how were the writing and the scrolls managed by various performers who worked from memory or who did a public reading? To what extent did scribes function as performers in contributing creatively to developing traditions?

8. Establishing criteria and developing methods for garnering the traces of orality from the extant writings we have in the New Testament and related literature—traces including *oral arts* of speech, *memory arts* designed to assist both performers and audiences, and *performance arts* evident in cues for the performer. This will include mapping the patterns of sound that give order and organization to a composition. These endeavors will require a new generation of scholars to be trained not only in reading ancient Greek but also in listening and speaking.

9. Experimenting with performances (in Greek and in translation) as a means to get in touch with the dynamics of performance: intonation, gesture, facial expressions, movement, subtext, emotions, humor, and interaction with audiences. In this way, we can imagine the possibilities of ancient performance better and even experience the dynamics of oral expression—as performer and as audience. Most of all, performing places us in the rhetorical position of seeking to have an impact upon an audience, thereby shifting the center of gravity in interpretation from a focus on semantic meaning to a focus on rhetorical force. This step may lead some New Testament interpreters to be trained as oral interpreters of literature.

10. Constructing possible performance scenarios that give us concrete imaginative contexts for performances of the documents we now have: the nature of performance, the social location and role of the performer, the audience, the venue, the life world or cultural context, the sociohistorical circumstances, the implied aural impact on the audience, and other factors. For example, we can imagine a messenger of Paul who has brought the slave Onesimus back to his master Philemon performing the letter to Philemon in front of the community that gathers in his house. Or we can imagine Mark being performed in its entirety in the marketplace of a northern Palestinian village with a mixed audience of Judeans and Gentiles, taking place shortly after the Roman Judean War of 66 to 70 CE. Such scenarios provide concrete contexts for us to imagine the performances of various New Testament writings as a basis for our reinterpretation of them.

11. Rethinking current New Testament methodologies in light of this paradigm shift. In so far as these disciplines employ or mimic the mentality of our modern print culture, we need to reorient and reframe them for study of the New Testament in a predominantly oral world. In addition, scholars are exploring secular disciplines new to New Testament studies that are relevant to this paradigm shift, such as theater studies, oral interpretation of literature, performance studies in general, social-memory theory, and speech-act analysis. All these are helpful for understanding the dynamics of performance events.

12. Translating the New Testament texts for performance as a means to enable us to discern in the Greek oral features such as word order, alliteration, assonance, rhythm, and so on, and challenging us to find ways to replicate these in modern languages. In turn, the experience of performing leads the performer to discern possibilities for translation that might not otherwise come to mind. The interaction of translating and performing are critical methods for interpretation.

13. Providing fresh interpretations of the New Testament writings as performance literature in the context of an oral/aural culture.

14. Grappling with theories of media studies. They help us understand the different communications media in history and the way the various media have shaped worldviews. We can be aware of changes that the electronic (digital) culture is making to the print culture in which many of us were raised. As scholars, we can become aware of the anachronistic print-culture mentality that has shaped and informed our methods and interpretations; we can recognize the flaws and limitations resulting from our print mentality; and we can become trained in the use of disciplines that engage the ancient media involving a combination of orality, memory, scribality, and performance.

Conclusion

Performance criticism is a new challenge and an exciting adventure in the field of biblical studies. It is important that we recognize it as a paradigm shift so that we embrace its revolutionary nature and grasp the transformations it requires of us. Everything looks somewhat different. Therefore it calls forth from us fresh methods, new information, and a great stretch of the imagination.

Bibliography

Achtemeier, Paul J. "*Omne verbum sonat*: The New Testament and the Oral Environment of Late Western Antiquity." *JBL* 109/1 (1990) 3–27.

Biblical Performance Criticism. http://www.biblicalperformancecriticism.org/.

Botha, Eugene, dir. *Orality, Print Culture, and Biblical Interpretation*. http://vimeo.com/44167508/.

Botha, Pieter J. J. *Orality and Literacy in Early Christianity*. BPCS 5. Eugene, OR: Cascade Books, 2012.

Boomershine, Thomas E. "Biblical Megatrends: Towards the Paradigm for the Interpretation of the Bible in the Electronic Age." In *SBLSP 1989*, 144–57. Atlanta: Scholars, 1989.

Carr, David M. *Writing on the Tablet of the Heart: Origins of Scripture and Literature*. Oxford: Oxford University Press, 2005.

Carruthers, Mary J. *The Book of Memory: A Study of Memory in Medieval Culture*. Cambridge Studies in Medieval Literature 10. Cambridge: Cambridge University Press, 1990.

Dewey, Joanna. *The Oral Ethos of the Early Church: Speaking, Writing, and the Gospel of Mark*. BPCS 8. Eugene, OR: Cascade Books, 2013.

Doan, William, and Thomas Giles. *Prophets, Performance, and Power: Performance Criticism of the Hebrew Bible*. New York: T. & T. Clark, 2005.

Dunn, James D. G. *Jesus Remembered*. Christianity in the Making 1. Grand Rapids: Eerdmans, 2003.

Elliot, John H. "A Dog, Shoes, and Subtabular Crumbthrowing: Gestural Communication in the Shift from Oral to Written Communication, with a Focus on the Gospel of Mark." Paper given at the Context Group, Portland, OR, March 13–14, 2009.

Eve, Eric. *Behind the Gospels: Understanding the Oral Tradition*. London: SPCK, 2013.

Foley, John Miles. *How to Read an Oral Poem*. Urbana: University of Illinois Press, 2002.

———. *The Singer of Tales in Performance*. Voices in Performance and Text. Bloomington: Indiana University Press, 1995.

Frei, Hans W. *The Eclipse of Biblical Narrative: A Study in Eighteenth and Nineteenth Century Hermeneutics*. New Haven: Yale University Press, 1974.

Gamble, Harry Y. *Books and Readers in the Early Church: A History of Early Christian Texts*. New Haven: Yale University Press, 1995.

Graham, William A. *Beyond the Written Word: Oral Aspects of Scripture in the History of Religion*. Cambridge: Cambridge University Press, 1987.

Harris, William V. *Ancient Literacy*. Cambridge: Harvard University Press, 1989.

Harvey, John D. *Listening to the Text: Oral Patterning in Paul's Letters*. ETS Studies 1. Grand Rapids: Baker, 1998.

Hearon, Holly E. *The Mary Magdalene Tradition: Witness and Counter-Witness in Early Christian Communities*. Collegeville, MN: Liturgical, 2004.

Hearon, Holly E., and Philip Ruge-Jones, eds. *The Bible in Ancient and Modern Media: Story and Performance*. BPCS 1. Eugene: OR: Cascade Books, 2009.

Hezser, Catherine. *Jewish Literacy in Roman Palestine*. TSAJ 81. Tübingen: Mohr/Siebeck, 2001.

Horsley, Richard A. *Text and Tradition in Performance and Writing*. BPCS 9. Eugene, OR: Cascade Books, 2013.

Horsley, Richard A., et al., eds. *Performing the Gospel: Orality, Memory, and Mark.* Minneapolis: Fortress, 2006.

Jaffee, Martin. *Torah in the Mouth: Writing and Oral Tradition in Palestinian Judaism, 200 BCE —400 CE.* Oxford: Oxford University Press, 2001.

Johnson, William A. *Readers and Reading Culture in the High Roman Empire: A Study of Elite Communities.* Classical Culture and Society. New York: Oxford University Press, 2010.

Kelber, Werner H. *Imprints, Voiceprints, and Footprints of Memory: Collected Essays of Werner H. Kelber.* SBLRBS 74. Atlanta: Society of Biblical Literature, 2013.

———. *The Oral and the Written Gospel: The Hermeneutics of Speaking and Writing in the Synoptic Tradition, Mark, Paul, and Q.* Philadelphia: Fortress, 1983.

Kirk, Alan, and Tom Thatcher, eds. *Memory, Tradition, and Text: Uses of the Past in Early Christianity.* SemSt 52. Atlanta: Society of Biblical Literature, 2005.

Kuhn, Thomas. *The Structure of Scientific Revolutions.* 3rd ed. Chicago: University of Chicago Press, 1996.

Lee, Margaret Ellen, and Bernard Brandon Scott. *Sound Mapping the New Testament.* Salem, OR: Polebridge, 2009.

Loubser, J. A. *Oral and Manuscript Culture in the Bible: Studies in the Media Texture of the New Testament—Exploratory Hermeneutics.* BPCS 7. Eugene, OR: Cascade Books, 2013.

Maxey, James A., and Ernst Wendland, eds. *Translating Scripture for Performance and Sound: New Directions in Biblical Studies.* BPCS 6. Eugene, OR: Cascade Books, 2012.

The Network of Biblical Storytellers. http://www.nbsint.org/.

Niditch, Susan. *Oral World and Written Word.* Library of Ancient Israel. Louisville: Westminster John Knox, 1996.

Ong, Walter J. *Orality and Literacy: The Technologizing of the Word.* New York: Methuen, 1982.

Oral Tradition. http://journal.oraltradition.org/.

Parker, D. C. *The Living Text of the Gospels.* Cambridge: Cambridge University Press, 1997.

Pelias, Ronald J. *Performance Studies: The Interpretation of Aesthetic Texts.* New York: St. Martin's, 1992.

Rhoads, David. "Performance Criticism: An Emerging Methodology in Second Temple Studies—Part I." *BTB* 36 (2006) 118–33.

———. "Performance Criticism: An Emerging Methodology in Second Temple Studies—Part II." *BTB* 36 (2006) 164–84.

Rhoads, David, et al. *Mark as Story: An Introduction to the Narrative of a Gospel.* 3rd ed. Minneapolis: Fortress, 2012.

Richards, E. Randolph. *Paul and First-Century Letter Writing: Secretaries, Composition, and Collection.* Downers Grove, IL: InterVarsity, 2004.

Rodriguez, Rafael. *Oral Tradition and the New Testament: A Guide for the Perplexed.* Guides for the Perplexed. London: Bloomsbury Academic, 2014.

———. *Structuring Early Christian Memory: Jesus in Tradition, Performance, and Text.* LNTS 407. European Studies on Christian Origins. London: T. & T. Clark, 2010.

Schweitzer, Albert. *The Quest of the Historical Jesus.* Translated by W. Montgomery et al. Minneapolis: Fortress, 2001.

Shiner, Whitney. *Proclaiming the Gospel: First-Century Performance of Mark.* Harrisburg, PA: Trinity, 2003.

Small, Penny Jocelyn. *Wax Tablets of the Mind: Cognitive Studies of Memory and Literacy in Classical Antiquity.* London: Routledge, 1997.

Thatcher, Tom, ed. *Jesus, the Voice, and the Text: Beyond "The Oral and the Written Gospel."* Waco, TX: Baylor University Press, 2008.

Ward, Richard F., and David J. Trobisch. *Bringing the Word to Life: Engaging the New Testament by Performing It.* Grand Rapids: Erdmans, 2013.

Weissenrieder, Annette, and Robert Coote, eds. *The Interface of Orality and Writing: Speaking, Seeing, Writing in the Shaping of New Genres.* WUNT 260. Tübingen: Mohr/Siebeck, 2010.

THOSE SITTING AROUND JESUS

Situating the Storyteller within Mark's Gospel

Philip Ruge-Jones

FOR ONE WHOLE SEMESTER A COMPANY OF FOURTEEN STU-
dents had memorized portions of the Gospel of Mark in order to perform
it. A few days after the public performance, the storytellers gathered in a
small room to tell each other our favorite stories. We were so close that
knee pressed upon neighbor's knee. Tommy told the story in which Jesus'
mother and brothers sent word to him that he was out of control and would
get himself in trouble. Tommy assumed the persona of Jesus, saying, "Who
are my mother and my brothers?" He shrugged and his eyes met the eyes
of each of his fellow learners in turn as words reinforced this engagement:
"And looking around at those seated about him in a circle, he said, 'Look,
here are my mother and my brothers!'" His sweeping gesture included each
member of our tiny community. And smiling at those who had journeyed
through a semester of struggles with him, Tommy brought forward Jesus'
words to us: "Because those who do God's will, they are my brother and sister and mother." Gathered together, listening to Tommy, we found ourselves
involved in the story.

Dimensions of Mark 3:31–34 come out in this encounter, which are absent—or at least muted—on the written page. As a silent reader, when I allow the scene to unfold in my mind's eye, I find myself looking down on the events, watching as if from above, and overhearing what happened for those gathered around Jesus. But as Tommy moved the text into a live performance, he also moved his listeners into the story world. The words Mark's Jesus had spoken to his followers in a room long ago echoed through time to become words spoken to us as brother, sister, and mother. This rhetoric of involvement—present in individual reading, but more directly and intensely present in performance—requires that the storyteller reflect on how to situate him- or herself within the narrative in order to support this audience inclusion. As a text that had its origins as a performance piece, the inherited script of Mark's Gospel must be negotiated in ways different from the methods we have learned from narrative criticism.[1] An effective way to help you imagine these distinctive dynamics is to invite you to step into the role of the storyteller and to ask you to engage an imaginary audience. (Assuming the role of the storyteller is the best way to understand what dynamic storytelling entails.) Therefore, throughout this chapter I will address you, the reader, as a willing storyteller whom I will direct into this role.

The Omnipresent Storyteller

Narration functions according to particular, identifiable dynamics when it is in the medium of oral storytelling. Unfortunately, beginning storytellers often import assumptions from literary studies about narrators and end up skewing their performance of texts.[2]

Within a performance understanding of Mark's Gospel, the storyteller is best understood as one of the characters moving within the story world. Since this character gets more stage time than any other, we must think through the location of the storyteller in order to understand this role. The stance of the storyteller will tell the audience where to take a stand in terms of the norms developed in the story. *Stance*, in this context, is a thick word implying responses to the following questions: Where do you as the storyteller stand in relation to the audience? In a world of competing interpretations of reality, where do you locate your position? In terms of each of the events that occurs in the narrative, where emotionally do you locate yourself? In

---

1. While many authors have maintained that Mark is a performance piece, the most extensive argument is found in Wire's *The Case for Mark Composed in Performance*.

2. I have devoted a whole chapter in another book to the conclusions I will only summarize here. See Ruge-Jones, "Omnipresent, Not Omniscient," 29–43.

terms of the characters who appear, with whom are you aligned, and against whom do you position yourself? In terms of the status and social locations of various characters who appear, where are you in relation to them? In terms of temporal dimensions of the story, how does a particular event you are performing relate to those that came before it or come after it? How does who you are as storyteller relate to the actual audience who stands before you? Finally, how will you use posture, gestures, and movement to convey the gospel? Our thick understanding of stance includes these spatial, ideological, emotional, temporal, relational, and physical dimensions.[3]

In the storyteller role, your job is to engage the audience at every point in the story. You have several tools available to assist you in this task. You report and sometimes embody the actions of the other characters. You also deliver the lines of all the characters who speak in the story. Unlike in literary works where the narrator cedes the stage to the other characters when they are quoted, in performance you as the storyteller are always present as the unique medium communicating all that happens in the course of a story, including the quotation of each character's lines.

The dimensions of this omnipresent role become quite clear when watching an experienced storyteller in the act of storytelling. But they also are apparent when you get together with a friend and tell her what just happened to you. While reporting the event, you never leave the presence of the friend (who is your audience) because then the story would come to a stop. Your friend hears you narrating what happened, but also sees you portray—at least at some level—the other people key to your story. You say,

> So Margo slammed the door obnoxiously, walked up to Angie, and said, "I don't like your attitude." And then Angie calmly responded, "Well, I don't much appreciate yours!"

In telling this story, you present Margo, and you present Angie. You mimic Margo's actions like her slamming the door. You deliver the lines of both Margo and Angie, and you speak the brief narratives that lead into their lines. You are there throughout the entire account, communicating all that happened and was said.

The same dynamic occurs in other kinds of storytelling. An example from within the Gospel of Mark makes the omnipresence of the storyteller clear. When Jesus told the parable of the Vineyard Owner (Mark 12:1–12), his audience knew that they were listening to Jesus even when they heard the

---

3. This list of different dimensions of stance was created through engagement with Yamasaki's *Perspective Criticism*. While I find his terminology for different dimensions of perspective helpful, my understanding of how each element is constructive in a narrative differs from his proposal.

tenants saying, "This is the heir; come, let us kill him, and the inheritance will be ours" (12:7). The audience knew that when they heard Jesus speak the tenants' lines, they were not hearing the tenants themselves but rather Jesus' portraying the tenants saying those words. The same dynamic is present when Jesus presents the vineyard owner's words: "They will respect my son" (12:6). Jesus tells the whole story, portraying what is happening and delivering the lines (what in a written text we might call direct speech) of each speaking character in turn. Jesus is ever present throughout the storytelling. He is an omnipresent narrator when telling this story.

This glimpse of Jesus telling that parable provides an analogy for how the Gospel's storyteller relates to the whole, more extensive narrative. If we expand the scope of our pericope slightly, we hear the storyteller's introduction to Jesus' storytelling is included: "And [Jesus] began to speak to them in parables" (12:1). Taking this single narrative step back from Jesus' parable, we see that Mark's storyteller is telling the story of Jesus, who is himself telling a story. That inner story includes Jesus presenting the lines of the tenants and the landowner. The storyteller negotiates and performs the whole telling. As we will see throughout this chapter, this radically directs the way multiple aspects of a performed story function; the omnipresent storyteller presides over the delivery of the entire narrative.

The Character of Mark's Storyteller

As you assume the role of storyteller in the Gospel of Mark, part of the stance that you unfold for your audience is your own character. In this role you assume the character of a faithful witness to the events associated with Jesus.[4] You tell the story in order to proclaim your character's confession regarding "the good announcement" or gospel that has come with "Jesus, the Christ, the Son of God" (Mark 1:1). While many interpreters have argued about whether this is a title introducing the prologue, or whether it speaks of the whole gospel proclamation, you know that in a storytelling medium the opening words serve a particular function in addition to these possibilities.

The first phrase uttered by any storyteller, and therefore the first one of Mark's account, establishes the initial, direct contact between the storyteller and the audience. In this moment, you speak in order to move your listeners out of everyday life into a story world. This first contact matters because it initiates the relationship between storyteller and audience. Mark's narrative

---

4. My use of the language of witness varies from that used by Bauckham in *Jesus and the Eyewitnesses*. I see the storyteller presented as a witness but recognize that this narrative strategy may not reflect historical actualities.

facilitates this transition with a soundscape that sets this story off from ordinary speech: Ἀρχὴ τοῦ εὐαγγελίου Ἰησοῦ Χριστοῦ υἱοῦ θεοῦ. The six repetitions of the οῦ sound creates a distinctive rhythm that is dominated by a
particular sound. The soundscape of this phrase functions like the hook of a
catchy bass line in a song. It syncs the listener to the storyteller's storytelling.
The introduction marks the boundary between normal, everyday speech
and that of the storytelling event; at the same time, the soundscape also
stands out from the rest of the narrative that follows. Thus the storyteller
stands within an orchestrated moment of liminality connecting with the
audience and guiding them into the story world.

What is more, the speaking of this first phrase does what it says. While
gospel conjures up notions of a literary genre for us, for those inventing this
new narrative form *gospel* still meant a "good announcement." Therefore
the words actually narrate what the storyteller is doing; he or she is beginning the announcement of the good news. This phrase carries out multiple
functions simultaneously. It syncs the storyteller-audience relationship; it
transitions the audience out of everyday life; it begins the announcing of the
good news; it points the audience toward Jesus, providing them essential
clues to his identity; and, it moves the synced and gathered audience into
the rest of the good announcement.

So who is the character that makes this good announcement? Whom
are you to become as you share this witness? At no point in Mark's Gospel
does the storyteller pause to share a personal resume. Neither masculine
nor female pronouns are ascribed to this character. No self-description in
any other form is explicitly offered. This allows for diverse people to play
the role of storyteller without awkward contradictions as long as they speak
as one giving witness to this good announcement. In addition to creating
openness to various faithful storytellers, this lack of focus on the storyteller's
identity also serves a testimonial function. By avoiding self-referential language, the recorded storyteller does not draw attention to him- or herself
but rather allows the good announcement of Jesus and of God's coming
reign to be central.

As I suggested earlier, while you clearly are omnipresent, you should
not assume that you are omniscient, as narrative critics sometimes do.[5] Your
character is well-informed about events that, within the conventions of the
story, have already transpired by the time you report them. You provide
accounts of what the other characters have done and said, and even some
commentary on the motivations that lie behind their actions. Often this last
element is referred to as "an inside view"; however, in performance you,

---

5. I find myself both agreeing and disagreeing with Rhoads et al., *Mark as Story*, 41.

as the storyteller, will often reveal the external clues that make public this inside view. You externally manifest the internal state of the character in your portrayal. So, for example, you report that Jesus was "moved by compassion" (Mark 1:41)[6] toward a leper, but compassion is not hidden away as a mystery in the soul of Jesus. Rather, it leaves clear traces upon his face and in his body language as you portray him. While the introspective consciousness of the modern world might describe this as an inside view, the understanding of emotions in the ancient world was bound to externals. One source from the same century as the Gospel of Mark celebrates the verbal art of a particular poet by stating, "Sappho, for instance, never fails to take the emotions incident to the passion of love from the symptoms that accompany it in real life. And wherein does she show her excellence? In the skill with which she selects and combines the most striking and intense of those symptoms."[7] Your success as storyteller will be to accomplish this same portrayal of external signs of a character's state that this commentator referred to as symptoms.

Authority within This Stance

Recognizing that the storyteller need not be omniscient to tell this story changes the understanding of how the authority of the storyteller is realized. Often in literary criticism the omniscient narration is understood to establish the authority of the narrator by providing the semblance of objectivity that makes the story feel true.[8] The adjective *omniscient* suggests that God's perspective is channeled through the narrator. However, the storyteller in the early Jesus movement established authority not by being above the audience in some position of assumed neutrality, but precisely by being with the audience and taking seriously their daily concerns and interests. This does not mean that the storyteller did not challenge the audience in very intense ways, but that the challenge offered through the storytelling occurred within terrains that were deeply important to the audience.

As a contemporary storyteller, you have a similar challenge. You will not connect with your audience in precisely the same ways that the storyteller recorded in the Gospel of Mark did. You are addressing a different audience for whom, for example, Galilee and Jerusalem have not been home. However, that you connect in at least small ways with the daily life of

---

6. Or "anger," depending on the textual variant one chooses. The externalizing dynamic described would be true regardless of the particular emotion.

7. Cited in Shiner, *Proclaiming the Gospel*, 62.

8. Rhoads et al., *Mark as Story*, 41.

your particular audience will be essential to the success of the storytelling. Storytelling in the first century or in the twenty-first requires establishing a trusting relationship between storyteller and audience, and one mechanism to establish this is taking seriously what matters to the audience.

Let me cite some examples of the kinds of connections that support this dynamic of storytelling for a contemporary audience. In the region of Texas where I live, there is an area referred to as "the hill country." It never fails to bring a smile to the audience when I say that "Jesus went up into the hill country to pray" (Mark 6:46). While the translation "mountain" would have worked in terms of the narrative flow, invoking this element of every-day Texas life into the story world draws the audience deeper into the story.

Or again, when telling the story of the mustard seed that becomes a large shrub I have developed the habit of saying "shrubbery" in the manner used in *Monty Python and the Holy Grail.* Many in the audience spontane-ously laugh at this odd conjunction of another story they love with the Jesus story. They do this at a moment in the Gospel when I believe Jesus was also going for a laugh by comparing God's reign to out-of-control weeds rather than to a magnificent, stately tree. So my *Monty Python* allusion re-creates something of the surprising moment that Jesus created. Yet it does this in a way that connects to my audience rather than to the ancient audience mem-bers, who never show up at my performances. The shrubbery moment's familiarity breeds contentment and strengthens the storyteller's connection with the actual audience.

Both the invocation of local vocabulary (hill country) and the brief, surprising moment of intertextuality (shrubbery) remind the audience that through this story God meets them in the stuff of their daily life, in their own Galilee and Jerusalem. The medium of storytelling strives toward this rhetoric of involvement. Where specifically you as storyteller orchestrate the interweaving of daily and storied life has flexibility, but interweave you must. These moments allow you as storyteller to bring the good news of God's gracious reign to the place where your audience dwells.

Directing the Cast of Characters

You as storyteller have various techniques to demonstrate the relationships between characters within the story. You become the stage for multiple per-spectives as they rub against each other in the narrative. You will need to preserve the distinctiveness of multiple characters' voices as you perform the story if you want your audience to follow what occurs. This interplay of voices communicates much that a solitary perspective could not get across to an audience. A story is not a creed. Its claims are made through the complex interplay of various voices that are given a place within the story.

Some of this variety is obvious, but not all are immediately apparent to us. While the contradictory perspectives held by Jesus and Pilate may be obvious, other stances are more subtly distinct. Narrative critic Elizabeth Struthers Malbon has made a provocative discovery that is very useful in performance. Using literary terminology, she has noted that the narrator in Mark speaks of Jesus as the Christ or Son of God and thus makes Jesus the center of the narrative. In contrast to this, the Markan Jesus in his speech and action deflects attention from himself, toward God. The Markan Jesus does not embrace the titles of Christ or Son of God. Again, using categories of literary analysis, Malbon writes,

> [These] tensions in a narrative need not be "resolved" at all. By means of the tension between the Markan narrator, who proclaims Jesus the "Christ, the Son of God" but mostly talks about Jesus, and the Markan Jesus, who proclaims the coming kingdom of God and the "Son of Humanity" and mostly talks about God, the Markan implied author offers the implied audience a powerful portrayal of one truly and obediently focused not on himself but on God.[9]

In performance, you speak directly to the audience in your storyteller persona, but then provide useful dramatic tension by embodying the speech of diverse characters whose perspectives may be at odds with that of the storyteller. In order to see this interplay more clearly, we turn now to the complexity of your stance as you portray multiple characters who speak and act within the story.

Your Stance While Portraying Other Characters in Speech

You as the storyteller portray the activity of other characters in a variety of ways. Sometimes you embody a character in their action; other times you report their activity as though it occurs offstage or at some other place within the room. Figuring out your stance (that is, where to locate yourself in relation to the unfolding events) can be challenging, so it is helpful to discover those places where the narrative *requires* specific location and then to work out the rest of your stance from those anchor points.

---

9. Malbon, *Mark's Jesus*, 255.

The clearest place where the dynamics of storytelling dictate the story-teller's narrative location is in the act of portraying characters as they speak their lines. With very rare exceptions, direct quotation demands the embodiment of the speaking character.[10] Unless one engages in ventriloquism, the voice that speaks a character's lines comes out of the storyteller, who is portraying the character. The storyteller must portray the words and accompanying external state of the speaking character to some degree.

As you map out your stances within a story's flow, the places where a character speaks provide the anchor points from which you lay out the rest of the narrating. Locating characters' lines actually takes care of this sense of your stance in a great portion of Mark's story since direct quotations are about 48 percent of the narrative. Breaking that 48 percent down even further, we see that the storyteller portrays Jesus speaking lines for a third of the total narrative. All other characters *combined* spend about half the time that Jesus does speaking lines. Through this disproportionate voicing of Jesus' words, the storyteller makes Jesus central to the story and provides ample opportunity for the audience to hear and see Jesus in his many expressions in order for the audience to bond with him. Having the audience listen to Jesus speak also structures a relationship like that of teacher to disciple between the character of Jesus and the actual audience members. Theologically, I would claim that these encounters are key moments when Jesus becomes incarnate and addresses the audience in, with, under, and through the storytelling; this will be addressed in depth later in the chapter.

The recorded storyteller could have structured the lines quoted within the narrative in another manner for different effect. For example, indirect quotations (that is, the reporting of speech without portraying its actual declaration) is at times used in Mark's Gospel. Indirect quotations convey similar information to that carried in direct quotations, yet conveying information is but one concern in storytelling. Characters who speak for themselves construct a particular communicative dynamic with the audience. For example, you as storyteller must become Jairus when he says to Jesus, "My little daughter is at the point of death. Come and lay hands on her so that she might be restored and live" (Mark 5:23). You demonstrate the *pathos* of the father bodily as you voice his plea. Hearing Jairus speak these words in the presence of the audience creates a direct connection with the man and his plight. The moment is quite different than if you had reported the request in an indirect way. Imagine yourself saying: *the father said to Jesus that his little daughter was at the point of death and begged him to lay hands on her so that*

---

10. The portrayals of the voice of God (1:11; 9:7) provide two exceptions to this general rule. I know of no other within the Gospel of Mark.

she might be restored and live. The information conveyed is the same, but the immediacy of the communication and much of its pathos are diminished by indirect quotation.

In the direct quotation, you orient the plea toward Jesus as you have placed him, but also toward the audience since a single storyteller cannot embody Jesus and Jairus simultaneously. Physics will not allow this.[11] The audience experiences the plea as though they were standing around Jesus and Jairus. What is more, this immediacy is magnified in your direct quotation because the audience watches it unfold in present-tense, real-time embodiment. The indirect indication of Jairus's plea that I posed above had to use past tense verbs: "*was* at the point of death" and "*begged* him." In direct quotation everything is more immediate ("My little daughter *is* at the point of death"), and the audience is not only told that he begged, but we see him in the act of begging as he says, "Come and lay hands on her so that she might be restored and live." The requirement of embodied portrayal allows the audience to be engaged as directly by the character of Jairus as possible. Direct quotations create a situation for more direct engagement between the distinct character whom the storyteller portrays and the audience.

Through moments like this one and the healings that follow, the audience becomes caught up in what Jesus is doing. They experience the reign of God that unfolds before them through the rhetoric of involvement. The whole first hour of the storytelling of this Gospel is designed to align the audience with Jesus and his announcement and demonstration that the reign of God is breaking in. Through empathy with various supplicants, the audience is drawn into the reign of God. They experience the solidarity of Jesus with those who are broken.

A Caveat

My use of some theater terms like *lines*, *direct*, and *offstage* is not meant to invoke every aspect of theatrical performance. The fact that the storyteller has to portray in an embodied way the diverse characters who have lines does not mean that the storyteller becomes the characters in the same way an actor does. While acting out this story with multiple actors might facilitate such identification, in a single-teller performance you will not become each of the characters as fully as an actor does. It is essential to remember

---

11. Richard Swanson has opted for finding out what a company of actors discover when improvising on a biblical text. His method has different goals than mine, but I find his approach helpful in preparation for storytelling, even if my goal is not to create such a multiple-actor performance. See Swanson, *Provoking the Gospel: Methods.*

that you are always the omnipresent storyteller even as you portray the various characters in the narrative.

The normative stance of the narrative that comes out of the storyteller's narrating shapes your portrayal of various characters' speech and actions. You never step outside the storyteller's commitment that "Jesus is the Christ, the Son of God," no matter whom you are portraying. Your challenge will be to portray each character's speech, actions, and accompanying physical states so that the audience recognizes that character's values, motivations, and emotions. Yet at the same time, you also embed the storyteller's response to what is portrayed; for example, you portray those who challenge Jesus about healing on the Sabbath even as you make clear that you as storyteller find yourself on Jesus' side.

This sounds like a very complex task, and at times it can be. However, if you first enter into and develop as fully as possible who you believe you are as the storyteller, and then also remember that you are omnipresent in the storytelling event, the rest flows quite naturally. As you tell the story of the Pharisees challenging Jesus' healing on the Sabbath, you are describing the moment, knowing that you as storyteller want to communicate the offense at what you describe, and that this requires a clear portrayal of their challenge to Jesus. Yet as storyteller you speak as one deeply grieved that they do not hear what Jesus says.

Let's return to the story of Margo I shared earlier:

> So Margo slammed the door obnoxiously, walked up to Angie, and said, "I don't like your attitude." And then Angie calmly responded, "Well, I don't much appreciate yours!"

Let us assume that your stance as the one telling the story is that Margo acted inappropriately. The adverbs already indicate this bias. Following that trajectory, you want the one listening to the account to understand how harsh Margo's words were. So you portray her words and what happened before them vividly. Maybe you even exaggerate them for effect. Yet, what happened is so insulting that at the same time as you portray actions and words, you find ways to communicate to your friend, "Can you believe Margo said that! That is so wrong!" Thus, your listeners know how you feel about Margo's words before they hear Angie's response. The end result you are going for as you share this account is to align your friend's perspective with your own stance about what had happened. In like manner, as you tell the Gospel of Mark, you tell the story in such a way that the audience might align their values with your stance as the storyteller.

As you can see, the need to embody a character in speech does not imply that you as storyteller fully identify in that moment with the speaker.

This is why it does not come across as appropriate when a storyteller takes on another character's speech—especially one whose point of view is dramatically different from that of the storytelling character—in actor mode rather than according the storytelling dynamic I have described. If you act out each character independent of the values of the storyteller, the narrative begins to feel disjointed by the radical mood shifts.

A Caveat to the Caveat

At this point, however, I need to invite you into yet one more level of complexity. Any perspectives present in the narrative that conflict with the storyteller's overall stance are voiced for a reason. The recorded storyteller was addressing through these other voices the continued questions of the gathered audience. Some interpreters see the other voices as opportunities the storyteller has created to distinguish the gathered community from other communities (for example, the Jesus followers from the Pharisees). However, I see the conflicts as embodiments of real, continued tensions that occurred *within* the early community that called itself by Jesus' name. Those in the Jesus movement continued to wonder about changes in dietary and Sabbath practices, about the nature of greatness, about how God could allow the temple to be destroyed, about the authority of the Human One to forgive sins, about divorce practices, about stances toward wealth and poverty, about how to respond to so-called sinners, about the role of children in the reign of God, and about the validity of a crucified messiah. These questions are given voice and taken seriously even as the storyteller invokes Jesus' presence to address them again.

This does not mean that you drain the story of conflict or portray everyone as well-intentioned. The point is to show that the conflict is real, and that legitimate, passionate concerns were aired on both sides of the conflict. In fact, showing the distinctive perspectives actually heightens the agonistic elements of the story. The sympathetic presentation of each character's struggle becomes the midwife to new life and transformation for the gathered community. If the goal of the narrative were to solidify Christian identity over and against the religious leadership, then the recorded storyteller would not have included episodes that portray religious leadership in a positive light, as do the story of Jairus, the story of the scribe not far from the reign of God, and the mentions of Joseph of Arimathea.[12] In all of these episodes, the recorded storyteller subverts any authorial project that could otherwise be construed as setting up a clear us/them relationship.

12. Rhoads et al., *Mark as Story*, 131.

Discovering this sympathetic portrayal in the early storytelling of this narrative is a challenge for us because in later contexts the story was forced into the service of us/them constructions. We know that this conscription of the text resulted in death and destruction for Jewish people. Yet we must not impose later history anachronistically back onto the original telling.

Contemporary Performance of the Caveats

In many cases contemporary audiences have moved on from the struggles of the early Jesus movement. Dietary laws and Sabbath practices do not seem to divide churches as they once did. Yet, your portrayal of these conflicts must be such that the contemporary audience, who does not have a stake in those struggles, senses that they were not about triviality, pettiness, or outright hypocrisy. The audience must understand that they were real, deep struggles like the conflicts that run through our own communities. In fact, undoubtedly individual members in the ancient context often felt divided *within* themselves about some of these issues. To portray these struggles trivially, dismissively, or stereotypically encourages the same banal drawing of battle lines today, whether in church or society. It also often reinforces the heinous Christian hatred of Jews that has soaked our history blood red.

Other issues that arise in Mark's story are not trivial today; they are perennial struggles for those seeking to follow Jesus. Are we ready to relinquish our possessions in order to care for the poor? Are we ready to abandon our own search for status? Are we really ready to drink the cup that Jesus came to drink? Are we ready to seek alternatives to violence when encountering our enemies? Do we see God do amazing things in our lives only to bury ourselves in fear a bit later when we encounter the same challenges afresh? Again in episodes related to these issues, vividly portraying the struggles of the characters introduces the possibility of transformation to contemporary listeners—a transformation that we will certainly need again and again. We identify with the characters as they struggle with what Jesus requires.

Bringing the Storyteller into Direct Quotations

We have just explored the complex portrayal of characters in the act of speaking lines, but this takes place within a larger narrative flow. Now I will suggest steps that will help in situating your stance within the flow of the narrative in general. Then we will explore one example in which I will flesh out the shifts within the storyteller's stance as I personally portray them. In order to reinforce that understanding, I will ask you to physically try out the stances I have mapped out as though you were the storyteller. And finally, we will explore the same performance from the audience's perspective.

In terms of interpreting the flow of the story throughout Mark's Gospel, I find it helpful to break any given text into sections with clear indications of even small narrative shifts. I create a visual representation of the relationship of components within a text. A shift within a scene marks a new section. A quotation of a character's lines usually brings one section to a close and sets up the beginning of another section even when that next section begins with Mark's additive "and." The story of Jesus and his family members that Tommy told, which I mentioned at the beginning of this chapter, would look like this:

> His mother and his brothers come, and standing outside,
>> they sent someone to him.
>
> And a crowd was sitting around him, and they say to him,
>> "Look, your mother and your brothers are outside seeking you."
>
> And answering them, he says,
>> "Who are my mother and my brothers?"
>
> And looking around at those seated about him in a circle, he says,
>> "Look, here are my mother and my brothers!
>> Because those who do God's will,
>> they are my brother and sister
>> and mother."

General Stance Dynamics in Mark

As I noted above, embodying characters when presenting lines addresses almost half of Mark's narrative. But what is the storyteller's stance within the rest of the story? A general pattern persists in the whole Gospel. Each direct quotation is preceded by a section that establishes who the speaker is before they speak. In its shortest form, the storyteller says, "And he said," followed by the character's lines. Other times the setup is rather extensive. During the prologue, John the Baptizer has one of the most elaborate setups (1:4–7). The man possessed by Legion also is introduced rather extensively (5:2–7). The storyteller also embodies the woman with the flow of blood before the audience overhears her speaking to herself (5:25–28).

The general rule for your preparation as a storyteller is to locate the place where you will present a character's lines and work your way backwards into the other part of the narrative. Find out how much of the episode before the lines functions to set up the character who eventually speaks. Most often the nominative place (either the subject or participles that modify the subject in an introductory clause) sets up the speaker. You as storyteller begin morphing into characters as you describe them or their activity. Sometimes you merely suggest their actions; at other times you move toward miming the actions; on still other occasions you *nearly* become them, albeit briefly, in the manner of an actor. In any case, you ease into showing or at least suggesting their external characterization as you move towards their lines. By the time you reach the quotation, you will have become the one who is speaking.

A crisp and clear division between the parts of the story where the storyteller narrates about a character and where the storyteller actually portrays a character does not exist. Rather, a transition takes place that is the storytelling equivalent of a movie crossfade. Even characters who do not speak are suggested along the way when they become the grammatical subject of a clause. When that connection is most intense, you yourself embody the character in a manner that is *similar* to an actor.

Often in this process a phenomenon occurs that parallels the musical dynamic of doubling. In music, *doubling* refers to a technique in a composition that requires two different instruments to simultaneously play either the same part or a musical line transposed at a consistent interval. (For example, a melody played on a violin is matched in a lower register by a doubling viola.) I wish to appropriate that term for storytelling dynamics by saying that there are times when a storyteller uses the instrument of the voice to say what is happening, while at the same time the storyteller uses the body to enact precisely what is being narrated in the third person. Doubling means that the storyteller as narrator explains what is happening to a character in the third person ("he bent down"), while becoming that character and doing what is reported (bending down). In times when the embodiment of the character is less intense and only suggested, we will refer to this as a muted doubling.

Let's observe these general dynamics as they occur in a particular story: the story of Jesus and his family.

His mother and his brothers come, and standing outside,
 they sent someone to him.

And a crowd was sitting around him, and they say to him,
 "Look, your mother and your brothers are outside seeking you."

And answering them, he says,
 "Who are my mother and my brothers?"

And looking around at those seated about him in a circle, he says,
"Look, here are my mother and my brothers!
Because those who do God's will,
they are my brother and sister
and mother."

In the first section of this story, no character has lines, although the Gospel composer could easily have provided the lines in a direct quotation: "His mother and brothers sent someone to him, saying, 'Tell Jesus we are outside.'" The quotation would have demanded from the storyteller a momentary full embodiment of either Jesus' mother or one of his brothers to represent the family; a more intense presentation of them to the audience would result. Instead, the content of the message is reported but not portrayed, so the storyteller will become the character in a more muted way than in the following three sections of the story, since each of the other three contains direct quoting of characters' lines. Let me describe how I would step into this text.

I would portray the opening of this story while taking a half step forward in order to suggest the movement of the characters, as I say, "His mother and brothers come," and then I would mutedly portray them, perhaps indicating by bringing a hand to my chest that I as storyteller have become them. Next, I would do a muted doubling of the words "they sent someone to him," gesturing to indicate that the family character is shooing one of their own in Jesus' direction. The historical present "come" provides an indication that a bit of vividness is called for, but the lack of direct quotation indicates that you as storyteller are suggesting the family members' actions rather than fully becoming the family members.

For the next three parts of this story, we will apply the principle of backing out from the direct quotations since each part of the story has a direct quotation. First we locate the lines spoken by a character. Three times we hear a character speak: first a representative of the crowd, then Jesus, and then Jesus again. Moving back from the lines spoken by the crowd's representative, we read that "a crowd was sitting around [Jesus]." I move into the quotation in this way: As I narrate the phrase above, I lean in as though I am a member of the crowd listening to Jesus. I continue, "and they say to him," as I place my hand on my chest to indicate that I am at this moment playing the role of a crowd member. Then, with a gesture, I move toward the teacher who sits in front of me. The use of a historical present "say" creates a sense of immediacy in what is said. I continue: "Look, your mother and your brothers are outside seeking you." I accompany these words with a gesture pointing toward the family members as I've located them. If they sent the messenger to Jesus from stage left, I point toward the place where they are located. I'm indicating the spatial relationship between the family's location and those seated in the house, but I'm doing this without even moving my feet between the muted portrayal of the family in the first section of the story and this section's portrayal of the crowd.

With this part completed, I scout out the next set of lines. The space in between the first quotation and the next one is where a crossfade occurs. In some manner, probably with body posture, I offer an indication to the audience that a new speaker, Jesus, will be the next one to address them. So, for example, the leaning-in posture I assumed as the crowd representative might smoothly shift toward a more erect posture for Jesus as I say, "And answering them, he says." Those seated before me see me move out of the first quotation (where I as a member of the crowd was leaning in and speaking to Jesus) and then move into becoming Jesus himself: upright, ready to speak. I am not suggesting that I have figured out the definitive stances that early storytellers used for these characters or the ones we must use today. I am claiming that in both the first and the twenty-first century, a storyteller found and will find ways to use the body to indicate character distinctions in order to communicate the narrative flow clearly to the audience.

Having brought Jesus forward in my embodiment, I speak as if I am Jesus. I glance to the left, toward where my family has been situated for the audience, and then shake my head. Then I look first directly in front of me where the established spatial relationship suggests that Jesus' questioner sits. I speak the quotation with the first few words to that person, and then as I finish the sentence, I speak as Jesus to the whole group I imagine sitting around him/me. So my eyes look to the left and right of where I indicated that the questioner is sitting.

Now that you have this much of the description, I would ask you to do an exercise that will make what I am saying more clear. I will give you the text we have just covered with brief stage directions reminding you of what we have just discussed. (Stand up. No, really. You. Stand up!) Speak out loud the biblical text and physically do the stage directions I give you:

His mother and his brothers come [*half step forward, hand to your chest*], and standing outside, they sent [*subtle shooing motion toward your right*] someone to him.

And a crowd was sitting around him, and [*lean forward*],
they [*hand to chest*] say to him,
"[*be the crowd member*] Look, [*point toward your left, talk to*

Jesus who is front of you, lean toward him]
your mother and your brothers are outside seeking you."

And [*execute the crossfade from leaning in to standing erect*]
answering them, he says [*look to the left toward your family and shake
your head. Start speaking to someone directly in front of you, and then
speak to the other members whom you imagine sitting around you*],
    "Who [*look first at your questioner in front of* you]
    are my [*look to left and right*] mother and my brothers?"

I realize that the last section of the story remains; we will return to that
shortly. Now I've described what I do as a storyteller and you have tried it
for yourself. So let's pass through the same material from your audience's
perspective.

- The audience sees you "come."

- The audience observes you suggesting the family and the message they
  sent to Jesus as the audience hears you narrate these activities.

- The audience sees someone shooed to the left toward the place where
  Jesus is as you simultaneously talk about that happening.

- The audience sees you facing them and hears you telling them about
  the crowd gathered even as the audience sees you become a member
  of the crowd.

- The audience sees you lean toward them and speak to Jesus as though
  Jesus were seated right in front of them, as though Jesus faces the same
  direction as the audience.

- The audience hears you as the character who reports the message sent
  to Jesus, speaking directly toward them, although the audience knows
  in this moment that the character you have assumed is addressing
  Jesus.

- The audience hears your words as they see you point to their right,
  where they know the family has been located.

- The audience senses you spin the imagined room 180 degrees as you
  say, "And answering them, he says." The audience intuits what is happening without deeply thinking about it as you morph from being the
  one conveying the message "your mother and brothers are outside"
  into the Jesus character suddenly facing them.

- The audience imagines that the messenger now sits in their front
  row as you face them as Jesus. The audience sees that your stance has

changed from leaning toward them to standing up straight. If this were a performance of the whole Gospel, the audience would already have seen the first twenty minutes of storytelling and would recognize your portrayal of Jesus when he returns once more to the stage.

- The audience sees Jesus glance to where his family has been situated to their right, and sees him shake his head. They see Jesus look at someone at the front and center and hear you speak Jesus' words. The audience member at whom you look feels like Jesus is first looking at and speaking to him or her.

- The audience hears Jesus ask the question, "Who are my mother and brothers?" as your eyes meet the eyes of those seated around Jesus. As that question is asked, the audience in fact, realizes that Jesus is and you are looking not at imagined characters but directly into their own eyes.

You should have a clear sense of the flow up to this point in the narrative. Now let's return to the story, analyzing the final section. Jesus' first lines in this story demonstrate an essential dynamic within this section—a dynamic repeated throughout Mark's narrative. As you look at your actual audience members, through the rhetoric of involvement they merge with the crowd within the narrative; they become "those seated around [Jesus]." The twenty-first-century people you are addressing as storyteller become a part of the story world itself. The question Jesus asks now addresses them: "Who are my mother and my brothers?" The followers in the narrative world who sat around Jesus merge with those in the present audience, who sit before the storyteller portraying Jesus. The historical present "says" (which introduces the quotation) facilitates the shift from past to present listeners. Having Jesus ask a question invites the audience into their own active reflection. They respond with an internal dialogue to the question with thoughts such as, "Aren't those people outside his family? Yet he seems to be setting us up for someone else to be his mother and brothers by asking the question. But whom?"

Thus the final section is cued. We scout ahead in the section and see that the next character to speak is again Jesus. In the structure of the sentence, he continues in the nominative position, so we know that you as storyteller will be identifying with Jesus and portraying Jesus while he speaks. In this way, the body posture remains the one you have led the audience to associate with Jesus. You double the narrative clause that introduces the final section; you describe Jesus' action and at the same time perform it: "And looking around at those seated about him in a circle." Your storyteller's eyes that are at the same time Jesus' eyes meet the eyes of your audience members as words and actions double to communicate what is happening through the instruments of your voice and your body. The narrative crowd remains merged with your present audience.

You make eye contact and a sweeping gesture which arcs across the gathered audience. It is as if Jesus has returned to address the present audience. They are not listening to what happened once upon a time, but now are participants in what is happening. The historical present again facilitates this liveliness: "he says, 'Look, here are my mother and my brothers! Because those who do God's will, they are my brother and sister and mother.'" You as storyteller have brought Jesus forward into the present in order to address those assembled, to affirm them, and also to call upon them to enact God's will. Something incarnational or sacramental has occurred in the midst of the telling. Jesus appears in, with, under, and through the proclamation. Through this rhetoric of involvement, those seated around you become those seated around Jesus as he speaks to them.

The Crucifixion of Jesus

The interpretation thus far has focused on the shape of the first two-thirds of the Gospel. The dynamics shift toward the end of the Gospel, not because the principles we have discussed no longer hold, but because they are carried out in a different narrative context than the earlier parts. The Passion Narrative deserves a chapter of its own, but I will briefly make suggestions about what occurs there in the context of this chapter.

In Mark 13, Jesus has his longest unbroken set of lines. For a whole chapter the storyteller abandons narration and speaks as Jesus. This stretch of speech is rivaled only by the Parables Discourse in Mark 4, but even there the storyteller interrupts Jesus' speech with regular comments like, "And he said to them," thus reminding the audience with frequency that the storyteller is telling us what Jesus said. In chapter 13, the storyteller becomes Jesus without interruption and places the audience in the intimate role of the four disciples who listen to him speak. With grief, Jesus compassionately addresses them, warning them of the trials that await them in the future.

In the next couple of chapters, Jesus speaks intimately to his disciples. Yet once he is brought to trial, his speaking nearly comes to a stop. If Jesus' lines dominated the first two-thirds of the narrative, his silence lurks in the ending. One time he responds to the high priest's interrogation, and once to Pilate's. Beyond those brief responses, Jesus does not speak; in fact, the storyteller comments on his surprising silence in each of these trials (Mark 14:61; 15:5). After his trials, Jesus only speaks once more, crying out, "My

God, my God, why have you abandoned me?" (15:34). If speaking indicates the need for embodiment, and Jesus is mostly silent, the storyteller only momentarily embodies Jesus in his trial and death. This nonembodiment is verified by grammar that moves Jesus out of the nominative place. He becomes the object of others' actions. The guidelines we discussed earlier for embodiment of characters suggest that the storyteller portrays all that is happening around Jesus, but does not portray Jesus himself for most of the Passion Narrative. The audience sees the storyteller, who sees what happens to Jesus. They see the agony on the face of one who believes that "Jesus is the Christ, the Son of God" as the storyteller describes what is happening to Jesus.

The success of this part of the story depends upon many things that have already transpired in Mark's telling of the story. The earlier part of the narrative facilitates bonding with Jesus so that the audience has been drawn into the reign of God. They have learned to trust the storyteller, who stands with them in their struggle and concerns. In the earlier part of the Gospel story, which we have already explored, the narrative generates a stance of excitement about Jesus and the rule he brings, as well as suspicion of those who resist Jesus. Unlike Mel Gibson's movie *The Passion of the Christ*, which does not portray Jesus' life and ministry, Mark's Passion Narrative needs the context of the life and ministry of Jesus in order to make sense. In a recent essay, David Rhoads, Joanna Dewey, and Donald Michie reverse Kähler's observation that Mark is a "passion narrative with an extended introduction." They astutely note it is actually a story about "the arrival of the reign of God with an extended dénouement."[13]

In the embodied performance of the Passion Narrative, the storyteller stands on the same ground as most of the other characters watching with us what happens to Jesus. The gaze of the audience is directed over and over again to the imaginative space above them, where Jesus hangs. The audience members themselves become spectators within the story world; they stand on the same ground as you, the storyteller, as you describe what you see. The rhetoric of involvement that results in the inclusion of the audience in the story world comes with the storytelling medium. In a film like Gibson's *The Passion of the Christ*, the camera zooms in on Jesus. Yet in storytelling, even as you focus the story on what happens to Jesus, you do not do this by portraying Jesus. Rather the audience members watch as you describe what you see, and they imagine what happens above them on the cross. You as storyteller are looking at the one hanging upon the cross, and describing what you see or enacting how others relate to him.

---

13. Rhoads et al., "Reflections," 277.

In the first two-thirds or more of the Gospel performance, Jesus has driven the story forward. He is the most prominent subject of sentences. Jesus comes and goes; he speaks; he commands; he calls; he teaches; he touches; he heals. His speech saturates the soundscape. But as he goes into his trial and execution, this is reversed. People testify against him; they condemn him to death; they beat him, they spit on him, they crucify him, and they mock him. Since the storytelling dynamic suggests portrayal of the characters in the nominative place, others take center stage and Jesus is pushed to the margin and up onto the cross. The voice that saturated the soundscape becomes silent except for a single shout of lamentation.

Why does this matter? In the crucifixion account, while Jesus is the center of attention, what is presented is not Jesus but rather people seeing Jesus' crucifixion. Unlike Gibson's film and others in the crucifixion genre that are almost pornographic in their portrayal of violence, Mark's Gospel portrays the Crucified One in a direct way during only two brief moments when he becomes the subject of sentences. First, when "he cried out a loud cry," we actually hear that cry. Since speech requires embodiment, here you must portray him. Then the other moment is when "Jesus let out a loud cry and died." Again, the structure suggests embodiment, although the absence of the actual cry in the narrative, combined with the inherent passivity of that final verb ("died"), suggests a muted portrayal of what happens.

The result of this way of recounting the crucifixion is that the execution of Jesus is left largely to the imagination of the audience. I suspect the original audience unfortunately knew well Roman violence and probably even this particular form of Roman violence in the wake of the recent Jewish-Roman war so that imagining someone crucified was painfully easy for them. Their own experience of imperial violence filled in the gaps left in Mark's portrayal of Jesus' execution. Therefore, a fusion of the horizons of their own recent experiences of violence with the violence against Jesus occurs. In fact, this is facilitated by the repetition of Jesus' sole line. First his sense of abandonment is expressed in Aramaic; the different language makes the cry stand out from the rest of soundscape. In this moment the storyteller becomes Jesus, searching the heavens, coming up empty, and throwing his accusing words heavenward. But then you speak the same words as the storyteller, translating and explaining them to the audience. The quotation from Jesus is repeated in translation, but this time it is spoken in the storyteller's own voice. The storyteller looks not heavenward but toward the audience, offering a clarification. But even as, on one level, you are translating the words of Jesus, on another level, you repeat Jesus' question, but this time as the storyteller, in grief. Jesus' question becomes yours: "My God, my God, why have you abandoned me?" And in the wake of the

Jewish-Roman War, you ask this question on behalf of the audience. Jesus' question, becomes your question, which voices that question asked by the whole community. In a very experiential way, Jesus voices the lamentation as he hangs in the place of the grieving people.

In light of this observation, I would like to reframe the comment by Rhoads, Dewey, and Michie that I cited above—that the Gospel is about "the arrival of the reign of God with an extended dénouement."[14] In a strange way, through the storytelling of the passion, the dénouement is for the audience an experiential recapitulation of the first part of the story. In the wake of the Jewish-Roman War, the witness to Jesus' execution was a way for the early audience to experience the solidarity of Jesus as he hangs with them in their people's plight and suffering, just a they had experienced Jesus with the suffering supplicants who appeared in the first half of the narrative.

In suffering with the audience, Jesus provides some measure of healing solidarity. The witness to the crucifixion of Jesus thus becomes a crucible that holds a crucified people's grief together with the hope generated by the coming of God's reign. The telling of Jesus' crucifixion experientially leads to a sense of solidarity between Jesus and the imperially occupied audience members. This solidarity is experienced as a recapitulation of the narrative solidarity of Jesus with the broken people in the first sections of the Gospel.

This work of connecting takes place in a dense swirl of opposing dynamics, as I suggested earlier in this chapter. The storyteller has to embody the characters who mock Jesus. Yet the storyteller does not take them on in the same way as an actor does with a character. In your performance, you as storyteller do not fully become the detractors. Your portrayal of them, rather, is framed and mediated by the narrative stance you have established in the storytelling of the Gospel. Even as you enact the mocking of Jesus, you do not step outside the commitment as storyteller that Jesus is the Anointed One, the Son of God. You must portray the speech, actions, and postures of the detractors so that the audience recognizes that character group's values, motivations, and emotions, while at the same time you surround that portrayal with your response to what is portrayed. When those around Jesus are taunting him, you must portray their mocking, their relishing this moment, their contempt, while at the same time conveying the appraisal of this from the storyteller's perspective. You must show both their mocking and the pain their mocking causes you; you must show how much they are enjoying this moment of triumph even as it causes you anguish. This is what makes the narrative so complex in storytelling. You must show your contempt of their contempt during the performance of their contempt.

14. Ibid.

Finally, I'd like to repeat a level of complexity that I mentioned earlier. Any voices present in the narrative that conflict with the narrator's overall stance are there for a reason. The recorded storyteller was addressing through these other voices the continued questions of Mark's gathered community. While this may seem feasible when looking at the objections of the religious leaders about Sabbath or dietary practices, I believe it is even true for those contrary voices that speak in the crucifixion account. Those followers of Jesus in the early audiences continued to wonder about the validity of a crucified messiah. Their deep and troubling perplexity is given voice and taken seriously in the story through the voices of those who mock Jesus. This taunting at the crucifixion was obviously told with immense repulsion and grief. Yet it gave voice to the real shock that what happened to Jesus could actually occur to God's Anointed One. Those of us who know the story too well often forget the incomprehensible shock that Jesus' execution caused his original followers. The contemporary storyteller has the task of reminding people today of this scandal. I am asking you to portray simultaneously mockery of Jesus, your narrative disgust at that mockery, and the community's understanding that the mockery is not entirely unintelligible. So just as the crucifixion narrative became an embodied way to experience Jesus' solidarity with those in the audience who know suffering, so also the complex narration of his execution becomes a means for holding in tension the disparate elements inherent in this event (even for Jesus' followers). The story holds together the mysteries that the ancient audiences, and perhaps even our own, seek to penetrate, without providing a false and easy resolution.

Conclusions

Several dynamics have surfaced in the analysis of the performance of this story that show how the media dynamics that demand consideration are distinctive from the set of dynamics that narrative criticism considers. Let's review the elements that we have observed as a storyteller is situated within the narrative before a live audience. The storyteller never leaves the stage. He or she becomes various characters to lesser or greater degrees, based upon clues within the text. By the time a direct quotation is deployed, the storyteller has morphed into the speaking character and assumes the speaker's identity. Narrative moments leading up to a quotation move the storyteller into the character who eventually speaks. When no quotation anchors an episode, the actions of the character in the nominative are generally indicated, and those actions are often doubled with third-person narrative accompanied by muted or strong embodiment of the actions narrated. At key moments the real audience members become characters within the narrative, usually as Jesus addresses them. This dissolving of the world of the text into the world in front of the text is a fundamental dynamic of the Gospel narrative. Silent reading of a text also may draw a reader into a story to identify with characters, but in performance the physical embodiment of the story by design sets up the opportunity for this dissolving of worlds into each other to happen even more intensely. We also have found that grammatical structure helps us to understand what is put forward in the telling of the story. The narrative shifts at the end of the story so that Jesus no longer drives the action, but becomes the object of violence. Yet this creates a space where the audience who has known imperial violence can also experience the solidarity of Jesus as the reality of such violence is taken seriously.

I have shown you some of the skeletal structure of the narrative and have also introduced you to some of its complexity. If nothing else, I hope you realize how much is going on in a performance that is missed in the silent reading of the text. As we engage this material with greater and greater care, other dynamics like those uncovered here will become apparent to us, and our reconstruction of past performances will gain depth. I invite you to explore the text through performance of it. You are ready to enter into the narrative, make your own discoveries, and bring it in a creative and lively form to the audience. Where you find my observations are useful, run with them; where they hinder your own storytelling, feel free to modify them. For one trait that must come across in your portrayal of the character of the storyteller is authenticity. So make the recorded storyteller's story your story, a gift offered to a living audience. Trust the narrative and let it lead you toward engagement

Bibliography

Bauckham, Richard. *Jesus and the Eyewitnesses: The Gospels as Eyewitness Testimony.* Grand Rapids: Eerdmans, 2006.

Malbon, Elizabeth Struthers. *Mark's Jesus: Characterization as Narrative Christology.* Waco, TX: Baylor University Press, 2009.

Rhoads, David, et al. *Mark as Story: An Introduction to the Narrative of a Gospel.* 3rd ed. Minneapolis: Fortress, 2012.

————. "Reflections." In *Mark as Story: Retrospect and Prospect*, edited by Kelly R. Iverson and Christopher W. Skinner, 261–82. SBLRBS 65. Atlanta: Society of Biblical Literature, 2011.

Ruge-Jones, Philip. "Omnipresent, Not Omniscient: How Literary Interpretation Confuses the Storyteller's Narrating." In *Between Author and Audience in Mark: Narration, Characterization, Interpretation*, edited by Elizabeth Struthers Malbon, 29–43. New Testament Monographs 23. Sheffield: Sheffield Phoenix, 2009.

Shiner, Whitney. *Proclaiming the Gospel: First-Century Performance of Mark.* Harrisburg, PA: Trinity, 2003.

Swanson, Richard W. *Provoking the Gospel: Methods to Embody Biblical Storytelling through Drama.* Cleveland: Pilgrim, 2004.

Wire, Antoinette Clark. *The Case for Mark Composed in Performance.* BPCS 3. Eugene, OR: Cascade Books, 2011.

Yamasaki, Gary. *Perspective Criticism: Point of View and Evaluation.* Eugene, OR: Cascade Books, 2012.

3

CHARACTERS IN TEXT AND PERFORMANCE

The Gospel of John

Holly E. Hearon

WHEN I ASK STUDENTS TO NAME THE CHARACTERS THAT AP-
pear in any one of the four canonical Gospels, I am usually greeted by silence, followed by "Jesus" and the names of one or two apostles. I then ask
them to keep a list of all the different characters who appear in a Gospel
narrative. It quickly becomes apparent that each of the Gospels is richly
peopled, producing a cast that would rival any of Shakespeare's historical
plays. Indeed, it can be argued that characters are what drive the narratives
of the Gospels.

The Distinctiveness of Characterization in the Fourth Gospel

When the canonical Gospels are considered, the characters in the Fourth
Gospel stand out. This is in part because of the several characters who
engage in sustained and sometimes complex conversations with Jesus, giving them a high level of visibility and individuation. Yet there is more: the

presentation of characters in the Fourth Gospel includes elements that are suggestive of a stage production or drama.[1]

This becomes readily apparent when comparing John's account of the feeding of the five thousand with versions of the story narrated in the other Gospels. For example, Matthew and Mark say that Jesus "saw a great crowd" (Matt 14:14; Mark 6:34); John, in effect, says the same thing, but in a way that incorporates dramatic action. Thus, "saw a great crowd" becomes "then lifting up his eyes and seeing that a great crowd is coming towards him" (6:5).[2] John continues to "direct" the actions of the characters as the story unfolds. The narrator says Jesus gave to those reclining bread and fish "as much as they were desiring [imperfect tense, suggesting ongoing action] and when they were satisfied, he is saying [historical present] to his disciples, be gathering [present imperative emphasizing ongoing action] the remaining pieces in order that nothing be lost" (6:11–12).[3] The use of the present and imperfect tenses emphasizes the *action* being carried out by the characters, while the phrases "as much as they were desiring" and "in order that nothing be lost" describe *how* they are carried out (i.e., the level of intensity in the actions). The scene is closed out by Jesus' withdrawing; his motivation for this action is his perception that the crowd wants to seize hold of him (ἁρπάζειν αὐτόν) in order to make him king (6:15). Embedded in this perception is an implied action on the part of the crowd; thus Jesus' withdrawal is paired with the (presumed) movement of the crowd towards him. In the other Gospels, the episode is brought to a close with the disciples gathering the remnants (i.e., in midaction). John's attention to the characters' actions not only describes but also enacts the scene.

In addition, John tends to populate the stage with many characters by individuating characters within groups. In the other Gospels, the disciples function in this scene as a character group, speaking en masse; John individuates the disciples by assigning lines to Philip and Andrew: "Philip

---

1. See the recent study by Jo-Ann A. Brant in her book *Dialogue and Drama*.

2. All translations of the Greek are my own. Here I draw attention to John's use of the historical (dramatic) present by translating it as a present tense, giving the story a "you are there" quality. Daniel B. Wallace describes it as "preeminently the storyteller's tool" and notes that, of all the Gospels, it occurs most often in John: 162 times (*Greek Grammar Beyond the Basics*, 528). This is an example of the many observations that can be made only on the basis of the Greek text; they are often masked in translation.

3. The verb ἀπόλλυμι ("be lost" v. 12]) occurs elsewhere in the gospel consistently in contexts that speak to the saving role of Jesus (e.g., "This was to fulfill the word that he had spoken, 'I did not lose a single one of those whom you gave me'" [18:9; see also 3:16; 6:27, 39; 10:10, 28; 11:50; 12:25; 17:12]). Thus, it serves a theological function within the narrative world of the gospel. Nonetheless, it also functions as a performance cue within this narrative.

answered him, 'Two hundred denarii of bread would not be enough for them each to receive a small amount.' One of his disciples, Andrew, the brother of Simon Peter, said, 'A boy child is here who has five barley loaves and two fish, but what are these things among so many?'" (6:7–8). These lines spoken by the two disciples reveal additional characters on stage, introducing a boy child who has sufficient food to feed himself but not the many, and calling attention to the individuals who make up the crowd ("enough for *each of them* to receive a small amount"). Whereas the narrative space in the other Gospels is inhabited by Jesus and two character groups (the disciples and the crowd), in John, there are four individuals (Jesus, Philip, Andrew, the boy) in addition to two character groups: the "disciples" (vv. 12–13) and the "crowd." The narrative stage (so to speak) in the Fourth Gospel is very crowded; from a dramatic perspective, this makes the stage a complex space and invites careful attention to the actions of and interactions between characters.

This extended illustration demonstrates that there is a distinctly dramatic thread woven into the narrative of the Fourth Gospel. Indeed, Jo-Anne Brant observes that "speaking of the Fourth Gospel as drama has become a habit for Johannine scholars."[4] Yet it is not a drama in the sense of actually being a play; it is without doubt a narrative, albeit a complex one. It is this complex nature of the narrative that I want to engage here by comparing and contrasting narrative and performance criticism as applied to character in the Fourth Gospel.

Characters in Narrative and Performance

Before proceeding, a few introductory words about narrative and performance criticism are in order.[5] (More will be said about each below.) Both engage the text in its final form and focus on the world within the text.[6] This "world within the text" is always a contrived world: that is, it is a construction of the implied author.[7] Yet "contrived" does not mean arbitrary; to the contrary, it is contrived in order to bring into sharp focus particular

4. Brant, *Dialogue and Drama,* 4.

5. For "performance criticism" I am drawing primarily on the work of Rhoads, "Biblical Performance Criticism," 157–98; Rhoads, "Performance Criticism: An Emerging Methodology," 118–33, 164–84.

6. Although what is presented in the text may sometimes need to be situated within its historical, social, or cultural context.

7. This is not to say that the "world within the text" necessarily bears no connection to a historical world. In the case of the Gospels, the distance between the implied author and the real author is assumed to be very small.

dimensions of that world and so present characters with particular questions, problems or tensions to be resolved. As a construct of the implied author, this "world within the text" is also shaped by the point of view of the implied author. This point of view evaluates some actions or decisions as better than others.

The characters who inhabit this world are also contrived; that is, they are a construction of the implied author. In both narrative and performance criticisms, the interpreter gains access to a character through an examination of direct evidence (what is specifically said about a character in the text) and indirect evidence (what can be inferred from a character's actions, interactions, associations, context and so forth).[8] The choices (questions, problems, or tensions) with which characters are confronted in the "world within the text" are created by the implied author, and it is this author who both determines and describes how each character responds to the choices presented. As will be shown, these responses are not necessarily simple or transparent. They are, however, limited by the parameters of the "world within the text" and the point of view of the implied author.

Because they are contrived, the "world within the text" and the characters who inhabit it are incomplete: that is, there are things left unsaid, presenting the interpreter with "gaps" and unanswered questions. In order to make sense of the characters and their world, the interpreter must attempt to fill in these gaps.[9] Both narrative and performance critics do this: in part by appealing to references in (the evidence of) the text; in part by filtering this material (consciously or unconsciously) through their own experiences, assumptions, values, and commitments—a process that actively engages the imagination. The result is a little like putting together a puzzle where the pieces can be aligned in different ways to create different pictures: this way a rooster, that way a frog. Which picture is constructed is determined by the interpreter working in league with the point of view of the implied author.[10] There is no single correct picture; there are only more compelling ones.

In the Fourth Gospel, the narrative world is constructed around an existential question: Will humankind recognize the one who makes God known and respond positively to this life-giving presence in the world?[11]

---

8. See Powell, *What Is Narrative Criticism?*, 52–54; Resseguie, *Narrative Criticism*, 121–22, 126–27, 130–32.

9. Burnett, "Characterization and the Reader Construction," 16.

10. The interpreter may resist the point of view of the implied author and even work against it. This, however, introduces additional critical tools and perspectives (e.g., deconstructionism, ideological criticism). Here, I understand that both the narrative and performance critic assent to the "world within the text" for the purposes of the task.

11. Scholars express this variously. Some place the emphasis on Jesus as revelation:

From the point of view of the implied author, this question has life-and-death consequences, filling the narrative world of the Gospel with intense conflict. This places the various characters in situations where they have to make choices with respect to the one who makes God known, that is, Jesus. Sometimes these choices are made on the spot. At other times, the choices emerge over a period of time (long or short) as characters interact with each other, Jesus, and their world.

Limitations of space preclude consideration of the many characters that appear in the Fourth Gospel. Because of the rich complexity of this Gospel, I have chosen to focus on a single character: Nicodemus. A variety of interpretations of Nicodemus's character are to be found, making him a particularly interesting character to explore from the perspectives of both narrative and performance criticisms.[12] Further, because he crosses paths with a number of other characters in the course of the Gospel, analysis of Nicodemus requires giving at least passing attention to these characters as well. In choosing depth over breadth, my hope is to give readers a sense of *how* each methodology works, *what is to be gained* from each approach, and how the two, at many points, *complement* each other.

Character Analysis in Narrative Criticism

From the perspective of narrative criticism, Nicodemus is a character in a written text. Readers encounter Nicodemus entirely through written words: the words of the narrator, who tells the reader about the character Nicodemus (who he is, what he does, how other characters respond to him); the words spoken by Nicodemus in the story; and the words spoken by other characters about Nicodemus or directly to him. The narrative critic, as a reader, engages in an analysis of the written text with respect to what it tells (by direct evidence) or shows (by indirect evidence) about Nicodemus.[13] If a narrative critic sees a pattern of persistent qualities exhibited in what

---

Schneiders, *Written That You May Believe*, 49; and Culpepper, *Anatomy*, 46–89. Warren Carter emphasizes how characters respond to this revelation (*John: Storyteller, Interpreter, Evangelist*, 25). Wayne Meeks focuses on the question of whether followers attain perfect faith in Jesus ("Man from Heaven," 54). Craig Koester sees the critical question revolving around humankind's estrangement from God (*Symbolism in the Fourth Gospel*, 287–99).

12. A summary of perspectives on Nicodemus in recent studies can be found in Hakola, "Burden of Ambiguity," 439–43. I regret that this chapter was completed before I was able to access the study edited by Skinner, *Characters and Characterization in the Gospel of John*.

13. Powell, *What Is Narrative Criticism?*, 52–54; Resseguie, *Narrative Criticism*, 121–22, 126–27, 130–32.

Nicodemus does and says, s/he may assign him character traits.[14] Alternatively, the narrative critic may focus on what happens to Nicodemus during exchanges with other characters in which a decision or response of some kind is required ("interindividuation").[15] At each step, the narrative critic is likely to encounter gaps to be filled, a process that engages both textual evidence and the imagination of the interpreter.[16] The goal of a narrative-critical analysis of character is to help readers of the Fourth Gospel gain knowledge of and insight into how the character Nicodemus functions within the world of the written text.[17]

Nicodemus appears three times in the course of the narrative: 3:1–10; 7:45–52; and 19:38–42. The first time Nicodemus is introduced the narrator tells readers three things about him: that he is a Pharisee, that he is a leader of the Jews, and that he came to Jesus at night (3:1). The first two statements locate Nicodemus within three other groups in the narrative world of the Gospel: Pharisees, leaders, and Jews. This not only provides information about him but also invites comparisons between Nicodemus and other members of these groups.

Nicodemus is the only Pharisee who is identified as an individual. As a group, the Pharisees are portrayed nearly consistently in opposition to Jesus. In 4:1, when Jesus learns that the Pharisees have heard of the success of his activity in Judea, he withdraws to Galilee (cf. 7:1). The Pharisees question the validity of Jesus' words (7:48; 8:13; 9:40) and are actively involved in efforts to arrest Jesus (7:32, 45, 47; 11:47; 18:3). Their opposition to Jesus is so strong that the narrator says even the religious leaders feared them (12:42). Yet the implied author introduces a crack in this construct. In 9:16 the Pharisees are described as divided: is Jesus a sinner because he does not observe the Sabbath, or from God since he performs signs?

This division has been anticipated in 7:45–52. Here the chief priests and Pharisees chastise the temple police for their failure to arrest Jesus. When the temple police respond, "Never has a person spoken like this!" (7:46), the Pharisees counter with a rhetorical question, "Has any one of the leaders or of the Pharisees believed in him?" (7:48), then dismissively declare that the crowds who are so taken with Jesus are ignorant of the

14. Chatman, *Story and Discourse*, 125.

15. McCracken, "Character in the Boundary," 30–33, 36–37. See also Conway, *Men and Women in the Fourth Gospel*, 57.

16. Burnett, "Characterization and Reader Construction," 16.

17. Powell, *What Is Narrative Criticism?*, 52. Rhoads, "Biblical Performance Criticism," 178. This brief summary, admittedly, fails to engage the many and varied theoretical issues that surround discussions of character. It is intended only as a description of basic practices.

law (7:49). Nicodemus, described here as having earlier gone to Jesus and also as "one of them" (i.e., a Pharisee as well as an "authority"), represents a second dissident voice in this gathering by raising a rhetorical question: "Our law does not judge a person unless it first hears from him and knows what he is doing, does it?" (7:50–51).[18] The description of Nicodemus is to the point: like the temple police and the crowds, he has seen and heard Jesus (the Pharisees, as yet, have only heard *about* Jesus [4:1; 7:32]); yet as a Pharisee, he is not ignorant of the law, as the crowds are said to be. The force of his rhetorical question places the other Pharisees on the defensive and elicits a rebuttal: "Surely *you* (emphatic σύ) are not also from Galilee, are you? Search [the law] and you will see that no prophet is to arise from Galilee" (7:52).[19] This challenge to Nicodemus's ethnic allegiance suggests that in the eyes of some he is moving dangerously close to the boundary between insider and outsider.[20] An earlier verse in this scene now appears to be ironic (7:48): perhaps there is one among the leaders and the Pharisees who does believe, or who is at least willing to give consideration to what Jesus says and does.[21] Yet precisely where Nicodemus's allegiance does reside remains ambiguous; he has raised a question on a point of law. This speaks to the process rather than the person (Jesus). Thus, while this scene reveals aspects of Nicodemus's character (he identifies as a Pharisee and a Judean, but is willing to differentiate himself from the group; he values both law and process), it also leaves a gap in terms of his relationship to Jesus.

Nicodemus is also identified as a "leader" (ἄρχων). The word for "leaders" (ἄρχοντες) occurs only a few times (3:1; 7:26, 48; 12:42),[22] but leaders clearly represent a group distinct from the Pharisees (7:48; 12:42). The very first use of this word is in 3:1, where Nicodemus is identified as a "leader of the Jews." Thus Nicodemus serves as the reference point for each subsequent use of this word. In chapter 7, Jesus goes up to Jerusalem during the Festival of Booths and is teaching in the temple. When he is not arrested, the crowds wonder, "Can it be that the leaders (ἄρχοντες) truly know that

---

18. Nicodemus's words, suggests Jouette Bassler, "unveil the hypocrisy of the Pharisees, who rebuke the crowd for their ignorance of the law (v. 49) yet fail to follow it themselves" (Bassler, "Mixed Signals," 640).

19. The NRSV reverses these lines; I follow the order in the Greek text.

20. On ethnic identity see Bassler, "Galileans," 243–56.

21. Bassler, "Mixed Signals," 640; Duke, *Irony in the Fourth Gospel*, 80–81; Michaels, *The Gospel of John*, 473.

22. The Greek word ἄρχων occurs in three additional texts where it is translated "ruler" (NRSV) and refers to "the ruler of this world," who is condemned and driven out (12:31; 14:30; 16:11).

this is the Messiah?" (7:26).[23] A few verses later the Pharisees ask (rhetorically), "Has any one of the leaders (ἄρχοντες) or of the Pharisees believed in him?" (7:48). Both questions receive an answer when the narrator reports, "Nevertheless, many, even of the leaders (ἄρχοντες), believed in him. But because of the Pharisees they did not confess it, lest they be put out of the synagogue" (12:42). Leaders, then, are shown to be a group divided; yet whereas the Pharisees never move beyond the point of debate (9:16), "many" of the leaders are said to cross over and believe in Jesus. This raises a question with respect to Nicodemus: he is identified as both a Pharisee *and* as a leader of the Jews; with which group does he align himself? From a narrative perspective, it is possible to read these few references to "leaders" as speaking directly to the characterization of Nicodemus. Precisely what is to be inferred, however, is not direct at all. Is Nicodemus among the authorities who believe in Jesus?

Nicodemus is identified, specifically, as a leader of "the Jews." This language is fraught with difficulties, not least, as Warren Carter points out, because almost all of the characters in the Gospel are Jews.[24] It is important to note the multiple contexts in which the phrase "the Jews" occurs. For example, Jesus says to the Samaritan woman, "salvation is from the Jews" (4:22). Many times the phrase is used in reference to festivals celebrated by the Jews or in reference to other distinctive practices, such as purification rites or burial customs (2:6, 13; 3:25; 5:1; 6:4; 7:2; 11:55; 19:40, 42). Some references appear to be neutral, indicating either curiosity or confusion but not necessarily animosity (1:19; 7:35; 8:22; 10:24; 12:9; 13:33; 18:20). A few are unquestionably positive from the point of view of the implied author (11:19, 31, 33, 36). In addition, "Jews" are, on three occasions, said to believe in Jesus (8:31; 11:45; 12:11) and once are described as divided in their response to Jesus (10:19). Most of the time, however, "the Jews" are disputing a teaching or action of Jesus (2:18, 20; 5:10, 15; 6:41, 52; 7:15; 8:48, 52, 57; 9:18; 19:31) or are actively engaged in persecuting Jesus, ultimately militating for his death (5:16, 18; 7:1, 11; 10:31, 33; 11:8, 54; 18:12, 14, 31, 36, 38; 19:7, 12; cf. 18:33, 35, 39; 19:3, 14, 19–21).[25] Carter suggests

23. It is possible that here the word refers to religious leaders generally, although in 7:45–52 the authorities and Pharisees are clearly distinguished.

24. Carter, *John: Storyteller, Interpreter, Evangelist*, 67.

25. Any complete analysis of the character group "the Jews" would need to examine what other characters, in particular Jesus, say about the Jews; this material compounds the negative presentation of "the Jews" exponentially, especially since Jesus is aligned with the ideological perspective of the implied author. On John and anti-Judaism see Rensberger, "Anti-Judaism and the Gospel of John," along with responses by Goodwin and Lea in Farmer, *Anti-Judaism and the Gospels*, 120–57; also Reinhartz, "Gospel of John: How the 'Jews' Became Part of the Plot," 99–116.

that the statement in 1:19 ("when the Jews sent priests and Levites from Jerusalem to ask him, 'Who are you?'") indicates that "the Jews" must refer to a distinctive group, rather than Jews in general, since John the Baptist is himself a Jew; further, since "the Jews" have the authority to send priests and Levites to John, they are people with power who are likely associated with the temple.[26] Thus, Carter reads the language of "the Jews" as a reference primarily to the religious leaders in Jerusalem.[27] Alternatively, Robert Kysar sees "the Jews" as a literary foil, representing "stylized types of those who reject Christ."[28]

Where do we locate Nicodemus in this complex picture? At a neutral level, he is among those who participate in the Jewish festivals and other religious practices. And he is a Jew who, like Nathanael (1:47), "comes" (ἔρχομαι) to Jesus (3:2)[29] and, like the crowds, has seen and heard Jesus. Nicodemus, however, is identified specifically as a "leader *of the Jews*." This is unlikely to mean that he is a leader of the religious leaders in Jerusalem; that role falls to the high priest (as indicated in the Passion Narrative [18:12–14]).[30] Is he, then, a leader among the religious leaders in Jerusalem? Or is he a leader of the Jews represented by various ordinary individuals as well as the crowds? There is a large gap in the narrative on this point. What is striking is that Nicodemus is presented as embodying all three character groups: Pharisees, leaders, Jews. Yet each of these groups, over the course of the narrative, exhibits different responses to Jesus. This makes Nicodemus a complex character indeed.

In addition to locating Nicodemus in these three groups, the narrator says that Nicodemus came to Jesus at night (3:2). This is the first time that the word "night" occurs in the Gospel. It will be used to identify Nicodemus

---

26. Carter, *John: Storyteller, Interpreter, Evangelist,* 68. Carter (ibid.) notes that in 1:24, these temple-based Jews are identified as Pharisees, a group that Josephus associates with the chief priests (Josephus, *J.W.* 2.411; Josephus, *Life* 189–198).

27. So also Brown, *Gospel according to John,* 1:lxxi; Keener, *Gospel of John,* 1:221. See the discussion in von Wahlde, "Johannine 'Jews,'" 33–60.

28. Kysar, *Maverick Gospel,* 82.

29. There may be a narrative connection between Nathanael and Nicodemus since, in these first chapters, only these two are described as "coming" to Jesus (cf. 1:39). Michaels notes that in 6:35 and 7:37–38, the language of "coming to me" and "believing in me" occurs in parallel construction (*Gospel of John,* 177). Because the verb "to come" occurs in many neutral contexts it is difficult to know how much significance to assign in selected contexts. Schneiders (*Written That You May Believe,* 118) sees Nicodemus as suspended between Nathanael (in whom there is no guile) and the Samaritan woman (an apostate Jew who believes in Jesus as the Christ).

30. Josephus describes the Pharisees as allies of the chief priests (*J.W.* 2:411; *Life* 189–198).

again in 19:39 ("who had at first come to Jesus at night") in his third and final appearance in the narrative.[31] In between these two appearances by Nicodemus, the word "night" occurs three more times. It is worth citing the texts in full:

> "It is necessary for us to work the works of him who sent me while it is day; night is coming when no one is able to work." (9:4)

> "If anyone walks during the day he does not stumble, because he sees the light of this world. If anyone walks at night he stumbles, because the light is not in him." (11:9b–10)

> "After receiving the piece of bread, then, [Judas] immediately went out. And it was night." (13:30)

These verses trace a trajectory that leads directly to Judas's betrayal, identifying him as one who stumbles in the night. The negative associations with "night" increase as "night" becomes metaphorically linked with "darkness" through the shared entailment of "light" (1:5; 3:19–21; 8:12; 12:35–36, 46; cf. 6:17 [20:1?]). This leads many to hear the reference to Nicodemus approaching Jesus at "night" in 3:2 as describing metaphorically Nicodemus's inability to grasp what Jesus is trying to tell him and characterizing him as obtuse.[32]

Yet it is possible to read this differently. Some view Nicodemus approaching Jesus in 3:2 as movement from the darkness towards the light.[33] Others place this movement later, in Nicodemus's final appearance following the crucifixion ("the one who *at first* came to Jesus at night" [19:39]).[34]

31. The word occurs one more time in the gospel, in 21:3: "Simon Peter said to them, 'I am going fishing.' They said to him, 'We will go with you.' They went out and got into the boat, but that night they caught nothing."

32. Duke writes, "The cumulative weight of the Gospel, however, and particularly the repetition of this detail in 19:39, leaves little doubt of the symbolic/ironic intent of this verse" (*Irony in the Fourth Gospel*, 186); see also Culpepper, *Anatomy*, 192. Bassler also seems to lean in this direction ("Mixed Signals," 638).

33. Brown, *Gospel according to John*, 1:130; Moloney, *Gospel of John*, 91; Munro, "Pharisee and the Samaritan in John," 716. Meeks allows that Nicodemus comes to the light but is depicted as "one who does not perceive that light clearly, and who is hesitant and unable to make the decisive step from darkness to light" ("Man from Heaven," 54). Michaels presents the reader with the possibility of reading the text either way (*The Gospel of John*, 178).

34. Keener, *Gospel of John*, 2:1161–62; Reinhartz, *Befriending the Beloved Disciple*, 64. Conway straddles the line (*Men and Women*, 92). Bassler ("Mixed Signals," 642) notes that, among the four gospels, the Gospel of John is the only one that *does not*

It is possible a contrast is being created between Judas, who literally is stumbling around in the night, and Nicodemus, who, in this final scene is paired with Joseph of Arimathea, described by the narrator as "a disciple of Jesus, though a secret one because of his fear of the Jews" (19:38). The pairing is striking because it aligns one who is a "leader of the Jews" with a "secret disciple for fear of the Jews." Since these two act in consort in preparing the body for burial, readers must in some way reconcile the tension created by their pairing. Although the language of "secret disciples" might suggest inadequacy, it is important to remember that other, known disciples have disappeared and will next be found behind closed doors "for fear of the Jews" (20:19). In this regard, all disciples seem to be equal.[35]

In this final scene, where Nicodemus joins Joseph of Arimathea in tending to the dead body of Jesus, he is described as bringing a mixture of spices, "weighing about a hundred pounds" with which to wrap the body in preparation for burial. This amount is extraordinary and mirrors the extravagance of Mary, who anoints Jesus feet with a pound of pure nard, valued at three hundred denarii, in an act that also anticipates Jesus' burial (12:3, 5, 7).[36] Yet the gesture that, on the one hand, seems to signify devotion, may, on the other hand, be viewed as extravagance born of a guilty conscience directed towards a dead body that can no longer cause anyone trouble.[37]

With its reference to Nicodemus as the "one who came first at night," this final scene circles back to the very first scene in which Nicodemus appears. In this first scene, following the brief introduction by the narrator, Nicodemus engages Jesus in a dialogue that consists of three short exchanges. Nicodemus's opening statement addresses Jesus as "Rabbi," a title used almost exclusively by disciples for Jesus (1:38, 49; 4:31; 9:2; 11:8; cf. 20:16).[38] The claim "We know that you are a teacher come from God" echoes the perspective of the implied author that in Jesus, God above (1:1, 14; 6:38; 12:28; 17:1) is made manifest on earth (1:1, 14).[39] As the dialogue unfolds,

---

describe Joseph of Arimathea retrieving Jesus' body *at night* (Matt 27:57; Mark 15:42; Luke 23:54).

35. Bassler, "Mixed Signals," 641–42.

36. Keener, *Gospel of John*, 2:1163–64. Michaels, *Gospel of John*, 982.

37. Duke reads it as a sign of remorse (*Irony in the Fourth Gospel*, 110). Meeks sees it as a ludicrous gesture indicating that Nicodemus clearly does not understand the "lifting up" of the Son of Man (*Man from Heaven*, 55). Culpepper similarly sees it as a vain gesture (*Anatomy*, 136).

38. Only in 3:2 and 6:25 (by crowds seeking Jesus, after they, like Nicodemus, have seen signs that he has performed) is it used by outsiders. In 3:26 it is used by John the Baptist's disciples in addressing him.

39. Michaels observes that Jesus says this of himself in 8:29 and 16:32 (*Gospel of John*, 179).

it becomes clear that Nicodemus does not fully understand the implications of what he has said. This comes back to him full force when Jesus declares in 3:10: "Are *you* [emphatic σύ] a teacher of Israel and do not know these things?"[40] Regardless of how Jesus' remark is heard (as sarcastic, compassionate, or humorous), it emphasizes the disparity between these two teachers: the one from God; the other a teacher of Israel who has been shown to not know the things about which the teacher from God speaks.[41]

Jesus responds to Nicodemus's opening address by redirecting the conversation toward humankind. This is not a complete non sequitur; the link is the very word that trips up Nicodemus: ἄνωθεν ("born from above/born again"). Unless people are, like Jesus, born from above, he says, from water and the spirit, they can neither see nor enter the kingdom of God (3:4, 5). The answer to Nicodemus's question, "how . . ." (3:4, 9) has already been given by the narrator in the prologue: "to whomever received him, he gave power to become children of God: the ones who believed in his name, who were born, not of blood or of the will of the flesh or of the will of man, but of God" (1:12–13).[42] Because it is language to which readers have access, but Nicodemus does not, Nicodemus is made to look foolish, an outsider who is unable to comprehend.[43] This is further emphasized by the use of the historical present to call attention to Nicodemus's line in 3:4, as if to say *"and then, if you can believe it, he says . . ."*

The dialogue is framed in a narrative context that further develops the characterization of Nicodemus. Chapter 2 concludes with the narrator's declaration that Jesus "did not entrust himself to them, because he knew all people and because he had no need for anyone to witness concerning humankind (ἄνθρωπος); for he himself knew what was in humankind (ἦν ἐν

---

40. Michaels notes that this question can from the perspective of grammar also be read as a statement (ibid., 189–90).

41. "Teacher" here is preceded by the definite article, which identifies Nicodemus as an important teacher, but by no means the *only* teacher of Israel (Moloney, *Gospel of John,* 100; see also Wallace, *Greek Grammar Beyond the Basics,* 222–23).

42. Winsome Munro sees the dialogue as undercutting Nicodemus's identity, which is dependent on ethnicity and social standing ("Pharisee and the Samaritan in John," 720). Schneiders, similarly, sees a link between the dialogue with Nicodemus and the discussion in 8:33–40 about being children of Abraham (*Written That You May Believe,* 120).

43. The one hint given within the dialogue may be in 3:8 where Jesus speaks of hearing the voice (φωνή) of the spirit, "yet you do not know from where it comes." Already, the voice (φωνή) of John the Baptist has been heard, crying in the wilderness (1:23). Following 3:8, the only voice (φωνή) that will be heard is the voice of Jesus (3:29; 5:25, 38; 5:37; 10:3, 4, 5, 16, 27; 11:43; 12:28, 30; 18:37). Thus, Nicodemus is the first to be specifically introduced to "the voice" (distinguished here from words simply spoken by Jesus). The voice of Jesus and the voice of the Spirit are linked in 14:26.

τῷ ἀνθρώπῳ)" (2:24–25). Chapter 3 begins with the very same language that concludes 2:25: Ἦν δὲ ἄνθρωπος ("There was a human being"). Thus, readers are led to conclude that Jesus, when he meets Nicodemus, knows what kind of an ἄνθρωπος he is: i.e., a human being who will not "know these things."[44] It is not wholly clear whether readers should further infer that Jesus does not entrust himself to Nicodemus (2:23–24); Jesus does, after all, engage Nicodemus.[45]

There is yet another link between the two passages (2:23-25; 3:1-10): the verb "know"(γινώσκω). Before the exchange with Nicodemus begins, Jesus is described as someone who "knows." That he next encounters someone who does *not* know serves the plot, already revealed in the prologue: "He was in the world . . . and the world knew him not" (1:10). Whether or not the encounter with Nicodemus should be heard in connection with the next line ("he came to his own, and his own did not receive him" [1:11]) is less certain. If 3:11 is read as a continuation of the scene with Nicodemus, the answer could be yes: "Truly, truly I say to you that we speak of what we know . . . but you do not receive our testimony." But is v. 11 a continuation of the scene?

Although v. 11 begins with a refrain that has twice punctuated the exchange with Nicodemus (3:3, 5), within the same verse Jesus immediately switches to the first-person plural ("we speak") as well as to the second-person plural ("you do not receive"), which continues through v. 12 (cf. 3:7). This raises the question of whether readers are intended to hear Jesus continuing to speak in these verses or whether they are intended to recognize a transfer to the voice of the narrator. Interpreters vary: some see Jesus' dialogue with Nicodemus continuing through v. 21;[46] others view vv. 11–12 as a bridge to a new scene.[47] If v. 11 is directed towards Nicodemus, then he becomes identified among those who do not receive Jesus' testimony and

44. In the same way, Jesus later knows that the Samaritan woman has had five husbands and that the one with whom she is now living is not her husband (4:16–18). This is the case whether or not one hears the reference to five husbands in literal terms or metaphorical terms.

45. Meeks assumes Jesus "does not entrust himself" (*Man from Heaven*, 55). So also Carter, *John: Storyteller, Interpreter, Evangelist*, 37; Rensberger, *Johannine Faith and Liberating Community*, 39. Munro disagrees ("Pharisee and the Samaritan in John," 716).

46. Brown, *Gospel according to John*, 1:145–49; Haenchen, *John*, 202; Meeks, "Man from Heaven," 52. Michaels sees Jesus as addressing those whom Nicodemus represents (*Gospel of John*, 193).

47. Howard-Brook, *Becoming Children of God*, 89–90; Moloney, *Gospel of John*, 90. Although Keener includes vv. 11–21 in his discussion of the Nicodemus episode, it is not at all clear that he views vv. 13–21 as addressed to Nicodemus but rather only as a discourse built on the dialogue with Nicodemus (*Gospel of John*, 560–74).

believe in him (cf. 1:11); if vv. 11–12 are viewed as a bridge to a new scene, then Nicodemus's role is ambiguous.

This narrative analysis of Nicodemus is far from complete, but it is sufficient to demonstrate some of the ways a narrative critic engages the written text when undertaking an analysis of character.[48] It also demonstrates that however much the implied author may tell or show about a character, there are questions or gaps for readers to resolve. I have intentionally emphasized some of these in order to highlight the ambiguities in the text. Depending on how these ambiguities are resolved, it is possible to characterize Nicodemus in at least three different ways:

- He can be read as a character who is fundamentally sympathetic to Jesus: who moves from the darkness to the light, raising questions if not fully comprehending the answers; who challenges his own people, and in the end aligns himself with a "secret disciple." In this role, he provides a presence and a voice that resists from within the almost overwhelming opposition of the Pharisees and "the Jews," a resistance that increases as the opposition to Jesus similarly increases until, at the end, Nicodemus appears to change sides completely.

- Alternatively, Nicodemus can be read as a flawed character who consistently fails to understand Jesus. In this role he gives face, as a representative character, to "the Jews" and Pharisees who oppose Jesus: "his own, who received him not" (1:11). Although Nicodemus raises questions, he never separates himself from the Pharisees, and while he accompanies Joseph of Arimathea, he is never said to believe in Jesus. He ultimately remains in the dark, uncomprehending and complicit by association.

- Finally, Nicodemus can be read as a character who continues to seek Jesus without ever arriving at full comprehension. He initially approaches Jesus as "one who knows," only to discover that he "does not know." When he reappears, he is seen distancing himself from the Pharisees by challenging their hasty efforts to arrest Jesus, revealing his uncertainty about what the Pharisees claim to know. Appearing alongside a "secret disciple" to honor Jesus in death, he is shown aligning himself with a different group, but not yet at a point of belief. In this role, he represents one of the many points along the way to belief.

---

48. I have not discussed, for example, comparisons that are invited by the implied author between Nicodemus and characters in the text with whom he does not interact (for example, the Samaritan woman or the man born blind).

What should be clear is that whichever characterization of Nicodemus is chosen, it will be intimately intertwined with plot as well as with Nicodemus's interaction and comparison with other characters. Character is not abstract, but always contextual.

Character Analysis in Performance Criticism

From the perspective of performance criticism, Nicodemus is a character in a story, who is personified by a storyteller in performance before a live audience.[49] The audience encounters Nicodemus not through words written, but through words spoken, gestures, facial expressions, tone of voice, proximity to other characters, spatial relationships and so forth.[50] The performance critic, as (potentially) performer, engages in an analysis of how to enact Nicodemus in real time and space. The following analysis will include consideration of how Nicodemus is presented in the written text, and how he may be perceived by a live audience (rhetorical impact). Unlike an actor in a play, who (normally) performs only one character, a storyteller performs"not only the character Nicodemus, but also the narrator who talks about Nicodemus, and the various characters with whom Nicodemus interacts.[51] This makes performance criticism a complex enterprise.

Performance criticism begins with the written text; thus, like narrative criticism, it is also interested in what the implied author shows and tells about the character Nicodemus. Enacting Nicodemus before a live audience, however, requires the performance critic to ask additional questions. For example, what will the audience have seen and heard prior to Nicodemus's appearance in the story that will shape their reception of him when he first appears? How does Nicodemus's voice or presence at particular points in the unfolding narrative contribute to the dramatic tension in the story? What performance cues (such as those identified in the story of the feeding of the five thousand above) have been written into the text for the character Nicodemus? What tones of voice, gestures, or postures will the storyteller employ in order to embody Nicodemus? In what kinds of space does the action take place, and where is Nicodemus located with respect to space? How

---

49. Rhoads, "Biblical Performance Criticism," 181. Arguably, writing may also be understood as a kind of performance. Here, I reserve the language of performance for performance by a solo performer. Oral performance could, of course, involve a cast (as in a play); this would open up more performance possibilities than can be entertained here.

50. Ibid., 165, 176–78.

51. Ibid., 181–82.

does Nicodemus interact with other characters in these spaces?[52] Above all, a performance-critical analysis requires filling in the gaps in order to achieve its goal: for a live audience to experience Nicodemus and his world in real time and space.[53]

Roughly seven scenes have transpired before Nicodemus enters the story: (1) the prologue (1:1–18); (2) John the Baptist's confession, to those sent from Jerusalem to him in Bethany beyond the Jordan, that he is not the Christ (1:19–28); (3) John the Baptist's testimony identifying Jesus as the "Lamb of God" (whom he did not know until God sent a sign) (1:28–34); (4) disciples of John follow Jesus; one of them, Andrew, brings along his brother Simon Peter (1:35–42); (5) Jesus goes to Galilee where he gains Philip and Nathanael as disciples (1:43–50); (6) a wedding in Cana of Galilee where Jesus, his disciples and Jesus' mother are present; after Jesus performs a sign revealing his glory, the disciples believe in him (2:1–12); (7) Jesus disrupts the temple (2:13–22 [23–25]).

These opening scenes alert the audience to three important storytelling patterns.[54] One is the function of geography or space. In these scenes, the four primary spaces of the narrative world are established, each associated with its own particular set of characters: the heavenly realm (associated with God; Jesus; John the Baptist, who is sent by God); Bethany beyond the Jordan (associated with John the Baptist and his disciples, some of whom become disciples of Jesus); Galilee (associated with Jesus, his disciples, and his mother); and Jerusalem (associated with the Jews, Pharisees, priests, and Levites).[55] The crossing of characters from one space into another is significant. The storyteller needs to have established these spaces within the performance area in preparation for Nicodemus's entrance. The second pattern is the function of direct discourse. Nothing that is spoken in direct discourse is superfluous; there are no throwaway lines. Direct discourse is used to witness to Jesus, point to his signs, articulate expressions of faith, and emphasize conflict. What Nicodemus says is important. The third pattern revolves around responses to Jesus. Of the seven scenes enumerated

52. William Doan and Terry Giles suggest similar questions: e.g., "What information is supplied beforehand that establishes the circumstances of the segment? What is the project of each character? What is the character moving toward, focusing his energy toward? What path does the tension follow? What kinds of resistance are present to provide increases and decreases in the tensions?" (*Prophets, Performance, and Power*, 78).

53. See Rhoads, "Biblical Performance Criticism," 175–76.

54. Other patterns are present as well; I highlight three that are particularly important for the present discussion.

55. Bassler rightly notes that it is the association of "space" with people, rather than land, that is of primary import ("Galileans," 254).

above, which precede Nicodemus's first appearance, in scenes 3 through 6 the response to Jesus is immediate and positive, resulting in a gathering of disciples who "believe." In scene 7, the responses are more complex. Jesus' actions and words in the temple create confusion. "The Jews" misunderstand, while the disciples remember and *later* understand, demonstrating that insight does not always come immediately.

Just prior to the scene in which Nicodemus appears for the first time, Jesus has moved from Galilee to Jerusalem (a space aligned with "the Jews," priests, Levites, and Pharisees [1:19, 24]) for the Passover Festival. This is not a neutral act, but a spatial transgression demonstrated through Jesus' disruption of the primary symbol of that space (the temple), a disruption that the audience both sees and hears. Following this act, the storyteller reports that Jesus remains in Jerusalem during the Festival, continuing to perform signs (2:13, 23). But the storyteller also says that Jesus did not entrust himself to those in Jerusalem who believed in his signs (2:23–24). This comment underscores the tension that has been created by Jesus' movement from one space into another.

The storyteller introduces Nicodemus before the audience sees him, describing him as an ἄνθρωπος from the Pharisees, named Nicodemus, a leader of the Jews. The audience has encountered "the Jews" only twice before in the course of the story: in scene 2, where they send a delegation of priests and Levites to John the Baptist asking, "Who are you?" (1:19)[56] and in scene 7, where they see Jesus overturning tables and driving the sacrificial animals out of the temple and ask, "What sign can you show us for doing these things?" (2:18). The audience has heard about Pharisees only once before. This was in scene 2 where, along with the Jews, they send a delegation to John the Baptist (1:24).[57] Neither of these encounters suggests animosity towards or rejection of Jesus, only curiosity and confusion. With the appearance of Nicodemus, the audience meets a Pharisee for the first time.

Following this brief introduction of Nicodemus, the storyteller says, "*This one* (οὗτος) came to him at night" (3:2). The demonstrative pronoun, οὗτος, generally translated as "he," functions as a pointer, drawing attention to Nicodemus as this particular Pharisee, and invites a gesture by the storyteller.[58] The specification "at night" introduces a secondary setting within

---

56. There is a direct link between these two scenes since scene 7 takes place in the temple where the priests and Levites from scene 2 serve.

57. There is some textual confusion here: are the Pharisees the ones sending the priests and Levites, or is a separate delegation of the Pharisees now questioning John? For a discussion, see Conway, *Men and Women,* 89.

58. Brant calls attention to the importance of demonstrative pronouns and personal pronouns from a performative perspective (*Dialogue and Drama,* 81–83).

"Jerusalem." This setting has already been discussed under narrative criticism, but performance criticism invites further consideration. This is the first reference to "night" in the story, and as yet there has been only one reference to darkness—in the prologue (1:5), where the narrator declares that the darkness has not κατέλαβεν the light. The verb καταλαμβάνω can be translated as either "overtaken" or "comprehended."[59] If the storyteller has used the translation "comprehend" an audience might hear "night" as a way of signaling that Nicodemus will not comprehend the "light," an image that has been linked to Jesus in the prologue (1:4–5, 7–9).[60] Yet there is at least one other possibility to consider. Scene 7, just prior to this, was a public scene, involving many people, and filled with action verbs (finding, making, driving out, overturning, destroying, raising up). This new scene, at night, is a private encounter, away from the crowds, between two individuals who belong to different spatial settings. As such, it dramatically alters the pace of the story and interjects a different kind of tension. As a setting within a setting, it creates a kind of liminal space where the boundaries that separate groups and people become blurred. The challenge for the storyteller is how to convey "night" in performance. Does Nicodemus carry a light of some kind? Do the characters stand in close proximity to indicate the intimacy of the encounter? Or is Nicodemus portrayed stumbling around in the night unable to see the figure of Jesus clearly, only hearing his voice? Performance requires a decision at this point: the nonverbal cues that are chosen will shape both the audience's perception of the character Nicodemus and the nature of his encounter with Jesus, thus they must be chosen not for effect but rather to create a coherent character.[61]

It is only with the reference to night that the storyteller *becomes* the character Nicodemus. The scene that follows consists entirely of dialogue. Although no physical action is described nor any physical characteristics identified, the storyteller must decide how Nicodemus carries himself and how he approaches Jesus. Is he old and bent (being "old" [3:4])? Upright and dignified (being "a leader" [3:1])? Does he come in secret, fearing the Jews? If so, this introduces an idea into the narrative that doesn't occur before 7:13.

59. BDAG, 519–20, s.v. καταλαμβάνω.

60. Separation by several scenes and coupled with complementary rather than repetitive language (i.e., "darkness" vs. "night") makes an immediate association unlikely in a performance context unless attention was drawn to the connection through exaggerated means.

61. Brant observes, "characters act; they do not behave" (*Dialogue and Drama,* 166). That is, in performance, motivation must be constructed from cues in the text. Doan and Giles similarly remark, "all presentation is doing, and from the spectator's point of view, doing consists of a sequence of perceptible signs created by the performer" (*Prophets, Performance, and Power,* 61).

Or does he approach Jesus displaying deference or respect, as one teacher might approach another (3:2, 10)? Whatever gestures, tone, proximity, and postures are employed, they are integral to characterization. Quintilian calls particular attention in this regard to the eyes: "of all the various elements that go to form the expression, the eyes are the most important, since they, more than anything else, reveal the temper of the mind."[62]

The dialogue is initiated by Nicodemus, who comes alone to Jesus. In thinking about presentation and tone of voice, the storyteller must keep in mind the trajectory of Nicodemus's character over the course of the narrative. For example, if the storyteller adopts for Nicodemus a voice dripping with sarcasm ("Rabbi, we know that you are a teacher who has come from God"), it is only possible (logically) for Nicodemus to become increasingly irritated as Jesus runs circles around him. When Nicodemus next appears, the audience may have trouble believing that he would challenge the other Pharisees, even on a point of process, after being so thoroughly trounced. But there are a range of options available: Nicodemus could be curious, cautious, puzzled, even ingratiating. In choosing which tone to adopt, the storyteller must keep in mind several things. (1) The largely negative characterization of "the Jews" and Pharisees has not yet emerged in the story. (2) In the previous scene, "the Jews'" have questioned Jesus, perhaps even with a degree of provoked hostility, but no further discussion or action has taken place. (3) What kind of role does Nicodemus have as a leader of the Jews? On the basis of this, what might motivate Nicodemus to come forward at this particular point? For example, is he trying to gain more information, a motive perhaps suggested by his line in 7:51? (4) How does his appearance at this point further the story? (5) Where does the storyteller envision Nicodemus ending in terms of how he views Jesus, and what would make a compelling starting point?

Some performance cues in the scene suggest how the dialogue might be enacted. Nicodemus's opening line references one of the four primary spatial contexts (the heavenly realm), a context that is referenced again in the language of ἄνωθεν (anew/from above) (3:3). Pointing towards this spatial context would assist the audience in making the connection between Nicodemus's opening line and Jesus' response. It would also draw attention to Nicodemus's misunderstanding, particularly if Nicodemus points towards his belly for "womb" (3:4).[63] Jesus' remark to Nicodemus, "do not be astonished" (3:7), suggests that a somewhat exaggerated response by Nicodemus in 3:4 would be appropriate. Jesus' words in 3:5–8 are filled with

---

62. Quintilian, *Inst.* 11.3.75.

63. The use of the historical present in 3:4 was discussed earlier.

active imagery that engages the senses and invite corresponding gestures: "to be born of flesh," "to be born of water," "to hear and feel the wind."[64] In particular, action added to "but you do not know from where it comes or where it goes" would mirror Nicodemus's growing confusion. The use of the emphatic pronoun when Jesus says, "You (σύ) are a teacher of Israel and you do not know these things?" suggests that Jesus might point to Nicodemus, just as earlier Nicodemus might point at Jesus when he says, "no one is able to do these signs which *you* (σύ) do, unless God is with him." Such gestures would complement verbal emphasis and draw attention to how each character views the other.

There is also considerable verbal play in this dialogue, which can be exploited. This is best illustrated by scripting out the lines:[65]

Nicodemus: Rabbi, *we know* that from God you have come, *a teacher.* **No one is able** to do *these signs* which <u>you</u> do **unless** God is with him.

Jesus: Truly, truly I say to you, **unless** someone is **born** from above, **he is not able to see** the realm of God.

Nicodemus: **How is a person able** to be **born** already being old? **He is not able to enter** his mother's womb a second time and be **born**, is he?

Jesus: Truly, truly I say to you, **unless** someone is born of water and spirit, **He is not able to enter** the realm of God. The one **born** ... the one **born** ... it is necessary **to be born** ... Thus it is with everyone **having been born** of the spirit.

Nicodemus: **How are these things able to be?** ["to be" plays on the sound of "born"]

Jesus: <u>You</u> are *a teacher* of Israel and *these things do not know[?]*[66]

---

64. Kysar, "Making of Metaphor," 33–34.

65. This verbal play is even more pronounced in the Greek.

66. See footnote 40. Writes Brant, "The penchant for self-identification in the gospel tends to be subverted by Jesus' reidentification of himself and others in the course of their dialogues, and in this way, shifting identity becomes part of the action of the gospel" (*Dialogue and Drama*, 189).

How this is played will shape how the audience perceives Nicodemus. The way each character picks up on the language spoken by the other suggests a kind of verbal volley. It could be played with considerable humor, leaving Nicodemus in a state of wonderment. It could also be played in a way that makes Nicodemus appear to be a buffoon. While the audience is likely intended to laugh at Nicodemus, if he is made so comical as to not be taken seriously, his appearances in subsequent scenes will be undermined. Humor, of course, is only one option. This exchange could also be played with great earnestness, or even a touch of combativeness, leaving Nicodemus utterly perplexed. What is key is that an opening must be left for Nicodemus to return with credibility.

Why does the writer introduce a character such as Nicodemus at this particular point in the story? It is helpful to review again what has happened up to this point: Jesus has gained a following of disciples who, in Galilee, form an identity as a group, see Jesus perform his first sign, and come to believe. From Galilee Jesus travels to Jerusalem where he overturns the primary symbol of that space, the temple, and with it a primary identity marker of "the Jews." Jesus next meets Nicodemus, a Pharisee and leader of "the Jews." Nicodemus's very identity introduces an element of suspense into the story: what will he do? Nicodemus does not lash out at Jesus; he identifies him, correctly but without comprehension. When Jesus proposes that it is necessary to be born anew, Nicodemus wonders how this can be. Nicodemus, in this way, serves as a starting point for the rest of the story, which unfolds through a series of encounters with Jesus in which characters either take a step towards this "new birth" or pull back in incomprehension.

What happens to Nicodemus after 3:10? He will be visually present to the audience only if the storyteller continues to personify the character Jesus and direct vv. 11ff. to the space that has been occupied by the character Nicodemus. This means that the audience has no access to how the character Nicodemus responds to the lines spoken. Yet how the lines are spoken will continue to shape their perception of Nicodemus. If Jesus says to Nicodemus "you (plural) do not receive our testimony," then the uncomprehending teacher's confusion becomes a rejection. An option available to the storyteller is to translate "do not receive" (λαμβάνω) as "do not comprehend."[67] This would focus on Nicodemus's confusion rather than necessarily imply his rejection of Jesus.[68] Another option is for the storyteller to speak v. 11a to Nicodemus ("Truly, truly I say to you, we speak what we know and testify to

---

67. BDAG, 584.8, s.v. λαμβάνω. This would correspond to a possible translation of 1:5, mentioned earlier.

68. This matter of translation has more to do with English than with Greek. Yet for a performer, translation is a critical issue.

what we have seen") then to turn from Nicodemus at v. 11b and (with a hand gesture) incorporate an unseen group—perhaps even including the audience (consistent with the "you" plural), involving them actively in the scene.[69] This would also give the storyteller the interpretive option of turning back to Nicodemus at v. 21 ("But those who do what is true come to the light").

But does the character Jesus continue speaking in vv. 11–12? Or does the storyteller shift from personifying Jesus to personifying the narrator? If the latter, then the audience is addressed in vv. 11–21. In this case, the translation "comprehend" is likely to be preferred, the lines becoming a kind of challenge to the audience. Nicodemus, in turn, becomes a character with whom the audience is invited to compare themselves—presumably by recognizing that what he is unable to comprehend, they can (by virtue of what has been revealed to them by the narrator).

When Nicodemus next appears, the dramatic tension in the story has increased significantly. In 4:2 the audience sees Jesus withdraw from Judea and begin to move back to Galilee because he learns that the Pharisees have heard he is baptizing more disciples than John. When Jesus returns (secretly) to Jerusalem for the Festival of Booths, the audience knows that "the Jews" are looking for an opportunity to kill him (7:1), and shortly thereafter discover that the chief priests and Pharisees have sent temple police to arrest him (7:32). It is when the temple police return empty-handed that Nicodemus reappears, in a gathering of the chief priests and Pharisees. Since the audience has seen him before, they are poised to learn how he will act in this new context.

The storyteller re-introduces Nicodemus by describing him as "the one who came to him [Jesus] before, being one of them."[70] The audience may trip momentarily at this point, wondering whether "being one of them" means being a follower of Jesus or one of the Pharisees. Attention is (again) called to Nicodemus's voice by the use of the historical present (7:50). Regardless of the tone of voice used (is he pleading? angry? attempting to reason?) Nicodemus's words present a challenge to the other Pharisees, escalating the tension in the scene (7:51).[71] Quintilian suggests that exhorta-

---

69. Other lines in the gospel are clearly directed towards the audience: e.g., 19:35; 20:30–31 and 21:24–45. The lengthy monologue here seems intended for the audience as much as for Nicodemus.

70. The NRSV reads "and who was one of them."

71. Nicodemus's remark contains a verbal echo of his earlier dialogue with Jesus: "unless" (ἐὰν μή [7:51; see 3:2, 3, 5]). Jesus is the only character, apart from Nicodemus and Thomas (20:25) who uses "unless" and he does so repeatedly (3:5, 27; 4:48; 5:19; 6:44, 53, 65; 8:34; 12:24; 13:8; 15:4, 6; 16:7). When the audience hears Nicodemus counter the other Pharisees with an argument punctuated by "unless," and, moreover, an argument in support of gaining further information before passing judgment on Jesus,

tions or statements of fact are effectively accompanied by a gesture in which the middle finger is placed against the thumb and the remaining fingers extended as the hand is moved forward firmly. A more forceful gesture can be made by extending the index finger only and folding the other fingers under the thumb, the palm facing the ground.[72] The tension of the scene is heightened further when the other Pharisees sarcastically suggest Nicodemus is from Galilee. As the climatic conclusion to the scene, these remarks seal the impression that Nicodemus may not be "one of them." Notably, this scene occurs just before Jesus enters into hostile debate over the question of identity in chapter 8.

When Nicodemus appears for the last time, the story is nearly ended. Jesus has been arrested and crucified, and both the Pharisees and "the Jews" have been actively involved in bringing this about. However, as narrated, the audience does not see the Pharisee Nicodemus until following Jesus' crucifixion. In the audience's previous aural and visual encounter with Nicodemus, he has challenged the Pharisees and, in turn, has had his loyalty to the Pharisees challenged. Appearing now with Joseph of Arimathea, a "secret disciple," Nicodemus literally stands in a different place. This is underscored by the storyteller's description of Nicodemus as "the one who had *at first* come to Jesus at night" (19:39).

Nicodemus enters the scene, bearing a great quantity of spices, as Joseph removes the body of Jesus from the cross. The storyteller says that *together* they take the body, wrap it in linen with the spices, and lay it in the tomb (19:38–42). In narrative criticism, it is possible to envision two separate characters each carrying out individual actions. Thus, for example, Nicodemus can be imagined piling more and more spices on the body of Jesus, hesitating, then piling on more as perhaps a comic presentation of a guilty conscience. Or he can be envisioned quietly participating in the burial of Jesus, then dusting off his hands as if to put to rest this interesting but troublesome figure. Yet either of these scenarios would be difficult for a solo storyteller to enact while simultaneously narrating a story in which *they* (the two characters) are described acting in consort; it would not be impossible, but it would require a considerable amount of miming. A solo storyteller, however, enacting the story as narrated, embodies the unity of their joint action.

Like the narrative analysis in the first part of this chapter, this performance analysis is far from complete.[73] It is sufficient, however, to give a

---

they may identify this as movement by Nicodemus towards Jesus.

72. Quintilian, *Inst.* 11.3.92–94.

73. Optimally, no performance-critical analysis would be considered complete without an actual performance in front of a live audience.

sense of how a performance critic undertakes an analysis of character with a view to performance before a live audience. Attention to the temporal line of the unfolding story, to the importance of space and spatial contexts, to the ways characters interact with one another in those contexts, to where and how they appear in relation to the tension that drives the story, to the pace and place of dialogue, to the performance cues in the narrative, to what it means for a story to be communicated by a solo performer, to the importance of maintaining coherence in characterization and credibility in character: these are the distinctive concerns that performance criticism brings to analysis of character in an effort to make the character three-dimensional.[74] There are still many gaps to be filled and numerous decisions to be made by the performer, and in performance, there can be no equivocating.[75] The result is that each performance will be somewhat different. At the same time, performance criticism, like narrative criticism, establishes interpretive limits. If we return to the three proposals for characterizing Nicodemus offered at the end of the narrative analysis, I believe that this performance-critical analysis demonstrates that it would be difficult to sustain in performance a portrayal of Nicodemus as completely uncomprehending and complicit by association. That still leaves considerable latitude in terms of presentation, but it reveals that performance criticism brings to view elements and issues that narrative criticism may not.

Conclusion

Narrative criticism and performance criticism are, in many respects, complementary. It would be possible to fold much if not most of what is said under narrative criticism into the discussion of performance criticism, and vice versa, with the result that both would be enriched. Both pay attention to how the character interacts with other characters, to descriptive markers and actions performed; both also leave the interpreter with many choices to be made. I have resisted making final decisions here because I want to emphasize the number of choices the interpreter faces, and, in this way, show how great a role the interpreter plays, *regardless* of approach. Despite these efforts, my interpretive voice is still apparent, a further reminder that there is no presentation or performance of a text apart from the active voice of an interpreter or performer.

---

74. Rhoads, "Biblical Performance Criticism," 182: "Such personification makes it clear that characters are not simply stereotypes, nor are they reducible to mere plot functions."

75. Ibid., 175. "There is no way to do a performance without conveying a subtext message with every line, no matter how badly done or ill-informed it is" (ibid., 185).

Narrative criticism and performance criticism also differ, as I have endeavored to demonstrate. Narrative criticism tends to work something like a jigsaw puzzle, pulling verses from a variety of places to construct a whole picture. As a reader, it is possible to move back and forth with ease within a text, bringing to bear on earlier sections what is revealed only later. In contrast, performance criticism approaches the text in a far more linear way, ever attentive to how the story unfolds before an audience in time and space, and how each character is incrementally revealed within and in relation to the story.[76]

Performance criticism also differs from narrative criticism in terms of its goal. Narrative critics write for readers, who engage the text at the same time that they engage the observations of the narrative critic. The textual world is always before them. In performance, the textual world disappears and is replaced by a person, a storyteller who embodies the world of the story, translating it into real time and space—"a rhetorical act of communication designed to change/transform an audience."[77] As a consequence, the ethical obligation that accompanies every act of biblical interpretation is increased in performance criticism. Performance in real time and space cannot help but engage issues in our own particular time and place. Yet, in a sense, this is precisely what makes performance criticism so important and so necessary. It holds us to a level of accountability that is easily sidestepped in other forms of biblical criticism and reminds us of the tremendous power of stories to transform lives.

Bibliography

Bassler, Jouette M. "The Galileans: A Neglected Factor in Johannine Community Research." *CBQ* 43 (1981) 243–57.

———. "Mixed Signals: Nicodemus in the Fourth Gospel." *JBL* 108 (1989) 635–46.

Brant, Jo-Ann A. *Dialogue and Drama: Elements of Greek Tragedy in the Fourth Gospel.* Peabody, MA: Hendrickson, 2004.

Brown, Raymond E. *The Gospel according to John.* 2 vols. AB 29–29a. Garden City, NY: Doubleday, 1966.

Burnett, Fred W. "Characterization and the Reader Construction of Characters in the Gospels." *Semeia* 63 (1993) 1–28.

Carter, Warren. *John: Storyteller, Interpreter, Evangelist.* Peabody, MA: Hendrickson, 2006.

---

76. "Theatre, and more specifically the drama, is not a thing but an event, an experience meant to be shared between presenters and spectators" (Doan and Giles, *Prophets, Performance, and Power*, 51).

77. Ibid., 175.

Chatman, Seymour. *Story and Discourse: Narrative Structure in Fiction and Film*. Ithaca: Cornell University Press, 1978.

Conway, Colleen M. *Men and Women in the Fourth Gospel: Gender and Johannine Characterization*. SBLDS 167. Atlanta: Society of Biblical Literature, 1999.

Culpepper, R. Alan. *Anatomy of the Fourth Gospel: A Study in Literary Design*. Foundations and Facets: New Testament. Philadelphia: Fortress, 1983.

Doan, William, and Terry Giles. *Prophets, Performance, and Power: Performance Criticism of the Hebrew Bible*. London: T. & T. Clark, 2005.

Duke, Paul D. *Irony in the Fourth Gospel*. Atlanta: John Knox, 1985.

Haenchen, Ernst. *John: A Commentary on the Gospel of John*. Vol. 1, *Chapters 1–6*. Translated by Robert W. Funk. 2 vols. Philadelphia: Fortress, 1984.

Hakola, Raimo. "The Burden of Ambiguity: Nicodemus and the Social Identity of the Johannine Christians." *NTS* 55 (2009) 438–55.

Howard-Brook, Wes. *Becoming Children of God: John's Gospel and Radical Discipleship*. 1994. Reprinted, Eugene, OR.: Wipf & Stock, 2003.

Keener, Craig S. *Gospel of John: A Commentary*. 2 vols. Peabody, MA: Hendrickson, 2003.

Koester, Craig. *Symbolism in the Fourth Gospel: Meaning, Mystery, Community*. 2nd ed. Minneapolis: Fortress, 2003.

Kysar, Robert. *John, the Maverick Gospel*. 3rd ed. Louisville: Westminster John Knox, 2007.

———. "The Making of Metaphor: Another Reading of John 3:1–15." In *What Is John?* Vol. 1, *Readers and Readings of the Fourth Gospel*, edited by Fernando F. Segovia, 21–41. SBL Symposium Series 3. Atlanta: Scholars, 1996.

McCracken, David. "Character in the Boundary: Bakhtin's Interdividuality in Biblical Narratives." *Semeia* 63 (1993) 29–42.

Meeks, Wayne. "The Man from Heaven in Johannine Sectarianism." *JBL* 91 (1972) 44–72.

Michaels, J. Ramsey. *The Gospel of John*. NICNT. Grand Rapids: Eerdmans, 2010.

Moloney, Francis J. *The Gospel of John*. SP 4. Collegeville, MN: Liturgical, 1998.

Munro, Winsome. "The Pharisee and the Samaritan in John: Polar or Parallel?" *CBQ* 57 (1995) 710–28.

Powell, Mark Allan. *What Is Narrative Criticism?* GBS. Minneapolis: Fortress, 1990.

Reinhartz, Adele. *Befriending the Beloved Disciple: A Jewish Reading of the Gospel of John*. New York: Continuum, 2001.

———. "The Gospel of John: How the 'Jews' Became Part of the Plot." In *Jesus, Judaism and Christian Anti-Judaism: Reading the New Testament after Holocaust*, edited by Paula Fredriksen and Adele Reinhartz, 99–116. Louisville: Westminster John Knox, 2002.

Rensberger, David. "Anti-Judaism and the Gospel of John." In *Anti-Judaism and the Gospels*, edited by William R. Farmer, 120–57. Harrisburg, PA: Trinity, 1999.

———. *Johannine Faith and Liberating Community*. Philadelphia: Westminster, 1988.

Resseguie, James L. *Narrative Criticism of the New Testament: An Introduction*. Grand Rapids: Baker Academic, 2005.

Rhoads, David. "Biblical Performance Criticism: Performance as Research." *Oral Tradition* 25 (2010) 157–98.

———. "Performance Criticism: An Emerging Methodology in Second Temple Studies—Part I." *BTB* 36 (2006) 118–33.

————. "Performance Criticism: An Emerging Methodology in Second Temple Studies—Part II." *BTB* 36 (2006) 164–84.

Schneiders, Sandra M. *Written That You May Believe: Encountering Jesus in the Fourth Gospel*. New York: Crossroad, 1999.

Skinner, Christopher W., ed. *Characters and Characterization in the Gospel of John*. LNTS 461. London: T. & T. Clark, 2013.

Von Wahlde, Urban C. "The Johannine 'Jews': A Critical Survey." *NTS* 28 (1982) 33–60.

Wallace, Daniel B. *Greek Grammar Beyond the Basics: An Exegetical Syntax of the New Testament*. Grand Rapids: Zondervan, 1996.

4

AUDIENCE ASIDES AND
THE AUDIENCES OF MARK

The Difference
Performance Makes

Thomas E. Boomershine

THE REASSESSMENT OF MARK AS PERFORMANCE LITERATURE, rather than as a text read by readers, invites a reexamination of some details that have been foundational for the identification of Mark's audience in recent Markan scholarship. Two statements of Mark have had a central role in the definition of Mark's original historical context: the explanation of Jewish practices of washing food, hands, and cooking vessels (Mark 7:3–4) and the identification of Simon of Cyrene as the father of Alexander and Rufus (Mark 15:21). The thesis here is that these statements were not narrative comments by the author/narrator to readers, but were storytelling asides to the audiences to whom Mark's story was told. When these audience asides are heard in the context of ancient performance, the exegetical focus shifts from private communication for readers to public communication for multifaceted audiences and points to a larger setting and purpose for the whole story. Rather than conceiving of Mark as addressed to readers in a Gentile Christian congregation in Rome or Syria, this data points to audiences that included Jews and Gentiles throughout the Greco-Roman world. The horizon of Mark's vision for the public proclamation of his composition is much wider than most current interpretation envisions.

Narrative Comments in the Identification of Mark's Audience and Purpose

A characteristic feature of biblical scholarship is the dialogue between the big picture of the historical context of the documents and the details of the documents themselves. This is particularly true of Markan scholarship. When Mark is viewed as ancient literature read by readers, the translations and various explanations that are frequent features of Mark's story are seen as narrative comments addressed to readers. The prevalent image of the reading situation in which Mark's story is usually interpreted is a private context of a person sitting alone with a manuscript of Mark, reading the text. Sometimes the imagined reading situation will include Mark's manuscript being read aloud either by the reader for her- or himself or to a group of hearers. But, if for a group, it is usually conceived as a small, local group—that is, a local congregation of believers.[1]

This is the picture in the background of two major recent commentaries (in English) on Mark. Both Joel Marcus in the Anchor Bible commentary and Adela Yarbro Collins in the Hermeneia commentary, though not regarding it as "a mathematical certainty," have portrayed the Gospel as a document written for readers and, sometimes, hearers in a particular congregation. While Collins concludes that a local congregation in Rome or Antioch is possible, Marcus favors a Syrian provenance.[2] The exegetical context reflected throughout both commentaries is the reading of Mark's Gospel in and for a local congregation of believing Christians.

Richard Bauckham and a group of his British colleagues have challenged this picture of Mark and the Gospels in a collection of essays, *The Gospels for All Christians*. Bauckham and colleagues argue that the contemporary consensus about the local audiences and purposes of the Gospels is too small. They propose that the Gospels were encyclical documents that were addressed to the Christian churches throughout the Greco-Roman world. As Bauckham observes, the local-church interpretation has become

---

1. This picture of Mark is drawn with characteristic clarity by Marcus (*Mark 1–8*, 25): "Whoever the author of the Gospel was, he seems to have written his work first and foremost to the Christian community of which he himself was a member." The critique here of Marcus's description of Mark's receivers is set in the context of my deep appreciation for the quality of the commentary and his insight about Mark's connection with the Jewish War.

2. Collins, *Mark*, 101–2; Marcus, *Mark 1–8*, 36–37.

the characteristic feature of late twentieth-century scholarship on the four Gospels. The initial studies of Mark and John as documents addressed to local congregations by Weeden and Martyn have been extended to Matthew and Luke in subsequent scholarship.[3] In a variety of ways, the Gospels have been read as inner-church documents that were directed to local congregations. In this interpretive horizon, the Gospels are a kind of mirror of the congregations to which they are addressed. A predominant dimension of their original meaning was the interpretation of the struggles and beliefs of those local churches.[4] While these two reconstructions of the audience and purpose of the Gospels are not irreconcilable, all subsequent interpreters will have to decide which of these pictures is most historically accurate. Is it more historically probable that the Gospels were composed in and for a local congregation or for a much wider series of audiences?

Mark's Narrative Comments for a Local Church

For Marcus, the pivotal sign that Mark was composed for a local congregation is the narrative comment that names the sons of Simon of Cyrene who carried Jesus' cross:

> Mark's notice in 15:21 that the man who carried Jesus' cross, Simon of Cyrene, was "the father of Alexander and Rufus" is most plausibly explained by the theory that Simon's sons were known to Mark's audience. Since, however, Alexander and Rufus are not mentioned elsewhere in early Christian literature, they were probably people who were familiar to the Markan community, perhaps even members of it, but little known elsewhere.[5]

Marcus's conclusion is that this comment implies that Mark's local congregation knew Alexander and Rufus. Mark's reference to Alexander and Rufus is an "in-group" naming of persons who were known to him and

---

3. The initial studies that launched the local-church horizon of Gospel interpretation were Weeden, *Mark;* and Martyn, *History and Theology in the Fourth Gospel.* This local context for Gospel interpretation has been developed in a whole series of subsequent studies of all four Gospels.

4. For Bauckham's helpful survey of the origins and tradition history of the "local" theory, as well as the purpose of the Gospels, see Bauckham "For Whom Were Gospels Written?," 13–26. Marcus also sees the description of persecution in Mark 13 as being *first* about the persecution of his local church.

5. Marcus, *Mark 1–8,* 25. Brown (*Introduction,* 163 n. 91) also notes this as a probable dimension of the Markan audience's foreknowledge: "15:21 suggests that Alexander and Rufus, the sons of Simon of Cyrene, were known to them."

to his church. This argument against Bauckham's proposal has been persuasive to Adela Yarbro Collins:

> One of his [Marcus's] better arguments is that Alexander and Rufus are mentioned in 15:21 because they were known to Mark's audience. Since both Matthew and Luke omit these names, it is likely that they did not expect the two men to be known to any of their audiences.[6]

The presence of this narrative comment in Mark and its absence from the other Gospels is seen as a decisive sign of an "in-church" provenance for the Gospel.

Furthermore, Mark's narrative comment explaining Jewish customs has been seen as a sign of the predominantly Gentile character of Mark's church. The inference from this comment is that the readers did not know Jewish customs and were, therefore, non-Jews. As Brown states, "For the most part the recipients were not Jews since the author had to explain Jewish purification customs to them."[7] This Markan comment has also been seen as decisive evidence that the Gospel's receivers were located in a Gentile Christian church.[8]

Another element of Mark's story lies in the background of this picture. In Jesus' final extended speech, often called the Little Apocalypse, Jesus foretells what is going to happen in the future. In the middle of that speech, in the description of the great tribulation, the document reads, "When you see the abomination of desolation set up where it ought not to be, let the reader understand, then those in Judea must flee to the mountains . . ." (13:14). This address to "the reader" has been understood as a parenthetical comment (usually placed in brackets by contemporary editors of the text) by the author in order to alert the reader to pay particular attention to what is being said by Jesus.

The most natural conclusion for contemporary interpreters has been that this is an address to the receiver of the document who is privately reading the document. The assumption of "the reader" as the recipient of the Gospels is ubiquitous in commentaries and monographs. Following Robert Fowler's recommendation, I have begun to underline the references to "the readers" in works of biblical scholarship and have found it to be virtually

---

6. See Collins, *Mark*, 97.

7. Brown, *Introduction*, 163. In the context of this article's topic, it is worth noting that Brown, who is less certain of a Roman locale, also says the following of the audience: "Most likely they had heard a good deal about Jesus before Mark's Gospel was read to them" (ibid.).

8. Incigneri, *Gospel to the Romans*.

universal. Sometimes "hearers" are added, but "readers" is the common and most frequent term for the recipients of the Gospels.

There is a connection between this assumption about "the readers" as the most common description of the receivers of the Gospels and the local-church hypothesis. The media world of literature has become increasingly private over the centuries. In the modern world, reading has become associated with an individual reading in silence. On the relatively infrequent occasions when a document is read to a group, the group is usually small: one or two children, a class, or a local congregation. In the case of the Bible, it has continued to be read aloud in weekly congregational worship in local churches.

The assumption of a small horizon for the reception of Mark's Gospel is natural. Thus, the explanation of Jewish cleanliness and purity traditions in Mark 7 and the identification of Simon of Cyrene as the father of Alexander and Rufus in Mark's story of Jesus' crucifixion have been interpreted as internal communication between the author/narrator and the receivers/readers of the document. Describing these components of Mark's story as narrative comments is an integral dimension of the critical interpretation of Mark. Those essentially private comments have been seen as central clues to the setting and purpose of the Gospel as inner-church communication. When studied as an address to readers, biblical texts are associated with communication events that have a small horizon.

Mark and "the Reader" in the Communication Cultures of Western Civilization

A first step in the reexamination of these elements of Mark is to identify the relationship between the Gospel of Mark and the communication cultures of Western literature. Recent research on the communication culture of the ancient world has made it clear that the first century was an early literate culture in which 80 to 90 percent of the people were illiterate.[9] Written documents were scarce and relatively expensive, and so the primary means of publication of first-century literature was performance. To be sure, there were exceptions to this dominant pattern, as has been demonstrated since the initial recognition of the predominance of oral performance in early literate culture.[10] The preeminent historical fact is, however, that "the reader"

9. The foundation of the recent recognition of the limits of ancient literacy has been the explicit study of the communication culture of antiquity. See Achtemeier, "*Omne verbum sonat*," 3–27; Balogh, "Voces Paginarum," 84–109, 202–40; Carr, *Writing on the Tablet of the Heart*; Shiner, *Proclaiming the Gospel*; Hadas, *Ancilla to Classical Reading*; Harris, *Ancient Literacy*; Ong, *Presence of the Word*; Ong, *Orality and Literacy*.

10. See Slusser, "Reading Silently in Antiquity," 499.

as the *dominant* receiver and object of literary composition and distribution did not happen until the seventeenth century.

A representative example of this historical recognition is William Nelson's study of the practices of reading in the Renaissance culture of the fifteenth and sixteenth centuries: "From 'Listen, Lordings' to 'Dear Reader.'" Nelson concludes that while people doubtless read to themselves and evidence of reading habits is scattered, the dominant pattern is clear:

> Enough does exist to show that not only the long narratives of the Renaissance but also books of every conceivable kind, whether in prose or in verse, were commonly read aloud, sometimes by the author himself, sometimes by members of a household taking turns, sometimes by a professional reader or 'anagnost' as he was called in ancient times, the audiences ranging from the princely and sophisticated to the rustic illiterate.[11]

In the court of Francois I (1537), there was an official position of "reader-in-ordinary," who was employed to read to the king and the royal court. Even in the aftermath of the printing press and the accompanying increase in literacy, books were normally read aloud in part because of the sheer pleasure of the shared experience of hearing and then discussing great works of literature. Annotations and introductions gave instructions about how works were to be read.[12] Thus, after approximately 1500 years, the dominant practices of reading literature in the ancient world were still present. While there were undoubtedly silent readers in this period, it was only in the seventeenth century that addresses to the receiver of literary works as "the reader" became widespread.

The exploration of this private relationship between an author and a reader sitting alone and reading in silence is first developed into an integral dimension of the novel in the fiction of Henry Fielding (1707–54). Fielding's comments to the reader are an omnipresent dimension of his narration of his tale. These comments serve up a plate of ever-new possibilities for the relationship between an author and a reader. Early in his greatest novel, *Tom Jones*, Fielding establishes a sense of camaraderie between the author and the reader sliding down the hill together into their literary adventure and into the next episode of the story:

11. Nelson, "From 'Listen, Lordings' to 'Dear Reader,'" 110–24.

12. Nelson (ibid., 117–18) quotes Ronsard, who in a 1572 preface gives instructions as to how his *Franciade* should be read: "Je te supliray seulement d'une chose, lecteur, de vouloir bien prononcer mes vers & acommoder ta voix a leur passion, & non comme quelques unes les lisent, plustost a la facon d'une missive, ou de quelques lettres royaus que d'un Poeme bien prononce."

Reader, take care. I have unadvisedly led thee to the top of as high a hill as Mr. Allworthy's, and how to get thee down without breaking thy neck, I do not well know. However, let us e'en venture to slide down together; for Miss Bridget rings her bell, and Mr. Allworthy is summoned to breakfast, where I must attend, and, if you please, shall be glad of your company. (Bk. 1, ch. 4)[13]

Another function of these narrative comments to the reader is to provide inside information about what is happening to the characters:

The reader will perhaps imagine the sensations which now arose in Jones to have been so sweet and delicious, that they would rather tend to produce a cheerful serenity in the mind, than any of those dangerous effects which we have mentioned; but in fact, sensations of this kind, however delicious, are, at their first recognition, of a very tumultuous nature, and have very little of the opiate in them. (Bk. 4, ch. 3)

Fielding's elaborate comments also guide and, in the quote that follows, provoke the reader to align the reader's norms of judgment with the norms of the author in relation to the characters and elements of the plot:

Examine your heart, my good reader, and resolve whether you do believe these matters with me. If you do, you may now proceed to their exemplification in the following pages: if you do not, you have, I assure you, already read more than you have understood; and it would be wiser to pursue your business, or your pleasures (such as they are), than to throw away any more of your time in reading what you can neither taste nor comprehend. To treat of the effects of love to you, must be as absurd as to discourse on colours to a man born blind; since possibly your idea of love may be as absurd as that which we are told such blind man once entertained of the colour scarlet; that colour seemed to him to be very much like the sound of a trumpet: and love probably may, in your opinion, very greatly resemble a dish of soup, or a sirloin of roast-beef. (Bk. 6, ch. 1)

As one can see from these brief examples of reader address, the range of narrative possibilities associated with the development of silent reading has been immense. Since the seventeenth century, the silent reading of fiction has provided both authors and readers with ever-new dimensions of the reading experience to explore.[14]

13. Fielding, *Tom Jones*. Six different digital versions are available at Project Gutenberg: http://www.gutenberg.org/ebooks/6593/.

14. For a comprehensive survey of the development of the relationship between

This development, however, has been the end result of processes in communication technology and culture that have happened over sixteen centuries since the composition of Mark. The technologies and pedagogies associated with writing, reading, and cultural formation evolved gradually during those centuries.

The reading and interpretation of the Bible has been part of this evolution. When silent reading became the normative way of reading the Bible, new dimensions of the possibilities of meaning also emerged. Hans Frei's description of "meaning as reference" as the underlying assumption of biblical interpretation since the eighteenth century is a helpful description of this new discovery. The investigation of the Bible's "meaning as reference" has made possible the endlessly fascinating exploration of the Bible as a source of "ostensive" referential information about, for example, "the historical Jesus" and "ideal" referential information about the theologies of the Bible.[15]

The entire apparatus of historical criticism based on "the reader" is, however, a relatively late development in the history of literate communication. Reader-response criticism is an appropriate methodology for the study of Mark as read by Enlightenment readers, as Robert Fowler's book on Mark, *Let the Reader Understand,* reflects. Fowler, however, makes a strong and consistent distinction between the first-century reader in Mark 13:14 and the contemporary reader of Mark, whose reading experience is the subject of his study. As Fowler writes,

> The Gospel of Mark was probably written to be read aloud to an assembled audience, and one possibility for identifying 'the reader' of 13:14 would be to take the parenthesis as a kind of wink or stage direction to an *anagnostes,* a professional reader reciting the Gospel of Mark before an assembled audience.[16]

Fowler identifies the other possible references to "the reader" in Mark 13:10 as "an isolated, individual reader . . . reading the Gospel aloud to himself in private" or "an individual student of the Jewish Scriptures, who should be able to recognize and comprehend an allusion to Daniel."[17] But the purpose of his book is to explore the rich interpretive tradition that has developed with the silent reading of Mark as a text read by readers rather than the interpretation of Mark and its reader in the ancient world.

the reader and the complexities of narration in modern fiction, see Booth, *Rhetoric of Fiction.*

15. Frei, *Eclipse of Biblical Narrative*; see, in particular, "Hermeneutics and Meaning-as-Reference," ibid., 86–104.

16. Fowler, *Let The Reader Understand*, 84.

17. Ibid.

This distinction between "the reader" now and "the reader" then has not, however, been widely adopted in biblical scholarship. A reading of representative works of biblical scholarship leads to the conclusion that "the reader" in the first century is virtually the same figure as "the reader" from the eighteenth century to the twenty-first century. This is, however, a major blind spot in the ongoing work of biblical scholarship. *In relation to the goal of identifying the meaning of the Bible in its original historical context*, the enterprise of biblical scholarship has been based on a massive media anachronism. It has read back into the ancient world the communication culture of the readers of the Enlightenment sitting in studies examining the documents of the Bible in silence. An underlying assumption has been that the Gospel tradition, for example, moved more or less immediately from a predominantly oral culture to the high literate culture of the eighteenth and nineteenth centuries. The omnipresence of "the reader" in critical biblical commentaries and monographs is a reflection of this anachronistic character of biblical interpretation in the historical-critical era. The historical probability is that most of the persons in Mark's audiences could not read. Robert Fowler's decision to note every instance of "the reader" in his reading of the works of biblical scholarship is a good idea as is his celebration of the conscious pursuit of the reading possibilities that this way of reading has made possible. But he also recognizes that this understanding of "the reader" is different than it was for Mark.[18]

If, and in as far as, our goal is the identification of the meaning of Mark in its original historical context and if Mark was composed as performance literature, we need to listen to every detail of Mark's story in the context of the communication culture of the first century as a story that was performed for audiences.

Audience Asides in the Ancient Performance of Mark

If Mark's story was originally performed for audiences rather than read by readers, the so-called narrative comments of Mark to his readers need to be studied as asides to the audiences who were present at the performances of Mark in the first century. In a performance of a story, audience asides are one of the most important storytelling techniques, since they allow the storyteller to pause the account of what is happening, to lean in and speak directly to the audience. This may be a step toward the audience, a hand to the side of the mouth, a wink and a smile, or a change of tone. Whatever the

18. Ibid., 82–87.

particular move, the storyteller gives some sign that indicates the statement to follow is inside information that will help the members of the audience understand what is going on in the story.

These moments enable a storyteller to establish a close relationship with an audience. In a storytelling performance, there are two figures present: the storyteller and the audience. The relationship between a storyteller (or story reader) and any particular audience is extremely fragile. In virtually every moment of the story, it is possible for a storyteller to lose contact with or even alienate the audience. Individual members of the audience can turn off and go to sleep or start looking around for something else to do. Thus, at the end of the Little Apocalypse and in the Gethsemane story, the storyteller (as Jesus) addresses the audience (as the disciples) and tells them to "stay awake" (13:33, 35, 37; 14:35, 37, 38, 40). Other audience members may physically get up and leave. John addresses this possibility at the end of the bread-from-heaven discourse (6:67): "Do you also want to leave?" Others may start making negative gestures or verbal comments to others in the audience or to the storyteller. The loss of the audience is an ever-present possibility for a storyteller.

This is the reason why audience asides in storytelling are usually short, especially in comparison with narrative comments to a reader. Readers have lots of leisure time. They will happily read for hours. Therefore, Fielding's comments to the reader can be long and complex. Audiences, on the other hand, can easily lose interest and need constant reinforcement. If the audience is comfortable and interested, they will happily sit for hours. But if the story gets boring, an audience can be lost. It is thus essential in a long story to keep it moving. Interruptions to the flow of the action need to be brief.

In Mark, the audience asides are all short and have a variety of functions. Each instance of an audience aside, regardless of its function, can be a clue about the character and identity of the audiences that are projected for the story's performance. In the analysis that follows, representative examples of the major types of audience asides in Mark will be listed. For the purposes of this chapter, only representative examples of each type of audience aside will be listed. Mark's audience asides need to be heard in order to be correctly understood. Therefore, I would recommend that the readers of this chapter read aloud, or preferably tell the following examples of audience asides to an audience, or, if that is not possible, to themselves.

1. The Markan storyteller translates Aramaic words into Greek. The translations are usually introduced by the Greek phrase, ὅ ἐστιν μεθερμηνευόμενον. Examples are:

a. Ελωι ελωι λεμα σαβαχθανι; ὅ ἐστιν μεθερμηνευόμενον Ὁ θεός μου ὁ θεός μου, εἰς τί ἐγκατέλιπές με; ". . . which means 'My God, my God, why have you forsaken me?'" (15:34–35)

b. τὸν Γολγοθᾶν τόπον, ὅ ἐστιν μεθερμηνευόμενον Κρανίου Τόπος. ". . . which means 'the place of the Skull.'" (15:22)

c. ταλιθα κουμ, ὅ ἐστιν μεθερμηνευόμενον· τὸ κοράσιον, σοὶ λέγω, ἔγειρε. ". . . which means 'Little girl, I say to you, get up.'" (5:41)

These translations are indications that there are Greek speakers in the projected audiences who do not understand Aramaic.

2. The storyteller explains Jewish customs and practices. The most extensive is Mark's explanation of the cleanliness laws:

a. "For the Pharisees, and all the Jews, do not eat unless they thoroughly wash their hands, thus observing the tradition of the elders; and they do not eat anything from the market unless they wash it; and there are also many other traditions that they observe, the washing of cups, pots and bronze kettles" (7:3–4).

b. ". . . since it was the day of Preparation, that is, the day before the Sabbath" (15:42).

These explanations are signs that there are non-Jews in the projected audiences who do not know Jewish cleanliness laws.

3. The storyteller introduces characters by naming their children or their parents. These introductions happen throughout the story. Because this is the immediate context of the audience aside regarding Simon of Cyrene, I will list all of the characters who are introduced by the naming of members of their family:

a. James, the son of Zebedee and John his brother (1:19)

b. Levi, the son of Alphaeus (2:14)

c. James, the son of Zebedee and John, the brother of James (3:17)

d. James, the son of Alphaeus (3:18)

e. Bartimaeus, the son of Timaeus, a blind beggar (10:47)

f. Simon of Cyrene, the father of Alexander and Rufus (15:21)

g. Mary, the mother of James the younger (brother) and of Joses (15:40)

These introductions of new characters make the characters familiar and sympathetic. It's like getting to know somebody's family. It is a response to the audience's desire to get acquainted with the characters of a story.

4. The storyteller often explains things that are puzzling in the previous statement. For example, in the introduction to the Beelzebul conflict story, the storyteller reports the surprising and puzzling news that Jesus' family had come to seize him. The storyteller's explanation to the audience is, "Because they were saying, 'He's out of his mind'" (3:21). Other typical explanations are:

   a. The explanation of Jesus telling the disciples to get a boat ready for him: "Because many were healed so that they pressed in on him so that anyone who had diseases might touch him" (3:10).

   b. The reason the woman with a flow of blood touched his garment: "Because she said, 'If I can touch his garment, I will be made well'" (5:28).

   c. The explanation of the Sanhedrin's inability to find testimony to put Jesus to death: "Because many bore false witness against him and their testimony did not agree" (14:56).

   d. The reason why Pilate surprisingly offered to release Jesus to the crowd: "Because he recognized that it was out of envy that the chief priests had handed him over" (15:10).

These explanations are a basic technique of audience engagement. Rather than providing explanations before the description of an action or event, the composer describes something that is puzzling or surprising. These little incongruities invite the audience to wonder. The explanation that follows is then a moment of relationship between the storyteller and the audience in which the answer is provided for the question that has just been raised.

5. The storyteller will sometimes provide the audience with an inside view of the feelings or motives of a character, usually as an explanation of something puzzling. Thus, the storyteller gives the audience a double explanation of why Peter was speaking like a bumbling idiot when he asked about building three booths for Jesus, Moses and Elijah: "For he did not know what to say because he was afraid" (9:6).

These insights into the feelings of a character answer the audience's question about what is going on with a particular character. In this case, the explanation answers the question: Why is he acting like such a fool? The explanation also assumes that the audience will appreciate the fear and intimidation associated with finding oneself in the presence of Moses and Elijah.

6. Mark uniquely gives explanations that raise more questions than the puzzle he has just reported:

   a. The explanation of the disciples' amazement at Jesus walking on the water: "For they didn't understand about the loaves because their hearts were hardened" (6:52).

   b. The reason the women said nothing to anyone: "Because they were afraid" (16:8).

At the end of the walking-on-the water story, the composer assumes that the audience will know the stories of Pharoah hardening his heart and, therefore, will wonder what connection the disciples' hardened hearts might have to their inability to understand about the loaves. Furthermore, why would the disciples harden their hearts in response to Jesus walking on the water? During these moments in the story, the Markan storyteller is more of a provocateur than a helper. Nevertheless, in all of these instances of direct address to the audience by the Markan storyteller, a multifaceted, inclusive relationship between the storyteller and the audience of the story was formed.

The Audience Asides regarding the Purity Laws and the Sons of Simon of Cyrene

We can now address the specific audience asides that have had a central role in the identification of Mark's audience and purpose. The explanation of Jewish cleanliness laws has a markedly different impact as an aside to an audience than as a narrative comment. As a narrative comment, the explanation defines the readers. A natural inference is that the readers and, therefore, the intended recipients of the Gospel are Gentiles, who do not know the "traditions of the elders." And given the adversarial tone of the controversy, a further inference is that the readers are Gentile Christians who are invited to distance themselves from Jews. As an audience aside, however, the explanation has the function of audience *inclusion*. The explanation means that the composer presumes that there will be non-Jews in the projected audiences of the Gospel whom he does not want to exclude. But this aside does not limit or define the audiences as non-Jews. In fact, this is the only instance of an aside to Gentiles in a story in which there are many allusions addressed to Jews.[19]

Thus, to name three among many, the story of the Gerasene demoniac depends on a presumed Jewish norm of judgment that pigs are unclean animals (5:11–14) whose deaths are to be celebrated. The story of the woman who touched Jesus' garment is based on the assumption distinctive to Jewish law that by touching him she made him unclean and was fully justified in being afraid to admit what she had done (5:27–33). And Jesus' third passion prophecy climactically names "the Gentiles" as those who will mock him, spit on him, flog him and kill him (10:34).

The overall conclusion that emerges from a performance-critical analysis of the Markan audience is that the audiences of Mark were predominantly addressed as Jews. When heard in that context, the aside to the audience explaining Jewish cleanliness is a gesture of inclusion of Gentile minorities in the projected audiences of the story.

The naming of the sons of Simon of Cyrene also sounds different as an aside to the audience than it looks as a narrative comment to a reader. The names of Alexander and Rufus as a narrative comment to a reader imply private communication about two brothers who may have been known by a person or small group. It is fully possible to infer from the character of the comment that both the author and a local congregation knew Alexander and Rufus. This comment would create a personal connection with their father as well as between the author and the readers in his local church.

When assessed as an audience aside in a composition that was performed for wide-ranging audiences, the naming of Simon of Cyrene's sons has a different significance. It is one of a series of asides that introduce characters by naming members of their families. For example, Mary, the second witness of Jesus' death (15:40), is described as "the mother of James, the younger, and Joses." For audiences who are listening to the whole story at one time, these names are a verbal echo of the earlier story of Jesus' teaching in his hometown synagogue, in which the members of the synagogue ask themselves (6:3): "Isn't this the carpenter, the son of Mary and brother of James and Joses and Judas and Simon?" There is no possible implication that Jesus' brothers would have been known to the various audiences of the Gospel. Instead the implication of this sonic connection is that this woman is Jesus' mother. In all of the asides that introduce characters by naming members of their families, it is highly unlikely that these were heard as

---

19. For a systematic analysis of audience address in Mark, see Boomershine, "Audience Address and Purpose in the Performance of Mark," 115–42.

allusions to persons who would have been known to audiences some forty years after the events being described.

When heard as an integral element of a performance, the primary significance of these names is that the Markan storytellers are passing on a story that is linked with real persons who were known by the composer of the story. In the case of Simon of Cyrene, the naming of his sons, Alexander and Rufus, implies that the storyteller heard and learned the story from someone who knew Simon and his sons. The impact of this aside to the audience is to increase the credibility of the storyteller and his story about people whom the original composer knew by name. Furthermore, if we assume that Matthew and Luke knew and rewrote Mark's story, this implicit allusion to personal knowledge is also a possible explanation of why Matthew and Luke did not include their names. If they heard Mark's naming of Alexander and Rufus as reflecting personal knowledge, they may have left out the names because they did not want to imply that they knew them. However, regardless of the motives of Matthew and Luke, Mark's aside creates a sense of the authenticity of the storyteller and his story.

The Horizon of Mark's Audiences

The perception and interpretation of what have been called Mark's narrative comments is different when the words are heard as asides addressed to audiences. This is a specific dimension of the reconception of Mark as performance literature in the early literate culture of the first century. There are, however, broader possible implications.

Studying Mark's Gospel as performance literature suggests that we may reconceive what we mean by Mark. Rather than an author who is singularly present to a reader, Mark was the composer of a story who was made present vicariously by a series of performers who told Mark's story. The function of a composition for performance is to facilitate as many performances as possible by a whole range of performers. In music, for example, a composer may launch a new composition by directing or playing the first performance. But the composer's hope is that many orchestras or soloists will perform the composition over many years, hopefully many centuries. The writing and duplication of a musical composition makes it possible for a much wider range of performers to perform the work than if it were only distributed by oral transmission. Likewise, a primary function of the distribution of copies of Mark's manuscript was to enable storytellers to learn and tell Mark's story, sometimes from memory and sometimes by reading the manuscript aloud. In each performance, these new storytellers retold Mark's story and in a sense made Mark as the composer present. But each new evangelist also brought new dimensions to the performance of the story. Therefore, we can imagine varied performances of Mark's composition by a series of Marks, who told the story to various audiences. The original Mark was the composer who set the proclamation and performance of his Gospel in motion.

We also can think of audiences rather than readers as the context in which Mark's story was experienced. When seen in the context of ancient performance literature, the probability is that a composition such as Mark was composed for widespread performance to a variety of audiences. Mary Ann Tolbert's proposal that Mark is analogous to ancient novels such as Chariton's *Callirhoe* may be ambiguous as a description of Mark's genre.[20] But it is accurate as a description of Mark's communication horizon. The projected audiences of Mark were, if anything, larger and more inclusive than the audiences of the novelists.

Bauckham and his colleagues have proposed that the Gospels were composed for "all Christians." Their proposal is that the audiences of the Gospels were the local churches of the Roman world rather than individual, local congregations. Listening to the Gospel of Mark suggests that even this expanded vision of the horizon of the Gospels is too limited.

Two sayings of Jesus explicitly identify the horizon of the audiences of Mark's Gospel. In the apocalyptic discourse, Jesus says, "It is necessary that the good news/Gospel be proclaimed/told first to all the nations (καὶ εἰς πάντα τὰ ἔθνη πρῶτον δεῖ κηρυχθῆναι τὸ εὐαγγέλιον, 13:10)." That global horizon is reinforced in Jesus' commendation of the woman who anointed him with precious ointment: "Wherever in the whole world the good news/Gospel is proclaimed/told (ὅπου ἐὰν κηρυχθῇ τὸ εὐαγγέλιον εἰς ὅλον τὸν κόσμον) what she has done will be told in memory of her" (14:9). What then do these two sayings describe? The term εὐαγγέλιον is the name that is given to the whole composition: "The beginning of the Gospel/good news of Jesus Christ" (Ἀρχὴ τοῦ εὐαγγελίου Ἰησοῦ Χριστοῦ, 1:1). Thus, the proclamation of the Gospel is most naturally understood as a description of the performance or telling of the story for audiences.

In these two sayings, Jesus envisions a global horizon for the audiences of the Gospel. His statements suggest that the horizon of the audiences envisioned for the proclamation of Mark's story were not only a local church or only the Christian churches. The envisioned audiences were Jews

---

20. Tolbert, *Sowing the Gospel*, 70–73. The major problem with the genre of the novel as a description of Mark is that the novels were explicitly fiction. However, Tolbert's identification of a broad, popular audience is more congruent with the character of Mark as performance literature than is an audience of small local churches.

and Gentiles throughout the Greco-Roman world. An initial exploration of Mark as performance literature suggests that the composer of Mark envisioned performances of the Gospel in the whole world and used asides to the audience to include everyone in the story.

Bibliography

Achtemeier, Paul J. "*Omne verbum sonat*: The New Testament and the Oral Environment of Late Western Antiquity." *JBL* 109 (1990) 3–27.

Balogh, Josef. "Voces Paginarum." *Philologus* 82 (1926) 84–109, 202–40.

Bauckham, Richard. "For Whom Were Gospels Written?" In *The Gospels for All Christians: Rethinking the Gospel Audiences*, edited by Richard Bauckham, 9–48. Grand Rapids: Eerdmans, 1998.

Boomershine, Thomas E. "Audience Address and Purpose in the Performance of Mark." In *Mark as Story: Retrospect and Prospect*, edited by Kelly R. Iverson and Christopher W. Skinner, 115–42. SBLRBS 65. Atlanta: Society of Biblical Literature, 2011.

Booth, Wayne C. *The Rhetoric of Fiction*. Chicago: University of Chicago Press, 1961.

Brown, Raymond E. *Introduction to the New Testament*. ABRL. New York: Doubleday, 1997.

Carr, David M. *Writing on the Tablet of the Heart: Origins of Scripture and Literature*. Oxford: Oxford University Press, 2005.

Collins, Adela Yarbro. *Mark: A Commentary*. Hermeneia. Minneapolis: Fortress, 2007.

Fowler, Robert. *Let the Reader Understand: Reader-Response Criticism and the Gospel of Mark*. Minneapolis: Fortress, 1991.

Frei, Hans W. *The Eclipse of Biblical Narrative: A Study in Eighteenth and Nineteenth Century Hermeneutics*. New Haven: Yale University Press, 1974.

Hadas, Moses. *Ancilla to Classical Reading*. Columbia Bicentennial Editions and Studies. New York: Columbia University Press, 1954.

Harris, William. *Ancient Literacy*. Cambridge: Harvard University Press, 1989.

Incigneri, Brian J. *The Gospel to the Romans: The Setting and Rhetoric of Mark's Gospel*. Biblical Interpreation Series 65. Leiden: Brill, 2003.

Marcus, Joel. *Mark 1–8: A New Translation with Introduction and Commentary*. AB 27. New York: Doubleday, 2000.

Martyn, J. Louis. *History and Theology in the Fourth Gospel*. New York: Harper & Row, 1968.

Nelson, William. "From 'Listen, Lordings' to 'Dear Reader.'" *University of Toronto Quarterly* 46 (1977) 110–24.

Ong, Walter. *Orality and Literacy: The Technologizing of the Word*. New Accents. London: Methuen, 1982.

———. *The Presence of the Word: Some Prolegomena for Cultural and Religious History*. New Haven: Yale University Press, 1967.

Shiner, Whitney. *Proclaiming the Gospel: First-Century Performance of Mark*. Harrisburg, PA: Trinity, 2003.

Slusser, Michael. "Reading Silently in Antiquity." *JBL* 111 (1992) 499.

Tolbert, Mary Ann. *Sowing the Gospel: Mark's World in Literary-Historical Perspective*. Minneapolis: Fortress, 1989.

Weeden, Theodore J. *Mark—Traditions in Conflict*. Philadelphia: Fortress, 1971.

5

SOUND AND STRUCTURE IN
THE GOSPEL OF MATTHEW

Margaret E. Lee

THE FIRST STEP IN THE JOURNEY FROM TEXT TO PERFORMANCE
is sound. New Testament (NT) compositions reached their first audiences
through speech in public performances, but printed versions of the NT
obscure its spoken character. They display its compositions in predigested
forms accompanied by interpretive ideologies. Although important aspects
of its first performances have been lost, NT texts preserve their spoken
quality by encoding a compositions' sounds. Sound organizes these ancient
compositions, not logic or abstract ideas. Auditory signals create patterns
and define narrative structure. Mapping such acoustic features and displaying them graphically creates new interpretive possibilities. The Gospel of
Matthew exemplifies these dynamics because simple auditory structures
articulated early in the Gospel train an audience to hear subtler effects as
the Gospel progresses. Repeated sounds and parallel structure in the birth
narrative and the Sermon on the Mount provide a foundation for complex
acoustic effects that occur throughout the Gospel. Attention to such auditory clues releases the grip of printed arrangements of the Gospel with their
associated ideological implications and reveals the Gospel's organic structure. The Gospel's sound map mediates new insights for interpretation.

What Is a Sound Map?

Our Scriptures have fallen silent. Contemporary interpreters experience the NT primarily through silent reading of printed Bibles. Divisions between words, sentences, and paragraphs organize the reading experience. Chapters, verse numbers, and section headings added long after composition interpret the text and imply structural outlines. The human voice rarely animates the compositions of the NT except when they are read aloud in worship, extracted from their literary contexts. Nevertheless, our printed versions of the Greek NT preserve a crucial dimension of such performances: their spoken sound.

Sound mapping aims to restore the NT's original, performed dimension that has been largely lost to antiquity. A sound map is a response to the silence of print. It analyzes speech sounds and graphically displays auditory patterns. Sound mapping is an analytical technique that takes seriously the aesthetic value that ancient Greek-speakers placed on their language's sound. By presenting audible patterns in a visual display, sound mapping partially compensates for a modern reader's lack of listening fluency and reveals a composition's organic structure. Like the mental processing practiced by fluent listeners in real time, sound mapping is an inductive, interpretive endeavor that construes patterns as they are enunciated, syllable by syllable.

Grammar and Sound

Sound mapping relies primarily on the structure of Greek grammar, which Greek literary critics regarded as the science of spoken sound.[1] Because Greek is an inflected language, grammatically related words with rhyming endings cluster together. Because of its flexible word order, such rhyming word clusters can be arranged in various ways, elided and expanded, repeated and contrasted in parallel, and concatenated in elongated sequences for auditory effect. Such sound effects shape a listener's construction of meaning and imbue a composition with unique sound signatures that entail specific associations. Sound mapping plots such patterns and discerns a composition's organic structure.

To analyze patterns of spoken sound one does not necessarily need to know the precise pronunciation scheme in play for a composition's original performances. Debate continues regarding the pronunciation of Hellenistic Greek in the first centuries of the Common Era. At issue are accentuation and the extent to which the melodic accent of classical Greek had given

1. Dean, "Grammar of Sound in Greek Texts," 53–70.

way to accentuation based primarily on stress, during the period when the NT compositions were first performed. Vowel quantity and quality remain unclear, as does the pronunciation of certain consonants. Thus, it seems prudent to allow for considerable variation in pronunciation over time and from region to region. Nevertheless, since Greek pronunciation is phonetic, a performance would have employed a consistent pronunciation scheme, irrespective of the values assigned to each phoneme. Because the establishment of patterns relies on repetition, the consistency of phonetic pronunciation ensures a reliable basis for sound analysis.[2]

A sound map begins with a printed or electronic version of a Greek composition. Organizing marks that accommodate silent reading are removed, including titles, paragraphing, punctuation, and conventional versification, since these designations are extrinsic to the composition and were added after the NT was composed and performed, often to facilitate silent reading.[3] What remains is a graphic representation of a stream of sound, with phonemes arranged in a linear series. Sound mapping then applies analytical criteria derived from the same linguistic environment that produced the compositions under analysis.

To create a sound map, a printed or electronic version of the selected passage is organized into the breath units recognized in Hellenistic literary criticism: the colon (κῶλον) and the period (περίοδος). Greek critics define a period as a complete utterance and a colon as one of its component parts. A colon is necessarily incomplete; the word connotes a limb or member, part of a larger whole. A period implies a circular path: it connotes an utterance that begins from one place, proceeds along a line of discourse and returns at the end to its starting point. Its characteristic features are rounding and balance. Rounding refers to similarities between a period's beginning and end; balance refers to aesthetic equivalence among its components. Both periods and cola are described as breath units, even though periods consist of cola.[4]

According to Greek literary criticism, periods and cola function both as grammatical units and as stylistic features: all prose is composed of periods, yet some prose is not very periodic; its periods are not rounded and balanced but consist of several cola strung together. The technical definitions of cola and periods that appear in Greek literary criticism do not conform to the categorical boundaries set forth by modern linguistics because

2. Lee and Scott, *Sound Mapping the New Testament*, 81.

3. Accents and spaces between words were also supplied later but these are preserved in a sound map to facilitate word recognition by modern readers who lack listening fluency.

4. Ibid., 108–11.

they are rooted in the spoken character of their literature. For the purposes of a modern sound map, functional definitions based on grammatical characteristics can be useful. Functionally, a colon consists of a predicate (simple or compound, expressed or implied) and all words grammatically related to it. A period consists of one or more cola.

Sound and Structure

After a composition has been analyzed into breath units (cola and periods), audible patterns are plotted on a sound map to reveal a spoken composition's structure. In literature composed for print, read silently, and reread at will, discernment of structure depends on conceptual abstraction from the semantic load of a composition's words and on sustained reflection on their logical connections. By contrast, live performance is time bound; it does not allow opportunity to reflect on each word's full semantic load. A listening audience perceives one sound at a time; each sound strikes the ear as previous sounds fade away. Because audiences experience spoken performances in real time, they must discern patterns that render sounds meaningful and memorable. Established sound patterns organize audience expectation; departure from an established pattern draws audience attention. Thus both the establishment of patterns and departures from established patterns are structurally significant.

Patterns organize a listening experience by creating structural boundaries for a composition's component parts and by selecting sounds for emphasis. Listeners associate and remember repeated sounds. Repetition serves as sound's most fundamental structuring tool because it organizes isolated sounds into memorable patterns. Corresponding pattern components can be juxtaposed to highlight the sounds that change from one pattern iteration to the next. Listeners overcome sound's time-bound character by storing sequences of associated sounds in memory and recalling them as unified patterns.

Sound creates structure in spoken compositions by establishing, arranging, and modifying memorable sound patterns. The structure of a spoken composition must be audible, built up one syllable at a time. As with the comprehension of music, structures built from repeated sounds do not depend solely upon semantic meaning. Repetition of words or phrases is not always necessary to establish a pattern. Often, auditory patterns in spoken compositions build on repeated phonemes and syllables, not repeated words or phrases. Once created, auditory patterns communicate efficiently. A few key sounds can imply complete patterns; thus, listeners can "name that tune" after hearing only the first few notes of a melody. Similarly, sound's implications for meaning in spoken performance do not depend on semantics.

Sound shapes understanding by forming patterns that delineate a composition's component parts and furnish its organizational structure. Because structure organizes meaning, correct discernment of a composition's structure is fundamental to any interpretation of its meaning. The most fundamental product of sound mapping is the discernment of a composition's audible structural skeleton.

Structure and the Gospel of Matthew

In his important study of the structure of Matthew's Gospel, David Bauer states, "There is currently no consensus whatsoever on the structure of this Gospel."[5] Bauer classifies the various structural schemes that have been proposed throughout the modern history of the Gospel's interpretation into three categories: geographical-chronological structures, topical structures, and conceptual structures. Geographical-chronological outlines focus the Gospel's narrative plot. Emphasizing the frequent use of the title *Christ*, and Matthew's distinctive quotations from Scripture, such outlines highlight "the messianic role of Jesus in the fulfillment of prophecy."[6] Following the work of B. W. Bacon, topical outlines emphasize Matthew's redactional activity, seeking to interpret the incorporation of five discourses into the narrative plot.[7] Conceptual outlines construe the Gospel as a unique account of salvation history that reinterprets the history of Israel in terms of Jesus' life and death and the dawn of Christianity.[8] Bauer shows that while proposals in all three categories highlight important features of Matthew's Gospel, none of the categories adequately accounts for such features. Moreover, consensus concerning the Gospel's structure has not yet emerged, even among proponents within a single category of interpretation.[9]

---

5. Bauer, *Structure of Matthew's Gospel*, 7.

6. Ibid., 24.

7. Ibid., 26–45.

8. Ibid., 45–54.

9. Ibid., 21–55.

Bauer astutely observes that the diversity of proposals regarding the Gospel's structure derive from differences in interpretive methodology, not from the Gospel's inherent characteristics. Bauer roots his own structural proposal in observations of various kinds of repetition in the Gospel: repetition of comparison, repetition of contrast, and repetition of particularization and climax with preparation and causation. He finds three major divisions in the Gospel: 1:1—4:16, 4:17—16:20, and 16:21—28:20. These are the same divisions delineated in a subgroup of Bauer's "conceptual structures" category entitled "Topical Outline based upon 'Superscriptions' at 1:1, 4:17; 16:21."[10]

The strength of Bauer's analysis is twofold. First, Bauer squarely confronts methodologies that too often shape interpretation by imposing on the Gospel extrinsic ideologies that bend the Gospel's message to an interpreter's interests. Second, Bauer correctly observes that repetition serves as the Gospel's primary structural device. Privileging repetition's structural role entails at least implicit recognition of the linear character of auditory reception. It also serves as a corrective to the practice of imposing extrinsic meanings, by rooting the interpretive process in the Gospel's inherent characteristics.

Missing from Bauer's analysis is any observation of the actual sound of spoken performance, precisely the vehicle that implements the Gospel's structural organization and its dimensions of meaning. A comprehensive assessment of Bauer's own structural proposal lies beyond the scope of this essay, but sound mapping can suggest more precisely the pragmatic means by which structural devices are implemented through spoken sound. Important clues to the Gospel's organic structure emerge from sound maps of the Gospel's opening chapters.

Structure in Matthew's Birth Narrative

Beginnings are important in performed compositions because they teach audiences how to listen. The Gospel's opening narrative of Jesus' birth and the first major speech, the Sermon on the Mount, provide important clues to the Gospel's structure. Matthew begins with a genealogy organized into brief cola with repeating sounds. Its primary structural features stand out in a sound map, even for readers who lack fluency in Greek. Cola are numbered for reference.

---

10. Ibid., 40.

Matt 1:1–17

1	Βίβλος		γενέσεως Ἰησοῦ Χριστοῦ υἱοῦ Δαυὶδ υἱοῦ Ἀβραάμ.
2	Ἀβραὰμ		ἐγέννησεν τὸν Ἰσαάκ,
3	Ἰσαὰκ	δὲ	ἐγέννησεν τὸν Ἰακώβ,
4	Ἰακὼβ	δὲ	ἐγέννησεν τὸν Ἰούδαν καὶ τοὺς ἀδελφοὺς αὐτοῦ,
5	Ἰούδας	δὲ	ἐγέννησεν τὸν Φάρες καὶ τὸν Ζάρα ἐκ τῆς Θαμάρ,
6	Φάρες	δὲ	ἐγέννησεν τὸν Ἐσρώμ,
7	Ἐσρὼμ	δὲ	ἐγέννησεν τὸν Ἀράμ,
8	Ἀρὰμ	δὲ	ἐγέννησεν τὸν Ἀμιναδάβ,
9	Ἀμιναδὰβ	δὲ	ἐγέννησεν τὸν Ναασσών,
10	Ναασσὼν	δὲ	ἐγέννησεν τὸν Σαλμών,
11	Σαλμὼν	δὲ	ἐγέννησεν τὸν Βόες ἐκ τῆς Ῥαχάβ,
12	Βόες	δὲ	ἐγέννησεν τὸν Ἰωβὴδ ἐκ τῆς Ῥούθ,
13	Ἰωβὴδ	δὲ	ἐγέννησεν τὸν Ἰεσσαί,
14	Ἰεσσαὶ	δὲ	ἐγέννησεν τὸν Δαυὶδ τὸν βασιλέα.
15	Δαυὶδ	δὲ	ἐγέννησεν τὸν Σολομῶνα ἐκ τῆς τοῦ Οὐρίου,
16	Σολομὼν	δὲ	ἐγέννησεν τὸν Ῥοβοάμ,
17	Ῥοβοὰμ	δὲ	ἐγέννησεν τὸν Ἀβιά,
18	Ἀβιὰ	δὲ	ἐγέννησεν τὸν Ἀσάφ,
19	Ἀσὰφ	δὲ	ἐγέννησεν τὸν Ἰωσαφάτ,
20	Ἰωσαφὰτ	δὲ	ἐγέννησεν τὸν Ἰωράμ,
21	Ἰωρὰμ	δὲ	ἐγέννησεν τὸν Ὀζίαν,
22	Ὀζίας	δὲ	ἐγέννησεν τὸν Ἰωαθάμ,
23	Ἰωαθὰμ	δὲ	ἐγέννησεν τὸν Ἀχάζ,
24	Ἀχὰζ	δὲ	ἐγέννησεν τὸν Ἐζεκίαν,
25	Ἐζεκίας	δὲ	ἐγέννησεν τὸν Μανασσῆ,
26	Μανασσῆς	δὲ	ἐγέννησεν τὸν Ἀμώς,
27	Ἀμὼς	δὲ	ἐγέννησεν τὸν Ἰωσίαν,
28	Ἰωσίας	δὲ	ἐγέννησεν τὸν Ἰεχονίαν καὶ τοὺς ἀδελφοὺς αὐτοῦ
			ἐπὶ τῆς μετοικεσίας Βαβυλῶνος.

29	Μετὰ	δὲ	τὴν μετοικεσίαν Βαβυλῶνος
	Ἰεχονίας		ἐγέννησεν τὸν Σαλαθιήλ,
30	Σαλαθιὴλ	δὲ	ἐγέννησεν τὸν Ζοροβαβέλ,
31	Ζοροβαβὲλ	δὲ	ἐγέννησεν τὸν Ἀβιούδ,
32	Ἀβιοὺδ	δὲ	ἐγέννησεν τὸν Ἐλιακίμ,
33	Ἐλιακὶμ	δὲ	ἐγέννησεν τὸν Ἀζώρ,
34	Ἀζὼρ	δὲ	ἐγέννησεν τὸν Σαδώκ,
35	Σαδὼκ	δὲ	ἐγέννησεν τὸν Ἀχίμ,
36	Ἀχὶμ	δὲ	ἐγέννησεν τὸν Ἐλιούδ,

37 Ἐλιοὺδ   δὲ   ἐγέννησεν τὸν Ἐλεάζαρ,

38 Ἐλεάζαρ   δὲ   ἐγέννησεν τὸν Ματθάν,

39 Ματθὰν   δὲ   ἐγέννησεν τὸν Ἰακώβ,

40 Ἰακὼβ   δὲ   ἐγέννησεν τὸν Ἰωσὴφ τὸν ἄνδρα Μαρίας,

              ἐξ ἧς ἐγεννήθη Ἰησοῦς ὁ λεγόμενος Χριστός.

41 Πᾶσαι οὖν αἱ **γεν**εαὶ

              ἀπὸ Ἀβραὰμ   ἕως Δαυὶδ   **γεν**εαὶ δεκατέσσαρες,

42 καὶ ἀπὸ Δαυὶδ   ἕως

              τῆς μετοικεσίας Βαβυλῶνος   **γεν**εαὶ δεκατέσσαρες,

43 καὶ ἀπὸ τῆς μετοικεσίας Βαβυλῶνος ἕως τοῦ Χριστοῦ

                                      γενεαὶ δεκατέσσαρες.

Brief cola with repeating sounds organize Matthew's genealogy. Every colon iterates some form of γίνομαι, repeating the syllable -γεν- that occurs in the Gospel's first colon (γενέσεως, colon 1; δὲ ἐγέννησεν τόν, cola 2–40; γενεαί, cola 41–43). Cola are arranged in parallel. Cola 2–40 begin by repeating the name enunciated at the end of the previous colon.

Pattern variations occur in cola 4, 5, 11, 12 and 15 but even these variations occur in parallel (the endings of cola 4 and 5 are parallel, beginning with καί; the endings of cola 11, 12, and 15 are parallel, beginning with ἐκ τῆς). In cola 28–29, the phrases ἐπὶ τῆς μετοικεσίας Βαβυλῶνος and μετὰ δὲ τὴν μετοικεσίαν Βαβυλῶνος interrupt the pattern but also leave it intact. The phrases are set in parallel; in fact, they are almost identical. The extended ending of colon 28 begins with καί, like cola 4, 5, 11, and 12, and Ἰεχονίας at the beginning of colon 29 repeats its mention in the previous colon, following the general pattern of the genealogy. The elongated ending of colon 40 begins with ἐξ ἧς which rhymes with ἐκ τῆς in cola 11, 12 and 15 and ἐπὶ τῆς in colon 28.

Cola 41–43 also modify the established pattern while retaining its defining features: -γεν- occurs in the middle of colon 41; the element named in cola 41 and 42 repeats at the beginning of the subsequent colon (Δαυὶδ, cola 41 and 42; τῆς μετοικεσίας Βαβυλῶνος, cola 42 and 43); and a doubled occurrence of τῆς μετοικεσίας Βαβυλῶνος occurs in the middle of this passage as it does in the middle of the genealogy. Cola 41–43 introduce the novel element of γενεαί, a nominal form of γίνομαι that repeats the section's sound signature (-γεν-). This newly introduced element occurs within a parallel structure, with a repeated phrase (γενεαὶ δεκατέσσαρες) that concludes cola 41–43.

The structural arrangement of sounds in Matthew's genealogy holds little significance at the semantic level of meaning beyond the emphasis laid on the lexeme γίνομαι and its various forms, calling attention to the passage's theme. The same information could have been conveyed with different words, longer cola, and more syntactical variation. Early establishment of clear auditory patterns indicates an additional dimension of meaning beyond semantics, contributed through pattern recognition. This audible dimension of meaning supports the Gospel's primary themes. Frequent repetition of -γεν- emphasizes Jesus' connection to Israel's story, while interruptions of parallel structure suggest ruptures in that story. Many have noticed that pattern deviations in cola 4, 5, 11, 12, and 15 correspond with problematic characters in Israel's past.[11] Division of the genealogy into two parts, before and after the pattern interruption in cola 28 and 29, mirrors how the Babylonian captivity divided Israel's story into the time before and after the exile. The pattern deviation in colon 40 announces the genealogy's climax with the name of "Jesus, who is called 'the messiah'" (Ἰησοῦς ὁ λεγόμενος Χριστός). Reprisal in cola 41–43 of established auditory patterns, combined with the novel structural feature of repeated ending sounds in these cola (γενεαὶ δεκατέσσαρες), summarizes the genealogy and draws it to a close, leading the audience to anticipate a change in scene.

The expected change occurs in 1:18 where the sound signature changes, yet the structural devices implemented in the genealogy continue to guide audience attention as the narrative proceeds. The genealogy employs frequently repeated sounds in brief cola. Repeated beginning sounds contain the syllable -γεν- in every colon. These same signals mark the beginnings of all three component episodes of the birth narrative, 1:1, 1:18, and 2:1.

Beginning Cola of the Birth Narrative's Component Episodes

Episode 1   Βίβλος **γενέσεως** Ἰησοῦ Χριστοῦ υἱοῦ Δαυὶδ υἱοῦ Ἀβραάμ (1:1)

Episode 2   Τοῦ δὲ Ἰησοῦ Χριστοῦ ἡ **γένεσις** οὕτως ἦν (1:18)

Episode 3   Τοῦ δὲ Ἰησοῦ **γεννηθέντος** ἐν Βηθλέεμ τῆς Ἰουδαίας

ἐν ἡμέραις Ἡρῴδου τοῦ βασιλέως (2:1)

All three episodes articulate the name of Jesus (Ἰησοῦ [Χριστοῦ]) in their opening cola. The second and third episodes repeat in their opening cola the syllable -γεν-, which was emphasized in the genealogy. They also both begin with τοῦ δὲ Ἰησοῦ, even though this phrase serves different grammatical purposes in 1:18, where it functions as the genitive modifier of ἡ γένεσις, and in 2:1, where it functions as a genitive absolute construction.

11. Brown, *Birth of the Messiah*, 71–74.

Given that the genealogy has organized the listening experience through frequently repeated sounds, the similarity of opening sounds in 1:1, 1:18 and 2:1 signals narrative shifts and redirects audience attention.

A similar device subdivides the lengthy third episode of the birth narrative (2:1–23) into three narrative scenes.

Beginning Cola of Episode 3's Component Narrative Scenes

Scene 1   Τοῦ δὲ Ἰησοῦ **γεννηθέντος** ἐν Βηθλέεμ τῆς Ἰουδαίας
                             ἐν ἡμέραις **Ἡρῴδου τοῦ βασιλέως** (2:1)

Scene 2   **Τότε Ἡρῴδης** λάθρᾳ καλέσας τοὺς μάγους (2:7)

Scene 3   **Τότε Ἡρῴδης** ἰδὼν ὅτι ἐνεπαίχθη
                             ὑπὸ τῶν μάγων ἐθυμώθη λίαν (2:16)

The prominent mention of Ἡρῴδου τοῦ βασιλέως in 2:1 sets up Jesus and Herod as rival kings. Herod's name is repeated when the scene changes in 2:7 and 2:16: the first cola of both scenes begin with τότε Ἡρῴδης. Finally, repeated occurrences of ἰδού draw attention to instances of divine intervention throughout the birth narrative.

Evolving Structures in the Gospel Narrative

The next section of the Gospel's narrative signals a shift in 3:1 with a change of scene and a reversion to the use in 1:18 and 2:1 of the postpositive particle δέ to signal the beginnings of narrative episodes.

3:1   Ἐν   **δὲ** ταῖς ἡμέραις ἐκείναις παραγίνεται Ἰωάννης ὁ βαπτιστὴς
                        κηρύσσων ἐν τῇ ἐρήμῳ τῆς Ἰουδαίας

3:4   Αὐτὸς   **δὲ** ὁ Ἰωάννης εἶχεν τὸ ἔνδυμα αὐτοῦ ἀπὸ τριχῶν καμήλου

3:7   Ἰδὼν   **δὲ** πολλοὺς τῶν Φαρισαίων καὶ Σαδδουκαίων ἐρχομένους
                        ἐπὶ τὸ βάπτισμα αὐτοῦ

With the entry of Jesus into the narrative in 3:13, narrative scenes begin with τότε, the other indication of scene beginnings used in the birth narrative (2:7, 16).

The Baptism Story

3:13   Τότε παραγίνεται ὁ Ἰησοῦς ἀπὸ τῆς Γαλιλαίας

3:15b Τότε ἀφίησιν αὐτόν

The Temptation Story

4:1   Τότε ὁ Ἰησοῦς ἀνήχθη εἰς τὴν ἔρημον

4:5   Τότε παραλαμβάνει αὐτὸν ὁ **διάβολος** εἰς τὴν ἁγίαν πόλιν

Whereas in the birth narrative τότε Ἡρῴδης introduced component scenes, in Herod's story, repetitions of τότε with another actor's name introduce narrative scenes in 3:13—4:11 when Jesus enters the story. In the baptism story, Jesus is the named actor in 3:13; the actor is unnamed but implied in 3:15b. In 4:1–11, the temptation story, actors alternate: the actor is ὁ Ἰησοῦς in 4:1; the actor is ὁ διάβολος in 4:5. Scenes consist of brief cola, frequently connected by parataxis. Throughout the baptism and temptation scenes, repeated occurrences of ἰδού signal divine intervention, as in the birth narrative.

The temptation story concludes with two periods that begin with τότε.

4:10   **τότε** λέγει αὐτῷ ὁ Ἰησοῦς, Ὕπαγε, Σατανᾶ

4:11   **τότε** ἀφίησιν αὐτὸν ὁ **διάβολος**

The doubled occurrence of τότε at the end of the temptation story and the absence of supporting signals to indicate new narrative scenes suggest the continuing evolution of that auditory signal. The occurrences of τότε in 4:10–11 reprise the names of the story's alternating actors, ὁ Ἰησοῦς and ὁ διάβολος, referring to and suggesting a conclusion to that story rather than a new beginning. Confirmation of τότε as a concluding signal occurs in 4:12 with an elongated colon that changes the scene by introducing new place names and new sounds set in parallel.

4:12   Ἀκούσας δὲ ὅτι Ἰωάννης παρεδόθη   ἀνεχώρησεν
                                  εἰς   τὴν **Γαλιλαίαν**
       καὶ καταλιπὼν τὴν Ναζαρὰ ἐλθὼν   κατῴκησεν
                      εἰς   Καφαρναοὺμ   τὴν παρα**θαλασσίαν**
                      ἐν   ὁρίοις Ζαβουλὼν καὶ Νεφθαλίμ

Like the temptation story, this new narrative scene also concludes with a period that begins with τότε, repeating the previous scene's innovation on the use of this auditory signal.

4:17　Ἀπὸ **τότε** ἤρξατο ὁ Ἰησοῦς κηρύσσειν

In 4:12–22, the narrative again reverts to the use of the postpositive δέ to signal the beginnings of new component units, as in 3:1–16.

4:12	Ἀκούσας	**δὲ** ὅτι Ἰωάννης παρεδόθη ἀνεχώρησεν εἰς τὴν Γαλιλαίαν
4:18	Περιπατῶν	**δὲ** παρὰ τὴν θάλασσαν τῆς Γαλιλαίας εἶδεν δύο ἀδελφούς
4:19	οἱ	**δὲ** εὐθέως ἀφέντες τὰ δίκτυα ἠκολούθησαν αὐτῷ.
4:22	οἱ	**δὲ** εὐθέως ἀφέντες τὸ πλοῖον

Finally, another change of scene occurs in 4:23 that introduces new place names and new sounds set in parallel.

4:23	Καὶ περιῆγεν	ἐν ὅλῃ τῇ Γαλιλαίᾳ
	διδάσκων	ἐν ταῖς συναγωγαῖς αὐτῶν
	καὶ κηρύσσων	τὸ εὐαγγέλιον τῆς βασιλείας
	καὶ θεραπεύων	πᾶσαν νόσον
	καὶ	πᾶσαν μαλακίαν ἐν τῷ λαῷ

Cola composing 4:23–25 are connected paratactically, and they multiply geographic references. Reduction of structural signals quiets the performance before new structural arrangements emerge in the Gospel's first lengthy discourse in 5:3—7:27, the Sermon on the Mount.

Sound and Structure in the Gospel's Opening Narrative

Frequently repeated sounds yield an important advantage beyond their semantic meaning, especially when they recur in corresponding locations in parallel compositional components. Such repetitions alert an audience to structural signals and their potential for thematic significance. Both the establishment of patterns and departures from established patterns shape an audience's construction of meaning. Auditory signals evolve throughout the Gospel and thus expand their expressive quality and organizational potential.

Structural signals forged at the beginning of the Gospel train an audience to comprehend the unfolding story by dividing it into unified and coherent episodes. Frequent repetition of beginning sounds in cola that are set in parallel trains an audience to expect repeated beginnings and parallel structure as primary organizing features. The genealogy establishes structural devices through frequent repetition in short cola. The Gospel then employs these devices in modified forms in the birth narrative, baptism story and temptation story to organize the first narrative section. The utility and simplicity of these auditory clues invite an audience to anticipate their subsequent use as structural devices in the Gospel.

The Structure of the Sermon on the Mount

After the Gospel's first narrative section, its first lengthy discourse employs repeated beginning sounds and parallel structure as primary devices to organize the listening experience and direct an audience's attention. The Sermon on the Mount opens in a distinctive way, with the Beatitudes. Periods and cola are numbered; for example, 3.2 signifies the third period, second colon.

1.1   **Μακάριοι οἱ** πτωχοὶ τῷ πνεύματι
1.2   ὅτι αὐτῶν ἐστιν   ἡ βασιλεία τῶν οὐρανῶν

2.1   **μακάριοι** οἱ πενθοῦντες
2.2   ὅτι αὐτοὶ παρακληθήσονται

3.1   **μακάριοι** οἱ πραεῖς
3.2   ὅτι αὐτοὶ κληρονομήσουσιν   τὴν γῆν

4.1   **μακάριοι** οἱ πεινῶντες καὶ διψῶντες   τὴν δικαιοσύνην
4.2   ὅτι αὐτοὶ χορτασθήσονται

5.1   **μακάριοι** οἱ ἐλεήμονες
5.2   ὅτι αὐτοὶ ἐλεηθήσονται

6.1   **μακάριοι** οἱ καθαροὶ τῇ καρδίᾳ
6.2   ὅτι αὐτοὶ τὸν θεὸν ὄψονται

7.1   **μακάριοι** οἱ εἰρηνοποιοί
7.2   ὅτι [αὐτοὶ] υἱοὶ θεοῦ κληθήσονται

8.1   **μακάριοι** οἱ δεδιωγμένοι ἕνεκεν   δικαιοσύνης
8.2   ὅτι αὐτῶν ἐστιν   ἡ βασιλεία τῶν οὐρανῶν

9.1   μακάριοί ἐστε

9.2   ὅταν ὀνειδίσωσιν ὑμᾶς

9.3   καὶ διώξωσιν

9.4   καὶ εἴπωσιν πᾶν πονηρὸν καθ᾽ ὑμῶν [ψευδόμενοι] ἕνεκεν ἐμοῦ

10.1   χαίρετε καὶ ἀγαλλιᾶσθε

10.2   ὅτι ὁ μισθὸς ὑμῶν πολὺς   ἐν τοῖς οὐρανοῖς

10.3   οὕτως γὰρ ἐδίωξαν τοὺς προφήτας τοὺς πρὸ ὑμῶν

Matthew expands the beatitude form beyond its trifold articulation in Q by multiplying their number and thus reiterating their distinctive beginning sound (μακάριοι) and their common format (μακάριοι οἱ . . . ὅτι αὐτῶν/αὐτοί . . .).[12] Matthew's version of the Beatitudes is distinctive in that iterates μακάριοι οἱ eight times to Luke's three, and it expands ὅτι to ὅτι αὐτῶν/αὐτοί, thereby emphasizing both structural devices: repeated beginning sounds and parallel structure. A comparison with the Beatitudes in Luke's Gospel highlights the extent to which Matthew amplified these two features.

The Beatitudes in the Gospels of Luke and Matthew

Luke 6:20–22	Matt 5:3–12
Μακάριοι οἱ πτωχοί,	**Μακάριοι οἱ** πτωχοὶ τῷ πνεύματι,
ὅτι ὑμετέρα ἐστὶν ἡ βασιλεία τοῦ θεοῦ	**ὅτι αὐτῶν** ἐστιν ἡ βασιλεία τῶν οὐρανῶν
	μακάριοι οἱ πενθοῦντες,
	ὅτι αὐτοὶ παρακληθήσονται
	μακάριοι οἱ πραεῖς
	ὅτι αὐτοὶ κληρονομήσουσιν τὴν γῆν
μακάριοι οἱ πεινῶντες νῦν	**μακάριοι οἱ** πεινῶντες καὶ διψῶντες τὴν δικαιοσύνην
ὅτι χορτασθήσεσθε	**ὅτι αὐτοὶ** χορτασθήσονται

12. Although Q's version of the Beatitudes is disputed, scholarly consensus maintains that Matthew multiplied the number of Beatitudes, either by redaction or expansion of a source (Kloppenborg, *Q Parallels*, 26). Luke's version of Q material is generally considered more authentic, but the International Q Project judges Matt 5:11 to be closer to Q than Luke 6:22 (Robinson et al., *Critical Edition of Q*, 50–51).

Luke 6:20-22	Matt 5:3-12
	μακάριοι οἱ ἐλεήμονες ὅτι αὐτοὶ ἐλεηθήσονται
	μακάριοι οἱ καθαροὶ τῇ καρδίᾳ ὅτι αὐτοὶ τὸν θεὸν ὄψονται
	μακάριοι οἱ εἰρηνοποιοί ὅτι αὐτοὶ υἱοὶ θεοῦ κληθήσονται
μακάριοι οἱ κλαίοντες νῦν ὅτι γελάσετε	
	μακάριοι οἱ δεδιωγμένοι ἕνεκεν δικαιοσύνης ὅτι αὐτῶν ἐστιν ἡ βασιλεία τῶν οὐρανῶν
μακάριοί ἐστε ὅταν μισήσωσιν ὑμᾶς οἱ ἄνθρωποι καὶ ὅταν ἀφορίσωσιν ὑμᾶς καὶ ὀνειδίσωσιν καὶ ἐκβάλωσιν τὸ ὄνομα ὑμῶν ὡς πονηρὸν ἕνεκα τοῦ υἱοῦ τοῦ ἀνθρώπου	μακάριοί ἐστε ὅταν ὀνειδίσωσιν ὑμᾶς καὶ διώξωσιν καὶ εἴπωσιν πᾶν πονηρὸν καθ᾽ ὑμῶν [ψευδόμενοι] ἕνεκεν ἐμοῦ
χάρητε ἐν ἐκείνῃ τῇ ἡμέρᾳ καὶ σκιρτήσατε	χαίρετε καὶ ἀγαλλιᾶσθε
ἰδοὺ γὰρ ὁ μισθὸς ὑμῶν πολὺς ἐν τῷ οὐρανῷ κατὰ τὰ αὐτὰ γὰρ ἐποίουν τοῖς προφήταις οἱ πατέρες αὐτῶν	ὅτι ὁ μισθὸς ὑμῶν πολὺς ἐν τοῖς οὐρανοῖς· οὕτως γὰρ ἐδίωξαν τοὺς προφήτας τοὺς πρὸ ὑμῶν

Acoustic patterns in the Sermon on the Mount take on added signifi-cance when heard in the context of the opening narrative. With their repeti-tion of opening sounds in brief cola with parallel structure, the Beatitudes employ acoustic devices introduced in the genealogy and implemented in modified form throughout the birth narrative, baptism story and temptation story. The Beatitudes' distinctive sound signature supplies an auditory scheme that organizes the entire Sermon on the Mount. Repetition of beginning sounds (anaphora) and parallel structure serve as the primary devices that organize the Sermon on the Mount. The Sermon consists of eight sections of unequal length. Each section consists of component units that share the same beginning sounds and articulate a distinctive sound signature for that section.[13]

Sectional Boundaries of the Sermon on the Mount

Sections	Repeated beginning sounds	Occurrences of repeated beginning sounds
1 5:3–12	Μακάριοι οἱ . . . ὅτι αὐτοί (αὐτῶν)	5:3, 4, 5, 6, 7, 8, 9, 10, 11
2 5:13–16	Ὑμεῖς ἐστε	5:13, 14
3 5:17–20	Μὴ νομίσητε	5:17
4 5:21–48	Ἠκούσατε ὅτι ἐρρέθη τοῖς ἀρχαίοις	5:21, 27, 33, 38, 43
5 6:1–18	Προσ- . . . Ὅταν	6:1, 2, 5, 7, 16
6 6:19—7:6	Μή + [imperative verb]	6:19, 7:1, 6
7 7:7–20	[Imperative Verb]	7:7, 13, 15
8 7:21–28	Οὐ πᾶς / Πᾶς οὖν	7:21, 24

The number of component parts, and therefore the number of repeated opening sounds, differs from section to section in the Sermon. Understandably, the largest number of repetitions occurs in the Sermon's first section, in which μακάριοι οἱ . . . ὅτι αὐτοί (αὐτῶν) occurs nine times. Audible clues must be repeated frequently, especially at the beginning of a structural unit, to establish their organizing function. Fewer repetitions are required as the Sermon progresses, after the structural importance of

13. For a full analysis of the structure of the Sermon on the Mount, see Lee, "A Method for Sound Analysis in Hellenistic Greek"; and Lee and Scott, *Sound Mapping the New Testament*, 309–52.

anaphora has been established and the audience has been trained to attend to this signal. Section 2 contains only two component parts, both of which begin with the same opening sounds, ὑμεῖς ἐστε. Section 3 deviates from the pattern. The Sermon's two middle sections, sections 4 and 5, reestablish the use of anaphora and parallel structure to delineate their five component units. The Sermon's final three sections decrease the number of components and repeated opening sounds to three in sections 6 and 7 and to two in the Sermon's final section, section 8.

The Sermon's eightfold structure with parallel component units enables an audience to predict when to pay attention. Since parallel elements repeat throughout each section, audiences can focus their attention on each section's distinctive elements. Once stored in memory, repeated structures fall to the background and novel features stand out.

Evolving Structures in the Sermon

Just as the pattern of repeating sounds and parallel structure was established in the genealogy and modified throughout the Gospel's first narrative section, the Beatitudes reestablish similar patterns that continue to evolve throughout the Sermon on the Mount. As does the genealogy, the Beatitudes also iterate repeated sounds and parallel structure many times to establish the pattern's organizing effect. As in the rest of the Gospel's opening narrative, patterns established in the Beatitudes subsequently shift, retaining components of the original pattern while incorporating novel elements. This occurs first in the transition from Beatitudes to the Sermon's next section. Periods and cola are numbered.

5:10–14

1.1 **μακάριοι οἱ** δεδιωγμένοι ἕνεκεν δικαιοσύνης

1.2 ὅτι αὐτῶν ἐστιν ἡ βασιλεία   τῶν οὐρανῶν

2.1 **μακάριοί ἐστε**

2.2 ὅταν   ὀνειδίσωσιν   ὑμᾶς

2.3 καὶ   διώξωσιν

2.4 καὶ   εἴπωσιν   πᾶν πονηρὸν καθ' ὑμῶν [ψευδόμενοι] ἕνεκεν ἐμοῦ

3.1 **χαίρετε καὶ ἀγαλλιᾶσθε**

3.2 ὅτι ὁ μισθὸς ὑμῶν πολὺς ἐν   τοῖς οὐρανοῖς

3.3 οὕτως γὰρ ἐδίωξαν τοὺς προφήτας τοὺς πρὸ ὑμῶν

4.1   Ὑμεῖς ἐστε   τὸ   ἅλας τῆς γῆς
4.2   ἐὰν δὲ   τὸ   ἅλας μωρανθῇ
4.3   ἐν τίνι   ἁλισθήσεται
4.4   εἰς οὐδὲν ἰσχύει ἔτι
4.5   εἰ μὴ βληθῆναι ἔξω
4.6   καὶ καταπατεῖσθαι ὑπὸ τῶν ἀνθρώπων

5.1   Ὑμεῖς ἐστε τὸ φῶς τοῦ κόσμου

The final beatitude in periods 2–3 deviates from the section's established pattern, but it retains the pattern's essential elements: μακάριοί at the beginning, which reiterates the section's distinctive sound signature; and a ὅτι clause in 3.2, suggesting the Beatitudes' established parallel structure. In the elongated final beatitude, both structural elements of the beatitude pattern, μακάριοι and the ὅτι clause, are modified. Period 2 opens with μακάριοί ἐστε instead of μακάριοι οἱ, and the ὅταν clause in 2.2 echoes the ὅτι clause but modifies that structural feature. Although ὅτι and ὅταν are semantically unrelated, their similar sounds and their corresponding placement in the parallel structure signaled by μακάριοι facilitate a structural function for these syllables. This transition illustrates that structurally significant repetitions often consist of recurring phonemes and syllables and not necessarily of repeated phrases, words or even lexemes.

The final beatitude, beginning in period 2, is connected to the established beatitude pattern as articulated in period 1. In addition to the repetition of μακάριοι, the occurrence of ἐν τοῖς οὐρανοῖς in 3.2 echoes ἡ βασιλεία τῶν οὐρανῶν in 1.2, and the concluding sound ὑμῶν in 3.3 rhymes with the concluding inflectional endings in 1.2. Yet the pattern deviations in periods 2–3 are clearly set forth. A new parallelism occurs in period 2, organized around three finite verbs ending in –ωσιν. This parallel unifies the period and interrupts the beatitude's established structure. The shift from μακάριοι οἱ to μακάριοί ἐστε in 2.1 is reinforced by the sustained use of the second grammatical person in 2.2 (ὑμᾶς) and 2.4 (ὑμῶν) and with χαίρετε καὶ ἀγαλλιᾶσθε at the beginning of 3.1. Thus the occurrence of ὑμεῖς ἐστε in 4.1 can be recognized as a potential structural signal, even though it introduces novel sounds. The signal is confirmed when ὑμεῖς ἐστε is repeated in 5.1.

Section 2 creates its distinctive sound signature, repeating ὑμεῖς ἐστε at the beginning of its two component units, with frequent repetitions within each unit of phonemes that echo the topic introduced in its opening colon. Thus the first unit (5:13), beginning with ὑμεῖς ἐστε τὸ ἅλας τῆς γῆς, multiplies α/η/ει sounds, and the second unit (5:14–16), beginning with ὑμεῖς ἐστε τὸ φῶς τοῦ κόσμου, resonates with ως/ους/οις sounds. Nevertheless, section 2's distinctive sound signature is established on the basis of modifications to prevailing patterns in the previous section, the Beatitudes. In fact, the prevailing pattern of the Beatitudes itself builds on patterns of repetition forged in the genealogy and implemented in different ways in the birth narrative, baptism story, and temptation story, within the first narrative section.

Structure and Meaning

Sounds organize the Sermon on the Mount and Matthew's Gospel through frequent repetition and by associating sounds in corresponding parts of parallel structures. Sound's structural role depends only partly on semantic meaning. Acoustic signals contribute to the construction of meaning independently of semantics; in fact, audiences attend to specific words precisely because of their placement into patterns of repeated sounds. Thus, patterns of sound select certain words and phrases for emphasis, directing audience attention in real-time performances that cannot support sustained reflection on every word's semantic load.

Such sound effects shape audience perception. A complete catalog of sound effects lies beyond the scope of this essay, but three interrelated acoustic effects in the Sermon on the Mount can be shown to mediate fundamental themes in the Sermon and Matthew's Gospel. These effects include a tension between form and content, the emergence of an authoritative voice for Jesus, and the shifting identity of you in the Sermon on the Mount.

Clash of Form and Content

The occurrence of μακάριοι at the beginning of all nine Beatitudes emphasizes this word's importance and focuses audience attention on a state of blessing and approval, yet the blessed situations describe unenviable identities: οἱ πτωχοὶ τῷ πνεύματι (5:3), οἱ πενθοῦντες (5:4), οἱ πενθοῦντες (5:5). A similar disjuncture characterizes the Gospel's opening narrative, in which pattern disruptions in the genealogy name problematic figures in Israel's history (Judah, Tamar, Rahab, Ruth, Uriah), despite the fact that the establishment of an honorable pedigree is a genealogy's primary purpose.[14] Moreover, the Babylonian captivity, with all its trauma and disgrace, divides the genealogy's structure, just as the event ruptured Israel's history. The genealogy concludes with Joseph's righteous dilemma over Mary's illegitimate pregnancy.

14. Carter, *Matthew and the Margins*, 53; Luz, *Matthew 1–7*, 108.

Both the Gospel's opening narrative and the beginning of its first lengthy discourse share sound effects and key structural characteristics. Both the genealogy and the Beatitudes employ similar structural devices, including brief cola with repeated sounds and parallel structure. Both passages also employ these devices to set form and content at odds. Because effective Greek prose is supposed to employ a style that supports a composition's intended meaning,[15] a disjuncture between form and content suggests that meaning lies precisely within the discord, implying irony, burlesque, ambivalence, or another sort of disharmony.

A sound map shows that the Sermon on the Mount sustains the mismatch of form and content in Matthew's Gospel. In section 3 of the Sermon, Jesus uses elegant style to claim that he does not intend to impeach the authority of the law and the prophets, yet he makes this declaration on the basis of his own authority, not authority derived from the law. The first two periods of section 3 illustrate the point.

5:17–18

11.1	Μὴ νομίσητε			
1.2	ὅτι	ἦλθον	καταλῦσαι	τὸν νόμον ἢ τοὺς προφήτας
1.3	οὐκ	ἦλθον	καταλῦσαι	
1.4	ἀλλὰ		πληρῶσαι	

2.1	ἀμὴν γὰρ λέγω ὑμῖν,	
2.2	ἕως ἂν	παρέλθῃ ὁ οὐρανὸς καὶ ἡ γῆ
2.3	ἰῶτα ἓν ἢ μία κεραία οὐ μὴ	παρέλθῃ ἀπὸ τοῦ νόμου
2.4	ἕως ἂν πάντα	γένηται

Both periods balance brief beginning and ending cola (1.1 and 1.4; 2.1 and 2.4) with longer intermediate cola (1.2 and 1.3; 2.2 and 2.3). Intermediate cola employ repeated predicates set in parallel (ἦλθον, period 1; παρέλθῃ, period 2), and because the predicates have the same lexical stem, they rhyme. Parallel and rhyming infinitives also occur in period 1 where the parallelism extends to 1.4 (καταλῦσαι, cola 2 and 3; πληρῶσαι, colon 4). Such flourishes finesse the disjuncture between the passage's explicit message (affirmation of the authority of the law and the prophets) and its implicit message (Jesus' greater authority). The primacy of Jesus' authority functions as a major theme in the Sermon and the Gospel, culminating in its climactic scene (28:18). Sound effects that set form and content at odds advance this

---

15. Lee and Scott, *Sound Mapping the New Testament*, 119–21.

theme and mediate between the assertion of Jesus' authority and its affirmation of the hegemony of the heavenly Father, who gave Israel the Law and the Prophets.

Jesus' Authoritative Voice

Important examples of a continuing clash between form and content also occur in sections 4 and 5 of the Sermon on the Mount. Significantly, these sections also sustain the tension between authoritative voices in Israel's past and the authority of Jesus, a tension inaugurated in section 3. Sound effects help to establish Jesus' authoritative voice in the Sermon and the Gospel. The first antithesis exhibits the structural configuration employed in all five of the section's component parts.

5:21–26

1.1 Ἠκούσατε ὅτι ἐρρέθη τοῖς ἀρχαίοις

1.2 Οὐ   φονεύσεις

1.3 ὃς δ' ἂν   φονεύσῃ   ἔνοχος ἔσται τῇ κρίσει

2.1 ἐγὼ δὲ λέγω ὑμῖν

2.2 ὅτι πᾶς ὁ ὀργιζόμενος τῷ ἀδελφῷ αὐτοῦ   ἔνοχος ἔσται τῇ κρίσει

2.3 ὃς δ' ἂν εἴπῃ τῷ ἀδελφῷ αὐτοῦ   'Ρακά,   ἔνοχος ἔσται τῷ συνεδρίῳ

2.4 ὃς δ' ἂν εἴπῃ   Μωρέ   ἔνοχος ἔσται
                                           εἰς τὴν γέενναν τοῦ πυρός

3.1 ἐὰν οὖν προσφέρῃς   τὸ δῶρόν σου   ἐπὶ   τὸ θυσιαστήριον

3.2 κἀκεῖ μνησθῇς ὅτι   ὁ ἀδελφός σου   ἔχει τι κατὰ σοῦ

3.3 ἄφες ἐκεῖ   τὸ δῶρόν σου ἔμπροσθεν τοῦ θυσιαστηρίου

3.4 καὶ ὕπαγε

3.5 πρῶτον διαλλάγηθι τῷ ἀδελφῷ   σου

3.6 καὶ τότε ἐλθὼν πρόσφερε τὸ δῶρόν σου

4.1 ἴσθι εὐνοῶν τῷ   ἀντιδίκῳ   σου   ταχὺ

4.2 ἕως ὅτου εἶ μετ'   αὐτοῦ   ἐν τῇ ὁδῷ

4.3 μήποτέ σε παραδῷ ὁ ἀντίδικος τῷ   κριτῇ

4.4 καὶ ὁ   κριτὴς τῷ   ὑπηρέτῃ

4.5 καὶ εἰς   φυλακὴν   βληθήσῃ

5.1   ἀμὴν λέγω σοι
5.2   οὐ μὴ ἐξέλθῃς ἐκεῖθεν
5.2   ἕως ἂν ἀποδῷς τὸν ἔσχατον   κοδράντην

All five antitheses repeat the opening colon (1.1). The second, fourth and fifth antitheses (2, 4, and 5 below) abbreviate the pattern.[16]

Opening Cola in the Antitheses

1   Ἠκούσατε ὅτι ἐρρέθη τοῖς ἀρχαίοις (5:21)

2   Ἠκούσατε ὅτι ἐρρέθη (5:27)

3   Πάλιν ἠκούσατε ὅτι ἐρρέθη τοῖς ἀρχαίοις (5:33)

4   Ἠκούσατε ὅτι ἐρρέθη (5:38)

5   Ἠκούσατε ὅτι ἐρρέθη (5:43)

In subsequent cola, the first period of all five antitheses articulates one of the law's commands (οὐ φονεύσεις, 1; οὐ μοιχεύσεις, 2; οὐκ ἐπιορκήσεις, 3; ὀφθαλμὸν ἀντὶ ὀφθαλμοῦ καὶ ὀδόντα ἀντὶ ὀδόντος, 4; ἀγαπήσεις τὸν πλησίον σου καὶ μισήσεις τὸν ἐχθρόν σου, 5). The second period in all five antitheses modifies or overturns the stated command, based on Jesus' authority. The second period begins with the same colon in all five antitheses, ἐγὼ δὲ λέγω ὑμῖν (2.1), followed by instructions or illustrations set in parallel. Three of the five antitheses draw conclusions at the end, introduced by a repetition of the λέγω statement in the first two antitheses (ἀμὴν λέγω σοι, 5:26; ἐγὼ δὲ λέγω ὑμῖν, 5:32) and by the concluding signal οὖν in the last antithesis (5:48).

Although all the antitheses employ an orderly pattern with multiple parallel parts, the pattern is not employed to prescribe orderly behavior but outrageous actions, like gouging out one's own eye (5:29) and cutting off one's own hand (5:30), as well as impractical actions, like never becoming angry (5:22), refusing to swear (5:34), offering no resistance to evil (5:38), turning the other cheek (5:39), giving away one's cloak (5:40), and walking an extra mile (5:41). The legal-sounding antitheses conclude with the command to be perfect like the heavenly Father (5:48), whereas the very existence of law presumes that perfection is impossible. While in section 3, elegant language distracts from Jesus' claim to ultimate authority, formalistic language in section 4 anesthetizes listeners to his authoritative but immoderate commands.

16. Some commentators analyze the occurrence of ἐρρέθη δέ in 5:31 as the beginning of a new antithesis (Davies and Allison, *Gospel according to Saint Matthew*, 1:527), but a sound map suggests that 5:31–32 forms the conclusion to the second antithesis because it completes the parallel structure used throughout section 4.

Form and content remain in tension as the Sermon on the Mount continues and as Jesus' authoritative voice emerges. Structural devices evolve in section 5, yet λέγω statements recur and they sustain their role of setting form and content at odds, as they do in sections 3 and 4. Two alternating patterns organize the component parts of section 5, which includes the Lord's Prayer (6:1–18). Frequent repetitions of the syllable -προσ- characterize the first of these patterns, which emerges in the section's first period.

6:1

1.1	**Προσέχετε** [δὲ] τὴν δικαιοσύνην ὑμῶν
1.2	μὴ ποιεῖν ἔμ**προσ**θεν τῶν ἀνθρώπων **πρὸς** τὸ θεαθῆναι αὐτοῖς
1.3	εἰ δὲ μήγε, μισθὸν οὐκ ἔχετε
	παρὰ τῷ πατρὶ ὑμῶν τῷ ἐν τοῖς οὐραν<u>οῖ</u>ς

Repetitions of -προσ- also occur in the introduction to the Lord's Prayer in the same lexical stem, emphasizing the section's theme: prayer.

6:7–9a

1.1	**Προσ**ευχόμενοι δὲ μὴ βατταλογήσητε ὥσπερ οἱ ἐθνικοί
1.2	δοκοῦσιν γὰρ ὅτι ἐν τῇ πολυλογίᾳ αὐτῶν εἰσακουσθήσονται
1.3	μὴ οὖν ὁμοιωθῆτε αὐτοῖς
1.4	οἶδεν γὰρ ὁ πατὴρ ὑμῶν ὧν χρείαν ἔχετε πρὸ τοῦ ὑμᾶς αἰτῆσαι αὐτόν
1.5	Οὕτως οὖν **προσ**εύχεσθε ὑμεῖς

A different pattern governs the rest of section 5 (excluding the Lord's Prayer). The pattern in section 5 delineates three component units that exhibit the same structure. As in the pattern that organizes section 3 and the antitheses in section 4, λέγω statements introduce the second period of each unit of section 5, making explicit Jesus' claim to authority. But unlike the pattern employed in the antitheses, the pattern of parallel structure that organizes section 5 into three parallel units admits no variation. The first iteration of this structure in 6:2–4 illustrates section 5's alternative organizational pattern.

6:2–4

1.1   Ὅταν οὖν ποιῇς   <u>ἐλεημοσύνην</u>
1.2   μὴ σαλπίσῃς ἔμπροσθέν σου
1.3   ὥσπερ οἱ ὑποκριταὶ ποιοῦσιν ἐν ταῖς συναγωγαῖς καὶ ἐν ταῖς ῥύμαις
1.4   ὅπως δοξασθῶσιν ὑπὸ τῶν ἀνθρώπων

2.1   ἀμὴν λέγω ὑμῖν
2.2   ἀπέχουσιν τὸν μισθὸν αὐτῶν

3.1   σοῦ δὲ ποιοῦντος   <u>ἐλεημοσύνην</u>
3.2   μὴ γνώτω ἡ ἀριστερά σου τί ποιεῖ ἡ δεξιά σου
3.3   ὅπως ᾖ σου ἡ   <u>ἐλεημοσύνη</u> ἐν τῷ κρυπτῷ
3.4   καὶ ὁ πατήρ σου ὁ βλέπων ἐν τῷ κρυπτῷ [αὐτὸς] ἀποδώσει σοι

In all three component units (6:2–4, 5–6, and 16–18), the first colon begins with ὅταν and introduces each unit's topic (ἐλεημοσύνην, 6:2–4; προσεύχησθε, 6:5–6; νηστεύητε, 6:16–18), drawing negative examples from οἱ ὑποκριταί. Period 2 is identical in all three units: ἀμὴν λέγω ὑμῖν ἀπέχουσιν τὸν μισθὸν αὐτῶν (6:2, 5, 16). Each unit's third period begins with σοῦ δέ, heightening the contrast between "you" and οἱ ὑποκριταί. The final period repeats the unit's topic and gives positive instruction, based on Jesus' commands. The three-part structure of this repeating pattern reinforces each unit's message: the Sermon's audience is set apart from οἱ ὑποκριταί and held to a different standard of behavior.

Section 5 is unique in the Sermon for its use of two patterns that alternate throughout the section instead of a single pattern that organizes the entire section. Relying only on structural signals such as repeated syllables and parallel structure, the dual-pattern device in section 5 serves a larger purpose without resorting to conceptual abstractions based on the semantic load of particular words. The two component units characterized by repetitions of -προσ- direct audience attention toward ὁ πατὴρ ὑμῶν ὁ ἐν τοῖς οὐρανοῖς (6:1, 7–15) and away from other people (μὴ ποιεῖν ἔμπροσθεν τῶν ἀνθρώπων, 6:1), including Gentiles (οἱ ἐθνικοί, 6:7). The three units organized around Jesus' λέγω statements clearly distinguish "you" from οἱ ὑποκριταί, and outline a different standard of behavior for the Sermon's audience.

Section 5's two organizing patterns, with their different sound signatures, nevertheless remain integrated, unifying the section instead of dividing it. Although the two-unit -προσ- pattern employs a connected style and highlights the heavenly Father, it nevertheless contrasts "you" with other people (6:1) and with the Gentiles (οἱ ἐθνικοί, 6:7), consistent with the three-unit λέγω pattern that sets "you" apart from hypocrites (6:2, 5, 16). Correlatively, the three units organized around Jesus' λέγω statements also contain repetitions of -προσ- in each unit's first period (μὴ σαλπίσῃς ἔμπροσθέν σου, 6:2; ὅταν προσεύχησθε, 6:5, τὰ πρόσωπα αὐτῶν, 6:16), forging a connection with the section's alternate organizing pattern. Pattern integration softens the apparent contradiction of two distinct messages: while the three-unit λέγω pattern sets "you" apart and holds the audience to a higher standard, the Lord's Prayer, which deviates from section 5's organizational scheme, counsels the Sermon's audience to set aside the offenses that divide them from their enemies (6:14–15). Sound effects abet communication of this complex and apparently self-contradictory message. This effect is made explicit in the Sermon's narrative conclusion, which states that Jesus taught with authority and not like their scribes (7:28–29).

Having forged the device of the λέγω statement to establish Jesus' authoritative voice in the Sermon on the Mount, the Gospel employs this device subsequently, both in discourse and in narrative. In the fourth discourse (18:3–20), λέγω statements mark structural boundaries and highlight Jesus' authoritative voice. A λέγω statement introduces the discourse in 18:3 and also introduces the final periods in each of the discourse's component units (18:6–10, 12–14, 15–10). A doubled λέγω statement occurs at the end of the discourse (18:18–19). The λέγω statement functions effectively to depict Jesus as an authoritative teacher in the fourth discourse.

Later in the Gospel narrative, λέγω statements punctuate a sequence of three narrative scenes in 26:6–34. These scenes reverberate with distinctive sound effects first employed in the birth narrative, where quotations from Scripture interpret the unfolding story of Jesus' flight from Herod. In 1:18–23, τοῦ δέ introduces component episodes, and τότε introduces the narrative scenes that compose episode 3. In 26:6–34, the same introductory sounds introduce narrative scenes that conclude with λέγω statements.

Scene 1:	**The anointing at Bethany (26:6–13)**
Opening colon:	Τοῦ δὲ Ἰησοῦ γενομένου ἐν Βηθανίᾳ ἐν οἰκίᾳ Σίμωνος τοῦ λεπροῦ (26:6)
Closing λέγω statement:	ἀμὴν λέγω ὑμῖν, ὅπου ἐὰν κηρυχθῇ τὸ εὐαγγέλιον τοῦτο ἐν ὅλῳ τῷ κόσμῳ, λαληθήσεται καὶ ὃ ἐποίησεν αὔτη εἰς μνημόσυνον αὐτῆς (26:13)

Scene 2:	The betrayal and last supper (26:14–30)
Opening colon:	Τότε πορευθεὶς εἷς τῶν δώδεκα (26·14) καὶ ἐσθιόντων αὐτῶν εἶπεν, Ἀμὴν λέγω ὑμῖν ὅτι εἷς ἐξ ὑμῶν παραδώσει με (26:21)
Closing λέγω statement:	λέγω δὲ ὑμῖν, οὐ μὴ πίω ἀπ' ἄρτι ἐκ τούτου τοῦ γενήματος τῆς ἀμπέλου ἕως τῆς ἡμέρας ἐκείνης ὅταν αὐτὸ πίνω μεθ' ὑμῶν καινὸν ἐν τῇ βασιλείᾳ τοῦ πατρός μου (26:29)
Scene 3:	Jesus predicts Peter's denial (26:31–35)
Opening colon:	Τότε λέγει αὐτοῖς ὁ Ἰησοῦς (26·31)
Closing λέγω statement:	ἔφη αὐτῷ ὁ Ἰησοῦς, Ἀμὴν λέγω σοι ὅτι ἐν ταύτῃ τῇ νυκτὶ πρὶν ἀλέκτορα φωνῆσαι τρὶς ἀπαρνήσῃ με (26:34)

Sound effects in 26:6–34 evoke those that delineate episodes in the birth narrative, but whereas the birth narrative incorporates quotations from Scripture, the story of Jesus' anointing, betrayal, and denial incorporates Jesus' speech, introduced by λέγω statements. Thus by the end of the Gospel, the authority of Scripture that interprets Jesus' flight from Herod is replaced by Jesus' authoritative voice, which interprets the story of his impending death.

The Shifting Identity of "You"

In addition to the clash between form and content and the emergence of Jesus' authoritative voice with λέγω statements, a third acoustic effect advances crucial themes and mediates major transformations in the Sermon and the Gospel. The shifting identity of "you" begins in the Sermon's first section. At the end of the Beatitudes, their structure is modified in the transition to section 2. The final beatitude modifies the established anaphoric signal from μακάριοι οἱ to μακάριοί ἐστε. The shift to ὑμεῖς ἐστε as the anaphoric signal in section 2 focuses the second grammatical person. Prominent use of direct address at the end of the Beatitudes and in section 2's sound signature shifts attention to the Sermon's narrative audience and the implied audience of the Gospel.

Focusing "you" facilitates a shift in its meaning from the beginning to the end of the Sermon. In section 2, the audience is called the salt of the earth (5:13) and the light of the world (5:14). In section 5, the audience is contrasted with hypocrites (6:2, 5, 16) and Gentiles (6:7) and instructed to act better than they do—the presumption being that all hypocrites and Gentiles act in despicable ways. Yet in section 6, Jesus disapproves of the audience. They are accused of having little faith (ὀλιγόπιστοι, 6:30); Jesus calls them hypocrites (ὑποκριτά, 7:5). Similarly, the audience—and not the hypocrites or the Gentiles—is called wicked (πονηροί) in section 7 (7:11).

Finally, section 8 issues threats of future disapproval. The anaphoric signal introducing the section's component parts is οὐ πᾶς (7:21) / πᾶς οὖν (7:24).

Opening Cola of Component Units in Section 8

7:21   **Οὐ πᾶς** ὁ λέγων μοι Κύριε κύριε
7:24   **Πᾶς οὖν** ὅστις ἀκούει μου τοὺς λόγους τούτους

Although the particle οὐ and the conjunction οὖν are semantically unrelated, their rhyming sounds and placement at the beginning of section 8's component units confer a structural function to these sounds. Instead of duplicating the same phrase in both units, this section's anaphoric marker arranges its few syllables chiastically, with πᾶς in the center. These repeated sounds ambiguate the universal implications of "everyone" (πᾶς) by negating it with οὐ in 7:21, then by dividing "everyone" into two groups in 7:24–27, corresponding to the two periods that compose the unit (πᾶς οὖν ὅστις ἀκούει μου τοὺς λόγους τούτους καὶ ποιεῖ αὐτούς, 1.1; πᾶς ὁ ἀκούων μου τοὺς λόγους τούτους καὶ μὴ ποιῶν αὐτούς, 1.2).

7:24–27

1.1   **Πᾶς οὖν** ὅστις ἀκούει μου τοὺς λόγους τούτους
1.2   καὶ ποιεῖ αὐτούς
1.3   ὁμοιωθήσεται ἀνδρὶ φρονίμῳ
1.4   ὅστις ᾠκοδόμησεν αὐτοῦ τὴν οἰκίαν ἐπὶ τὴν πέτραν
1.5   καὶ κατέβη ἡ βροχὴ
1.6   καὶ ἦλθον οἱ ποταμοὶ
1.7   καὶ ἔπνευσαν οἱ ἄνεμοι
1.8   καὶ προσέπεσαν τῇ οἰκίᾳ ἐκείνῃ
1.9   καὶ οὐκ ἔπεσεν
1.10   τεθεμελίωτο γὰρ ἐπὶ τὴν πέτραν

2.1 καὶ πᾶς ὁ ἀκούων μου τοὺς λόγους τούτους

2.2 καὶ μὴ ποιῶν αὐτοὺς

2.3 ὁμοιωθήσεται ἀνδρὶ μωρῷ

2.4 ὅστις ᾠκοδόμησεν αὐτοῦ τὴν οἰκίαν ἐπὶ τὴν ἄμμον

2.5 καὶ κατέβη ἡ βροχὴ

2.6 καὶ ἦλθον οἱ ποταμοὶ

2.7 καὶ ἔπνευσαν οἱ ἄνεμοι

2.8 καὶ προσέκοψαν τῇ οἰκίᾳ ἐκείνῃ

2.9 καὶ ἔπεσεν

2.10 καὶ ἦν ἡ πτῶσις αὐτῆς μεγάλη

Emphasis laid on οὐ πᾶς and πᾶς οὖν by virtue of the structural placement of these sounds drives home the ambivalence articulated throughout
the Sermon over the identity of those who are included in the community.
Previously, the Sermon called the identity of "you" into question, using λέγω
statements to enforce Jesus' authority. Section 8 contrasts Jesus with another,
hypothetical speaker, ὁ λέγων μοι Κύριε κύριε, whom Jesus addresses as "you"
when he rejects that one: τότε ὁμολογήσω αὐτοῖς ὅτι Οὐδέποτε ἔγνων ὑμᾶς.
Ἀποχωρεῖτε ἀπ' ἐμοῦ οἱ ἐργαζόμενοι τὴν ἀνομίαν (7:23). Uses of the second-
person pronoun in the Sermon facilitate shifts in Jesus' approval of "you."

Echoes of the Sermon's shift in the meaning of "you" reverberate throughout the Gospel. Whereas the audience is distinguished from Gentiles as the
negative example in sections 4, 5, and 6 (5:47, 6:7, 6:32), the Gospel concludes
with the Great Commission that commands Jesus' followers to preach to the
Gentiles and baptize them (28:19). The Sermon erases distinctions between
friends and enemies, good and bad, righteous and unrighteous (5:43–47) and
the Gospel subsequently assures that God alone ultimately will make this distinction, not on conventional grounds but solely on the basis of the treatment
of "the least of these." Notable Matthean passages such as the parables of the
Weeds and Wheat (13:4–30) and the Last Judgment (25:31–46) drive home
this point. Such shifts implement the Gospel's narrative purpose: to change
the definition of who should be included in the audience's community. Both
the Sermon and the Gospel transform the meaning of "you" to enable its Jewish audience to envision inclusion of Gentiles.

Breaking the Pattern

Only one part of the Sermon, section 3 (5:17–20), fails to delineate component units through anaphora and parallel structure. Since this section

stands out from the rest of the Sermon stylistically it has correctly drawn interpreters' attention as a key to the Sermon's meaning.

5:17–20

1.1	Μὴ νομίσητε		
1.2	ὅτι	ἦλθον	καταλῦσαι	τὸν νόμον ἢ τοὺς προφήτας
1.3	οὐκ	ἦλθον	καταλῦσαι
1.4	ἀλλὰ		πληρῶσαι

2.1 ἀμὴν γὰρ λέγω ὑμῖν,
2.2 ἕως ἂν   παρέλθῃ ὁ οὐρανὸς καὶ ἡ γῆ
2.3 ἰῶτα ἓν ἢ μία κεραία οὐ μὴ   παρέλθῃ ἀπὸ τοῦ νόμου
2.4 ἕως ἂν πάντα   γένηται

3.1 ὃς ἐὰν οὖν   λύσῃ   μίαν τῶν ἐντολῶν τούτων τῶν ἐλαχίστων
3.2 καὶ   διδάξῃ   οὕτως τοὺς ἀνθρώπους
3.3 ἐλάχιστος   κληθήσεται ἐν τῇ βασιλείᾳ τῶν οὐρανῶν

4.1 ὃς δ᾽ ἂν   ποιήσῃ
4.2 καὶ   διδάξῃ
4.3 οὗτος μέγας   κληθήσεται ἐν τῇ βασιλείᾳ τῶν οὐρανῶν

5.1 λέγω γὰρ ὑμῖν ὅτι
5.2 ἐὰν μὴ περισσεύσῃ ὑμῶν ἡ δικαιοσύνη πλεῖον
                        τῶν γραμματέων καὶ Φαρισαίων
5.3 οὐ μὴ εἰσέλθητε   εἰς τὴν βασιλείαν τῶν οὐρανῶν

Section 3 coheres as a whole and is not subdivided into parallel units. It opens with the prohibition μὴ νομίσητε, and its repeated phoneme, η, reverberates throughout the period in η/α sounds. This first period has been discussed above, where attention was placed on verbs set in parallel, including predicates (ἦλθον, 1.2 and 1.3) and infinitives (καταλῦσαι, 1.2 and 1.3; πληρῶσαι, 1.4). Predicates and infinitives in cola 2 and 3 are identical (ἦλθον καταλῦσαι). Colon 4's predicate is implied but not expressed. Its infinitive rhymes with those in cola 2 and 3 by virtue of their identical inflectional suffixes (καταλῦσαι, πληρῶσαι). Standing outside parallel elements in cola 2–4 is the phrase, τὸν νόμον ἢ τοὺς προφήτας.

Period 2 is organized similarly. It opens with ἀμὴν γὰρ λέγω ὑμῖν, followed by two cola with identical predicates set in parallel (παρέλθῃ). Its final colon concludes with a predicate whose inflectional ending rhymes with the parallel infinitives in period 1 (γένηται). Period 2 applies rhetorical force to claims of authority for Jesus (ἀμὴν γὰρ λέγω ὑμῖν, 2.1) and the law (ἰῶτα ἓν ἢ μία κεραία οὐ μὴ παρέλθῃ ἀπὸ τοῦ νόμου).

Periods 3 and 4 are set in parallel. Both begin with conditional statements, employ the same predicates in corresponding cola, and conclude with ἐν τῇ βασιλείᾳ τῶν οὐρανῶν. Concluding phrases in 3.1 (μίαν τῶν ἐντολῶν τούτων τῶν ἐλαχίστων) and 3.2 (οὕτως τοὺς ἀνθρώπους) are implied in corresponding positions in period 4.

Period 5 begins with a modified version of the first colon in period 2 (λέγω γὰρ ὑμῖν) and ends with ἐν τῇ βασιλείᾳ τῶν οὐρανῶν, reiterating the phrase that occurred in the parallel period 3 and 4.

Many structural proposals for the Sermon have focused on the phrase ὁ νόμος καὶ οἱ προφῆται. Commentators have long observed that the phrase occurs both in 5:17 and in 7:12, with Jesus' articulation of the so-called Golden Rule. Based on the single repetition in the Sermon of this phrase, many have argued that it brackets the Sermon's primary message.[17] Others have amplified this scheme to locate the Lord's Prayer (6:9–13) at the Sermon's center, construing correspondences between material preceding and following the prayer. They propose a chiastic arrangement.[18] Both sets of structural proposals construe the Sermon as moral instruction and advice for personal piety.

The importance of 5:17–20 can be easily misconstrued when adequate account is not taken of the Sermon's sound. A sound map reveals a distinctive sound signature for section 3. It shows that the occurrence of ὁ νόμος καὶ οἱ προφῆται in 5:17 does not lie at a structural boundary. Although it occurs in section 3's first period, it does not occur in its first colon, which the Sermon and the Gospel have shown to be a favored position for structurally significant sounds. Although ὁ νόμος καὶ οἱ προφῆται serves as the first period's topic, it is not repeated; instead, attention is drawn to the contrast drawn between καταλῦσαι and πληρῶσαι in parallel cola, emphasized by the contrast drawn by οὐκ (1.3) and ἀλλά (1.4).

Taken as a whole, prominent sounds in section 3 include

- The section's opening prohibition, μὴ νομίσητε

- Repeated η/ει sounds that reinforce the prohibition throughout the section

17. Betz, *Sermon on the Mount*, 62.

18. Luz, *Matthew 1–7*, 212.

- Phrases highlighted by their structural placement (τὸν νόμον ἢ τοὺς προφήτας, 1.2; ὁ οὐρανὸς καὶ ἡ γῆ; τῇ βασιλείᾳ τῶν οὐρανῶν, 3.3, 4.3, 5.3; ἡ δικαιοσύνη, 5.2)

- Negative particles (μή, 1.1, 2.3, 5.2, 5.3)

- The doubled verbs ἦλθον (1.2, 1.3) and κληθήσεται (3.3, 4.3)

- Verbs in the subjunctive mood (νομίσητε, 1.1; παρέλθῃ, 2.2, 2.3; γένηται, 2.4; λύσῃ, 3.1 and 4.1; διδάξῃ, 3.2 and 4.2; περισσεύσῃ, 5.2; εἰσέλθητε, 5.3)

• The occurrence of τὸν νόμον ἢ τοὺς προφήτας outside the parallel elements of cola 1.2–1.4

• A λέγω statement in 2.1, repeated in 5.1

• Parallel conditional statements in periods 3 and 4

• The occurrence of ἐν τῇ βασιλείᾳ τῶν οὐρανῶν in 3.3, 4.3, and 5.3

The cumulative effect of section 3's distinctive sounds is to establish an authoritative voice for Jesus as an agent for the kingdom of heaven. Because of the emphasis that sound and structure place on Jesus' prohibition at the beginning of the section, on repeated λέγω statements, and on repetition of εἰς τὴν (ἐν τῇ) βασιλείαν τῶν οὐρανῶν at the section's end, the accent falls on Jesus' authority, not on the Law and the Prophets.

Nor does the mention of the Law and the Prophets in 7:12 lie at a structural boundary, according to a sound map of section 7. In fact, structural boundaries lie elsewhere, delineated by the same structural devices that organize the rest of the Sermon. The use of anaphoric signals at the beginnings of parallel component units has been demonstrated for sections 1, 2, 4, 5, and 8. Sections 6 and 7 employ the same structural device. Just as acoustic signals evolve throughout the Gospel's opening narrative and the first sections of the Sermon, so evolution continues in sections 6 and 7. There, repeated grammatical structures with rhyming components fulfill the structural function served in other sections by repetition of discrete phrases, such as μακάριοι (section 1) and ἠκούσατε ὅτι ἐρρέθη τοῖς ἀρχαίοις (section 4). As in all other sections of the Sermon (except section 3), similar sounds in opening cola introduce each of the section's component units. In section 6, the grammatical structure that repeats at the beginning of each component unit is a prohibition (a negated imperative verb) whereas section 7 is organized by positive imperatives at the beginning of each unit.

Opening Cola in Section 6

Unit 1　　Μὴ θησαυρίζετε ὑμῖν θησαυροὺς ἐπὶ τῆς γῆς (6:19)
Unit 2　　Μὴ κρίνετε (7:1)
Unit 3　　Μὴ δῶτε　　τὸ ἅγιον τοῖς κυσίν (7:6)

Opening Cola in Section 7

Unit 1　　Αἰτεῖτε καὶ δοθήσεται ὑμῖν (7:6)
Unit 2　　Εἰσέλθατε διὰ τῆς στενῆς πύλης (7:13)
Unit 3　　Προσέχετε ἀπὸ τῶν ψευδοπροφητῶν (7:15)

Sound mapping consistently has shown that repeated beginning sounds and parallel structures organize the Sermon, even though implementation of these devices varies throughout the Sermon, and even though component sections have unequal duration. The first component unit of section 6 contains a long discourse that interrupts its structure, the so-called prohibition of anxiety (6:25–34). Nevertheless, the structural significance of prohibition in section 6 is confirmed by its recurrence in 7:1 and 7:6. In section 7, further reinforcement of the structural significance of imperative verbs is implied by a tripled imperative in parallel cola in the first period of section 7's first unit.

7:7

1	Αἰτεῖτε	καὶ δοθήσεται	ὑμῖν
2	ζητεῖτε	καὶ εὑρήσετε	
3	κρούετε	καὶ ἀνοιγήσεται	ὑμῖν

Within the three-part structure that organizes section 7 and corresponds to the three-part arrangement of units in section 6, ὁ νόμος καὶ οἱ προφῆται occurs at the end of section 7's first component unit (7:7–12). Although this phrase occurs at the end of a component unit, it does not delineate a major structural boundary. Rather, 7:13–20 coheres with 7:7–12 and completes the section's three-part structure. Completion of this threefold structure is important because it confirms audience expectation of three component units and rewards audience attention to sophisticated structural clues. The first such clue is the innovation in the previous section of a repeated grammatical structure—a negated imperative verb—instead of repeated opening syllables. The extended prohibition of anxiety (6:25–34) in the first unit of section 6 confirms the structural importance of prohibition in this section. The second clue to audience expectation of a three-part structure occurs in section 7, where a tripled imperative in parallel cola composes the section's first period. The occurrence of three imperatives in quick succession reprises the previous section's three-part arrangement of prohibitions, and builds expectation for a corresponding arrangement of positive imperatives in section 7.

The difficulty with proposed organizational schemes for the Sermon based on the occurrence of ὁ νόμος καὶ οἱ προφῆται in 5:17 and 7:12 is that they cannot be executed in real time during performance. Such proposals fail to explain how these few syllables alone can organize three chapters of material that require roughly half an hour to perform. Moreover, they fail to account for the many distinctive acoustic patterns elaborated in the Sermon, such as the repetition of beginning sounds and parallel structure among the Sermon's component units, heard first in the Beatitudes (which stand outside the 5:17—7:12 bracket) and most extensively in the antitheses. Proposals that construe the Sermon as a ring composition around the Lord's Prayer fail to explain how an audience could remember the corresponding elements of the ring composition in the proper sequence before and after the Lord's Prayer. The proposal fails to advance any mnemonic strategy that would enable a listening audience to hold the entire ring composition in mind at one time.

A sound map suggests that section 3 of the Sermon, where ὁ νόμος καὶ οἱ προφῆται first occurs, is critical to the interpretation of the Sermon and the Gospel, but not because it introduces a phrase that is repeated in 7:12. The importance lies in the deviation of section 3 from established structural patterns and the reverberation throughout the Sermon and the Gospel of sound effects first employed in this exceptional section. The phrase ὁ νόμος καὶ οἱ προφῆται in itself does not serve a structural function; it does not de-lineate a structural boundary in either 5:17 or 7:12. Nevertheless, the first occurrence of this phrase in section 3 of the Sermon introduces structural innovations that profoundly shape the Sermon's meaning. Section 3 employs complex sound effects such as a disjuncture between form and content, and λέγω statements that contribute to the Gospel's fundamental themes: the emergence of Jesus' authoritative voice and the shifting identity of "you." Such themes implement the Gospel's purpose: to deliver Jesus' authoritative command to baptize the Gentile nations and include them in community.

Conclusion

Sound analysis suggests that the Sermon on the Mount employs auditory features forged in the Gospel's opening narrative to render its distinctive meaning. Correlatively, auditory features of the Sermon on the Mount help to provide an interpretive key to the Gospel. Auditory clues that function beyond the realm of semantics help to convey complex messages and teach audiences of performed compositions how to listen and understand. Sound effects in the Sermon and the Gospel transform a listening audience into a community prepared to reach beyond their boundaries and to accept the Great Commission: Jesus' command to preach the gospel to the Gentile nations.

Performance criticism opens new vistas of meaning by restoring the spoken, real-time dimension of NT compositions. Sound mapping captures the linear stream of sound that constitutes vocal performance. Since structure must be audible in performance, sound analysis can illuminate a spoken composition's inherent, organic structure. Sound furnishes important clues to the structure of Matthew's Gospel, inviting a broader and more comprehensive sound analysis that may yield a more convincing structural proposal than has yet been advanced. New structural observations generate new insights about the meaning of Matthew's Gospel.

Bibliography

Bauer, David R. *The Structure of Matthew's Gospel: A Study in Literary Design.* JSNTSup 31. Sheffield: Almond, 1988.

Betz, Hans Dieter. *The Sermon on the Mount.* Hermeneia. Minneapolis: Fortress, 1995.

Brown, Raymond E. *The Birth of the Messiah: A Commentary on the Infancy Narratives in Matthew and Luke.* Garden City, NY: Doubleday, 1977.

Carter, Warren. *Matthew and the Margins: A Sociopolitical and Religious Reading.* Bible and Liberation Series. Maryknoll, NY: Orbis, 2000.

Davies, W. D., and D. C. Allison. *A Critical and Exegetical Commentary on the Gospel according to Saint Matthew.* 3 vols. ICC. Edinburgh: T. & T. Clark, 1988.

Dean, Margaret E. "The Grammar of Sound in Greek Texts: Toward a Method of Mapping the Echoes of Speech in Writing." *ABR* 44 (1996) 53–70.

Kloppenborg, John S. *Q Parallels: Synopsis, Criticial Notes & Concordance.* Foundations and Facets: Reference Series. Sonoma, CA: Polebridge, 1988.

Lee, Margaret E. "A Method for Sound Analysis in Hellenistic Greek: The Sermon on the Mount as a Test Case." D.Theol. diss., Melbourne College of Divinity, 2005.

Lee, Margaret Ellen, and Bernard Brandon Scott. *Sound Mapping the New Testament.* Salem, OR: Polebridge, 2009.

Luz, Ulrich. *Matthew 1–7: A Commentary.* Translated by Wilhelm C. Linns. Continental Commentaries. Minneapolis: Augsburg, 1989.

Robinson, James M. et al., eds. *The Critical Edition of Q.* Hermeneia Supplements. Minneapolis: Fortress, 2000.

6

THE PRESENT TENSE OF PERFORMANCE

Immediacy and Transformative Power in Luke's Passion

Kelly R. Iverson

LIVING WITHIN THE BOUNDS OF TIME IS AN INEXORABLE COM-
ponent of the human experience. Calendars, clocks, and technology remind us of the ubiquitous presence of time, and despite attempts
to quicken or impede its progress, the relentless onslaught of time remains one of the assured features of our existence. We may ignore or resist the temporal world, but as Ridderbos observes, "what we cannot do
is break free from time."[1]

  Given its universality, one might assume that the discussion of time
is like a well-trodden path that has been thoroughly explored and mapped.
But as Moltmann suggests, although "we live in time and reckon with it
. . . we really do not know what time is."[2] What seems pedestrian is, in historical perspective, a complex discussion that has confounded scholars and
thinkers throughout the ages. Indeed, as Aveni notes, among "the family of
four-letter words" one is "hard-pressed to find a word [like *t-i-m-e*] that has

---

1. Ridderbos, *Time*, 5.
2. Moltmann, "What Is Time?," 27.

more descriptions or conflicting and confusing meanings than this innocuous member."[3]

Despite the inherent challenges, the discussion of temporal matters has not failed to captivate the imagination of scholars throughout the ages. In fact, dialogue has taken place across a host of disciplines, including physics, anthropology, psychology, biology, philosophy, psychoanalysis, and more.[4] This wealth of research, however, has not been reciprocated in the field of biblical studies where the analysis of time is relatively uncommon.[5] On those occasions when the conversation has been raised, it has seldom garnered widespread attention, no doubt, due to the ostensibly pedantic nature of the subject, as well as its perceived insignificance for the interpretation of the biblical texts.

In view of this lacuna, the purpose of this essay is to address "this consistently neglected . . . [and] disregarded" feature of the Gospel narratives.[6] More specifically, in keeping with the theme of the volume, this chapter explores the temporal character of the Gospels in conversation with literary and performance approaches to the biblical texts. Considering the complexity of the discussion, it is beyond the scope of this essay to provide an exhaustive treatment of the subject, particularly in relation to other scholarly works that have attempted to unravel this elusive concept. Rather, the objective of this essay is to understand how time functions within the dynamics of oral performance—a discussion that has been conspicuously absent in other treatments of the subject. Unlike previous studies, this essay will argue that not only does performance time unfold in a rhetorically sophisticated

3. Aveni, *Empires of Time*, 5. Augustine expresses a similar perspective (*Conf.*, 11.14 [Watts, LCL]): "For what is time? Who is able easily and briefly to explain that? Who is able so much as in thought to comprehend it, so as to express himself concerning it? And yet what in our usual discourse do we more familiarly and knowingly make mention of than time? And surely, we understand it well enough, when we speak of it: we understand it also, when in speaking with another we hear it named. What is time then? If nobody asks me, I know: but if I were desirous to explain it to one that should ask me, plainly I know not."

4. For a sample of the kinds of temporal studies, see Greene, *Fabric of the Cosmos*; Gell, *Anthropology of Time*; Winfree, *Geometry of Biological Time*; Wagner, *Enigmatic Reality of Time*; Canestri and Fiorini, eds., *Experience of Time*; Momigliano, "Time in Ancient Historiography," 1–23.

5. Notable exceptions include Cullmann, *Christ and Time*; Muilenburg, "Biblical View of Time," 225–52; Barr, *Biblical Words for Time*; Wilch, *Time and Event*; De Vries, *Yesterday, Today, and Tomorrow*; Deterding, "New Testament View of Time and History," 385–99; Brin, *Concept of Time in the Bible*; Schildgen, *Crisis and Continuity*; Estes, *Temporal Mechanics of the Fourth Gospel*; Palu, *Jesus and Time*.

6. Hickox (*Time*, 2) refers to the general neglect of the subject in the wider scholarly discourse, but his conclusions are equally applicable to the field of biblical studies.

fashion, but that the conceptual underpinnings are foundational to the ontology of the oral event. To appreciate the temporal dynamics of performance, the chapter will begin by exploring the theoretical foundations of the discussion, before considering possible implications within the context of Luke's Passion Narrative.

Time in Narrative-Critical Perspective

Performance criticism is a relatively new phenomenon within the field of biblical studies, and though it has rightly been described as a "paradigm shift" (subtly implying a break from the past), its roots lie within narrative-critical soil.[7] Indeed, many of the prominent voices in the movement (e.g., David Rhoads, Joanna Dewey, and Tom Boomershine) were foundational in the rise and development of narrative criticism. Because of this organic relationship, understanding the hermeneutics of performance requires, to some extent, a basic understanding of the narrative and literary theories that have shaped biblical studies and out of which performance criticism arises. As a prelude to the conversation, it is imperative to contextualize the discussion by charting a brief survey of the conceptual backdrop, based upon a narrative-critical perspective.

The rise of narrative criticism over the last three decades has had far-reaching implications. Beyond advancing a hermeneutical paradigm that bypassed numerous historical-critical issues (i.e., questions of authorship, provenance, etc.), narrative critics brought renewed focus to the creative and artistic features of the biblical texts. Drawing attention to the "final form," countless studies have explored and continue to explore narrative features such as characterization, plot development, and the means by which the reader is drawn into the rhetoric of the story. In addition to studying these elements, narrative critics have also advanced a new way of analyzing biblical time. Although not as widely appreciated as other components of the paradigm, the narratological analysis of time nonetheless offers a unique perspective for consideration.

Within the Gospels, the narrative discussion of time is indebted to the work of Alan Culpepper, whose analysis of the Fourth Gospel, while not the first to apply the insights of narrative analysis, was the first to offer an "eclectic thoroughness in the use of modern narratological techniques."[8] Drawing

---

7. On performance criticism as a paradigm shift, see Rhoads, "Biblical Performance Criticism," 157–98.

8. Quotation from the foreword to Culpepper, *Anatomy*, vi.

from the pioneering work of Gérard Genette,[9] Culpepper's landmark work devoted an entire chapter to the subject of time, beginning with a discussion of the seminal distinction between narrative time and story time. While the two terms share a common basis (i.e., time), they reference distinct aspects within the temporal flow of the narrative. Narrative or discourse time denotes the sequencing of events as described within the text. Story time, on the other hand, refers to the perceived chronology of events assumed by an author in the composition of a story.[10] What is important to note is that although narrative time and story time often overlap, they are not identical, since the recounting of events within the narrative may differ from the implied chronology of the story world. As a means of evaluating how these dynamics function within the biblical texts, narrative critics have brought attention to three temporal features within the narrative: order, duration, and frequency.

First, one of the primary means of differentiating narrative time and story time is by assessing the order of events. Whether in fiction or film, authors often utilize *analepses* and *prolepses* within the narrative. An analepsis is simply an explicit or implicit reference to an event after it has already occurred (what is often referred to as a flashback). In contrast, a prolepsis is any explicit or implicit reference to an event before it has happened: a flashforward or preview. Analepses and prolepses may be internal (referring to events that transpire within the narrative), or they may be external (referencing events that occur beyond the envisioned story world, either before inception or after its conclusion).[11]

For example, Mark 6:14–29 provides a classic illustration of where narrative and story time diverge. In 1:14, readers are informed that John the Baptist has been taken into custody, but the detail is left unresolved and given no further explanation until 6:14. In the pericope following the sending of the disciples, Herod begins to consider whether the powers that are at work in Jesus (and the disciples) are the result of John being raised from the dead (6:14). The litany of perfect- (ἐγήγερται, 6:14) and aorist-tense verbs (ἀπεκεφάλισα, ἠγέρθη, 6:16) suggests that the death of John has already taken place, despite the fact that the event has yet to be narrated within the story. In what literary critics would deem an (internal) analepsis that fills in the details surrounding the death of the Baptist (6:17–29), the narrator refrains from describing the account until after suggesting that John

9. Genette, *Narrative Discourse*.

10. Culpepper, *Anatomy*, 51–75.

11. Analepses and prolepses may also be "mixed," thus referring to events that begin (analepses) or conclude (prolepses) beyond the story world but nonetheless cross over into the temporal period of the story. See, ibid., 56–57.

has already died. Though there is debate about the precise function of this analepsis, there is little doubt that the distinction between narrative and story time is a rhetorical technique that creates interest and heightens the drama of the story.[12]

The second component of narrative-critical temporal analysis is duration. Culpepper suggests that the evaluation of duration seeks to explore "the length of the narrative to the length of the story." [13] The comparison focuses on the difference between the time required to narrate an event orally versus the time (i.e., hours, days, months, years) that is assumed to have elapsed during the story. To describe the relative duration of events and the relationship between the temporal features within and beyond the story, scholars often use terms such as *summary, scene, stretch, ellipsis,* and *pause.*[14] The aim in evaluating the duration is to ascertain the relative tempo of the narrative, since stories rarely, if ever, move at a consistent speed and often vary the rhythm of the narrative in order to accent particular episodes.

Culpepper provides a helpful example from John's Gospel that demonstrates how duration may be manipulated within the story.[15] He begins by observing that John's Gospel depicts a period spanning approximately two and a half years. Within the narrative, however, this time is expressed in an inconsistent manner and often changes pace or pulsates to draw attention to certain events. As a case in point, the first year of the Johannine Jesus is narrated in 116 verses (3:22—6:2). But the second year is depicted in 295 verses (6:66—12:50), and from there the story begins to slow down even more dramatically, focusing on a two-week period in John 12–20, with seven of the chapters (chs. 13–19) honing in on a single twenty-four-hour period of time. Culpepper concludes that the speed of the narrative and the distinction between narrative and story time emphasizes the most crucial features of the story. "Like Henry Fielding's ingenious traveler," the evangelist "does not jog 'with equal Pace through the verdant Meadows or over the barren Heath,' but 'always proportions his Stay at any Place to the Beauties, Elegancies, and the Curiosities which it affords.'"[16]

---

12. Some Markan scholars regard 6:14–29 as little more than an interlude while the disciples are on mission (e.g., Best, *Following Jesus*, 192). Others, however, view 6:14–29 within a broader Markan intercalation (6:7–30) that juxtaposes the disciples' self-proclaimed success with the self-sacrifice of John the Baptist (e.g., Moloney, "Mark 6:6b–30," 647–63).

13. Culpepper, *Anatomy*, 70.

14. For a summary of duration and a more expansive treatment of these terms, see Powell, *What Is Narrative Criticism?*, 38–39.

15. Culpepper, *Anatomy*, 72.

16. Ibid., 70.

Finally, the third temporal feature emphasized by narrative critics is the frequency by which an event is narrated. Culpepper argues that the relationship between the occurrence of an event and the frequency of its narration may be used to further differentiate narrative and story time.[17] In general, there are four possibilities to consider: (1) an author may provide a single account of an event that occurs once; (2) an author may narrate repeatedly an event that occurs repeatedly;[18] (3) an author may narrate once an event that happened repeatedly; or (4) an author may narrate repeatedly an event that happened once. As Powell observes, "the frequency with which events are referred to in the telling of a story is important to narrative criticism because it affects the reader's understanding of the narrative as a whole. . . . By controlling frequency of reference to events, the implied author is able to send signals to the reader that offer guidance in making sense of the text."[19]

In their own respective ways, the Gospels and Acts make use of the four frequency types. Perhaps most indicative of technique (1) are the many events that occur and are reported once. The Sermon on the Mount, for example, is one of the five major discourses in Matthew, and though there are numerous analepses that look back to the Sermon (e.g., Matt 26:39, 42, 48–50), the discourse is narrated on only one occasion. The Gospels also make significant use of repetition and frequently narrate scenes that happen repeatedly (2), as evidenced by Jesus' seemingly endless confrontations with the religious leaders (e.g., Mark 2:6–10, 16–17, 18–22; 3:1–6; 7:1–13; 8:11–12; 11:27—12:27). Likewise, there are frequent summaries that portray events that happened repeatedly (3), even making use of the imperfect to emphasize the iterative nature of the activities (e.g., John 3:22; 6:2).[20] Finally, though less common, is the repeated narration of a single event (4), perhaps best illustrated in Paul's Damascus road experience. Although the event is narrated in Acts 1:1–9, the scene is reiterated on two additional occasions (Acts 22:4–16; 26:9–18).

In summary, Culpepper is right to observe that when "we read a story, we sense the passage of time . . . [even though] we may become so absorbed in the passage of time within the story that we lose all awareness of the time

---

17. Ibid., 73.

18. Genette (*Narrative Discourse*, 113) notes that no event can occur repeatedly since every event is a unique experience. When Genette and Culpepper refer to the repeated narration of an event that occurs repeatedly, they have in view *similar* events or events that fall into a discernible category.

19. Powell, *What Is Narrative Criticism?*, 39–40.

20. It could also be argued that the summaries fall into category (2). These scenes narrate multiple-occurring events that collectively function as an event of a particular type.

we have spent reading."[21] By scrutinizing the order, duration, and frequency of the narrative's temporal flow, narrative critics are able to categorize and explain how the Gospels are artistically arranged, as well as how the rhetorical features of the story are intended to shape the reading experience.

Time in Performance-Critical Perspective

There is little question that narrative critics have advanced the temporal discussion and brought greater clarity to understanding the dynamics of biblical stories. Narrative-critical concerns have pushed scholarly discussion beyond traditional queries of time, which have typically revolved around historical-critical matters (e.g., salvation history). Even more than emphasizing how the temporal features within the story may be exploited, narrative critics exposed the multifaceted nature of time—that temporal matters are far more complex than is often assumed. Though it was not their intent, narrative critics demonstrated that time may be analyzed from any number of angles, further confirming the elusive nature of the concept.

While it is certainly true that narrative critics advanced the discussion, in other respects they unwittingly stunted the conversation. Most problematic was the limited scope of the analysis, which typically focused on the story world of the narrative and the imagined depiction of events, independent of the horizons beyond the literary artifact.[22] In his fine introduction to narrative criticism, for example, James Resseguie suggests that scholars must remain "alert to temporal settings that may be significant for the interpretation of a narrative." Taken in isolation this statement represents a concise and informed perspective regarding the importance of temporal matters. But, like other narrative critics, Ressequie restricts the discussion to the "temporal settings" within the narrative.[23] While this analysis is important for exegesis—as settings, though brief, are often highly suggestive in biblical literature—the underlying perspective underscores a shortcoming of the hermeneutical paradigm. Both the genius and limitation of narrative criticism is the focused return to the text, but this exclusive orientation reduces the analysis to the temporal mechanics of the literary artifact.

Neglected in these discussions is a recognition that time *does not* function within an autonomous story world, insulated from an audience's experience of the narrative. Such a view reflects an overreliance upon modern

---

21. Culpepper, *Anatomy*, 53.

22. Beer observes that "in narratology the study of time and tense *within* fictions . . . was emphasized" ("Storytime and Its Futures," 127, italics original).

23. Resseguie, *Narrative Criticism*, 21.

literary theories, as well as an inadequate understanding of how texts were typically experienced in the ancient world. Scholars have convincingly shown that only a small percentage of the first-century Mediterranean world was capable of reading with any degree of proficiency.[24] Rather than through "reading," in the modern sense of the term, stories were experienced in an oral context between a performer and audience. While these distinctions may appear semantic in nature (author vs. performer; reader vs. audience), the similar terminology shrouds distinctions that have important consequences for the interpretive process. There are points of convergence between the paradigms, but it would be reductionistic to ignore the hermeneutical particularities of the two media. If, as it seems, the Gospels were performed in an oral arena—whether a formal public reading or a memorized performance—then a host of interpretive and hermeneutical issues emerge, not the least of which is the nature of time.

The temporal perspectives reflected in the media are grounded in the experiential contexts of the two communicative systems. Due to their presuppositions, narrative critics have focused on the temporal mechanics within the confines of the story, but they have ignored the impact that performance has upon the *audience's perception of time*. To appreciate how this works, theater critics often draw an elemental distinction between two kinds of performance time: off-stage time and stage time. Off-stage time refers to the contextual period of the narrative (e.g., first-century Palestine), whereas stage time denotes the actual time of performance, in which the audience and performer assemble (e.g., in the twenty-first century).[25] Although in any given performance off-stage time and stage time may refer to temporal periods that are chronologically distant, *the temporal dimensions converge in the oral arena*. Despite the temporal distinctiveness of the narrative and performance worlds, the liveness of performance fuses the horizons, transforming the audience's perception of the drama. Because the story unfolds in the direct spatio-physical presence of the audience and performer, the relative distance between events and discourse is compressed. This proximity has the effect of seamlessly converging the off-stage and stage times so as to thrust forward (or backward) the world of the narrative into the world of the performance. As Gillian Beer explains,

> [In performance] at least two people, and very probably more, are in relationship at this moment, though what the tale tells

24. Harris, *Ancient Literacy*; Bar-Ilan, "Illiteracy in the Land of Israel," 2.46–61; Millard, *Reading and Writing in the Time of Jesus*; Hezser, *Jewish Literacy in Roman Palestine*.

25. Pavis, *Dictionary of the Theatre*, 409.

may be drawn from the remotest past. The past tense of the teller is intercalated with the present tense of his or her being . . . [and] [t]he story told aloud is embedded in the real time of its telling, as well as the place of its events.[26]

The implication is that in performance, "time unfolds in a continual present."[27] In fact, it is for this reason that scholars often refer to the theatrical event as taking place *hic et nunc* (here and now).[28] De Toro argues that "even when events take place in the past, they present themselves in the present, in the form of performative action."[29] While this is not to imply that performance is unable to reference a temporal period other than the one embodied at the moment of delivery, it does suggest that the default action of the story is made contemporaneous to the audience's experiential context. De Toro illustrates this phenomenon with an example that has notable parallels to the Gospel of Luke (σήμερον; 2:11; 4:21; 5:26; 12:28; 13:32–33; 19:5, 9; 22:34, 61; 23:43): "in theatre the utterance 'today' is a spatio-temporal co-reference" but in literary texts, "one must consider this utterance in relation to the mesurative [*sic*], directive or stative conditions, that is, to the chronological time of the calendar."[30] In the process of reading, "today" is grounded in specific, spatio-temporal realities that pertain to the story world of the narrative. But when the same announcement is uttered in a performative context, though the off-stage time may reference a period in ancient history or the eschaton, the immediacy of oral discourse has the effect of relativizing certain elements of the temporal pronouncement or, at the very least, imbuing them with a surplus of meaning that relativizes the strict historical roots. In performance, "today," though possibly referring to a period long since passed, is ushered into the present through the act of performance.

This phenomenon is in direct contrast with the reading process, which assumes a spatio-temporal distance between events and discourse, and furthers the inherent divide between narrator and reader. It may be that "fiction can freely traverse, re-assemble, and invoke past and future," but it is never "*taking place* (taking *space*, one might say) in the present. It is actual in the emotions, breeding potential outcomes in the reader's mind,

26. Beer, "Storytime and Its Futures," 132.

27. Pavis, *Dictionary of the Theatre*, 409.

28. Fischer-Lichte argues that "theatre—unlike the epos, novel, or a series of images—does not tell a story taking place at another time and place but portrays events that occur and are perceived by the audience *hic et nunc*. What the spectators see and hear in performance is always present. Performance is experienced as the completion, presentation, and passage of the present" (*Transformative Power of Performance*, 94).

29. Toro, *Theatre Semiotics*, 26.

30. Ibid., 27.

but never located in any outside," immediate expression of those events.[31] While stories may be provocative and stimulating, ensnaring readers in a powerful narrative web, the temporal mechanics of the story function differently, particularly when viewed in relation to the oral event.

Pushing these observations to their logical conclusion, some have suggested that the present tense of performance is a defining characteristic of the media type. Phelan, for instance, argues that the *hic et nunc* of performance is an intrinsic feature of theater and endemic to the very ontology of the oral event. As Phelan succinctly observes, "performance's only life is in the present."[32] This distinctive trait is what differentiates performance from literary texts and renders standard treatments of time—particularly as it pertains to the Gospels—incomplete. Thornton Wilder elaborates,

> Novels are written in the past tense. The characters in them, it is true, are represented as living moment by moment their present time, but the constant running commentary of the novelist, inevitably conveys to the reader the fact that these events are long since past and over . . . On the stage it is always now. This confers upon the action an increased vitality which the novelist longs in vain to incorporate into his [or her] work.[33]

It is the present-ness of performance that gives rise to the "magic,"[34] or as one writer describes, the "utopian" experience of performance.[35] Exactly how this "utopian" experience is achieved is dependent upon the notion of "presence"—a concept closely related to the *hic et nunc* of performance. Though the term has been broadly defined in theatre studies, referring to concepts ranging from a performer's aura to the mode of representation,[36] for the current discussion, it is important to emphasize the tangible and physical presence—that is, the shared spatio-temporal arena between the audience and performer. Unlike the act of reading whereby a separation or absence between the author and reader is assumed, the performance arena is defined, in part, by the co-presence of its participants.[37] Walter

---

31. Beer, "Storytime and Its Futures," 132, emphasis original.

32. Phelan, *Unmarked*, 147.

33. Wilder, "Some Thoughts on Playwriting," 114.

34. Barranger, *Theatre*, 9.

35. Dolan, *Utopia in Performance*.

36. On the various kinds of theatrical presence, see the important work by Power, *Presence in Play*.

37. Lavender, "Mise en scène: Hypermediacy and the Sensorium," 64. Presence is yet another layer of the present-ness of performance, but not merely between the audience and events. Presence denotes the temporal relationship between the audience and

Benjamin suggests in his famous essay "The Storyteller" that in contrast to the reader, who experiences the narrative in relative seclusion, storytellers experience companionship and proximity as hallmarks of the storytelling event.[38] Indeed, many have described the relationship between audience and performer as conferring a mutual exchange of "energy"[39] or a "contagious force."[40] Although the act of reading may also stimulate an affective response, the emotions generated through performance are magnified by the aesthetic experience between the audience and performer. This observation, long noted by both modern and ancient scholars (cf. Pliny, *Ep.* 2.14.5; Quintilian, *Inst.* 10.1.17–19) recognizes that it is the present-ness and presence among the participants that arouses and heightens audience response.[41] The dynamics that unfold among the group are triggered by the audience's collective reception and increase the emotional intensity of the performance.[42]

It is for this reason that the transformative potential of performance and theater are often described in lofty terms. At its best, Esslin notes, theater and performance "can produce a concentration of thought and emotion which leads to an enhanced degree of lucidity, of emotional intensity that

---

performer.

38. Benjamin, *Illuminations*, 83–109.

39. Fischer-Lichte, *Transformative Power of Performance*, 59.

40. Fischer-Lichte, *Theatre, Sacrifice, Ritual*, 81.

41. Pliny and Quintilian both note that this aspect of performance may have both positive and negative effects. In some contexts, individuals were invited and/or paid to participate for the purpose of swaying other audience members.

42. Pfister, *Theory and Analysis of Drama*, 37. The power of group dynamics to prompt heightened emotional experience is perhaps best illustrated in comedy. It is widely recognized that "laughter is infectious," and that one's desire to laugh is accentuated in a communal setting. What is striking is how producers tap into this phenomenon in different media, particularly in television and film. Recognizing that comedy's success hinges on its ability to spark laughter, television producers typically include prerecorded laughter during the humorous scenes. These laugh tracks function as backdrop to the comedy and provide the viewer with the false but necessary impression of participating in a communal setting. The overall effect is to accomplish in seclusion (i.e., in private viewing within homes) what freely occurs in corporate settings. With film an entirely different scenario transpires. Because films are viewed in theaters with captive audiences, the need to interject an artificial laugh track is unnecessary. The communal setting is already present, paving the way for the corporate response of laughter. Although film and television represent different media types from oral performance, they nonetheless attempt to harness the power of group dynamics inherent to oral performance. Whereas a humorous book might cause a person to chuckle or smile, television and film exploit the power of the communal setting, thereby intensifying a person's experiential response. On this characteristic of laughter, see Downs et al., *Art of Theatre*, 74.

amounts to a higher level of spiritual insight and can make such an experience akin to a religious one."[43] This magical quality of theater is a frequent point of discussion in performance studies but is seldom considered or appreciated in biblical studies. Though mysterious in certain respects, the dynamic power of the aesthetic experience is derived from the present-ness inherent to the performance arena.

An Absence of Emotion in Luke's Passion?

The subjects of time, performance, and emotion come into sharp relief in the examination of Luke's passion. Of concern is not the dramatic display of emotion, but the emotional control of the Lukan Jesus, particularly when compared to Matthew and Mark. Even prior to the actual trial and crucifixion, many have suggested, that there is a discernable shift in the tone of Luke's account. At Gethsemane, for instance, Matthew and Mark indicate that Jesus is anxious and distressed about the fate that awaits him (ἀδημονέω [Matt 26:37; Mark 14:33], ἐκθαμβέω [Mark 14:33]; λυπέω [Matt 26:37]). The depiction is made explicit by the narrator and is immediately reiterated by Jesus' acknowledgement that he is "deeply grieved" (περίλυπος; Mark 14:34; Matt 26:38), leading him—out of his fragile emotional state— to fall down in prayer (Mark 14:35; Matt 26:39). Remarkably, these references to Jesus' grief and distress are conspicuously absent in Luke's account (22:39–46). Although the appearance of the angel and the statement about Jesus' blood-like sweat in Luke 22:43–44 appear more in-line with the Synoptic counterparts, the inclusion of these verses is highly disputed and may reflect a later, second-century interpolation.[44] However, even if the details are retained, they do not necessarily alter this general portrayal. That Jesus was strengthened by an angel and sweating in an intensified fashion need not connote fear or excruciating pain but rather, according to Senior, the struggle undertaken by an athlete or warrior.[45] Thus in contrast to Matthew and Mark, where Jesus is dependent on the disciples to "keep watch" (Mark 14:34; Matt 26:38) during his time of emotional struggle, the Lukan Jesus is presented as "God's champion and obedient Servant," kneeling "with self-control and dignity, to pray for the strength and courage to follow God's will even into the jaws of death."[46]

---

43. Esslin, *Anatomy of Drama*, 26.

44. For a discussion of this *crux interpretum*, see Ehrman and Plunkett, "The Angel and the Agony," 401–16.

45. Senior, *Passion of Jesus in the Gospel of Luke*, 88.

46. Ibid., 87.

Peter Doble suggests that this "marked absence of emotion" in Luke is not a minor deviation in the presentation of Jesus.[47] The lack of emotion and heightened sense of composure exhibited by Jesus is a hallmark of the Lukan narrative. Reflecting on Luke's redaction of Mark, O'Toole concludes that the evangelist has systematically "dropped certain Marcan passages, which speak of Jesus' emotions."[48] Powell also concurs, arguing that the portrayal of the Lukan Jesus has been carefully "retouched" so as to significantly downplay the emotional volatility.[49] Likewise, in perhaps the most poignant statement regarding the Lukan Jesus, Fitzmyer argues that the Third Gospel evidences Luke's "delicate sensitivity" in eliminating "anything that smacks of the violent, the passionate, or the emotional."[50]

Literary Parallels in Luke's Passion

In an attempt to explain this dichotomous relationship with the Synoptics, many have suggested that Luke's passion must be understood in concert with ancient literary parallels. Neyrey, for example, after studying the use of λύπη (grief) in Stoic philosophy and Hellenistic Judaism, argues that the term carried a particularly negative connotation. Because the concept of grief, according to Neyrey, was "(1) one of the four cardinal passions [which were to be avoided], (2) a typical punishment for sin, and (3) an indication of guilt,"[51] the third evangelist made a deliberate choice to excise this emotion from the narrative. In order to avoid depicting Jesus as a distraught figure or one lacking moral courage, Luke redacts any unworthy trait that might diminish the character of Jesus. In contrast to Matthew and Mark, the resulting portrait of Jesus is one who exemplifies moral restraint and tranquility despite the looming shadow of the cross.

Still others have sought to explain Luke's characterization of Jesus by examining relevant Jewish parallels. Brown, for instance, draws attention to the martyrological literature—in particular, to the similarities that Luke shares with the Maccabean tradition and Antiochus's attempt to enforce the worship of pagan gods.[52] Brown argues that several phrases in 4 Maccabees 6 that depict the martyr Eleazar "flowing with blood" (4 Macc. 6:6) and

---

47. Doble, *Paradox of Salvation*, 200.

48. O'Toole, *Luke's Presentation of Jesus*, 26–27. See also Shellard, *New Light on Luke*, 269; Tannehill, *Narrative Unity of Luke-Acts*, 1:271.

49. Powell, *Introduction to the Gospels*, 90–91.

50. Fitzmyer, *Gospel according to Luke*, 1:94.

51. Neyrey, "Absence of Jesus' Emotions," 157.

52. Brown, *Death of the Messiah*, 1:187–89.

"bathed in sweat" (4 *Macc.* 6:11) bear a striking resemblance to the Lukan passion (cf. 22:44). In addition, just as Jesus is provided angelic assistance in Gethsemane (22:43) so too do many of the martyological accounts include the presence of divine beings as, for example, in the story of Shadrach, Meshach, and Abednego (Dan 3:28). Brown suggests that these textual and thematic links indicate that Luke may have been influenced by the accounts of the martyrs. Along these same lines, other scholars have attempted to demonstrate similar connections with figures such as Socrates, who was regarded as the "paradigmatic martyr of his society."[53] Although unique in their own respective ways, these propositions attempt to explain Luke's reserved emotional depiction of Jesus in terms of contemporary norms and/ or heroic figures.

These interpretations continue to be debated and offer intriguing parallels that may reflect points of intertextual exchange, but it is questionable whether these solutions adequately explain the complexities of the narrative.[54] The underlying assumption of these perspectives—that the evangelist was concerned to depict a more "manly," less-emotional Jesus (to use Neyrey's terminology)—ignores other scenes in the narrative. For example, in 7:12–17 Jesus is filled with compassion (σπλαγχνίζομαι, 7:13) for a widow whose only son has passed away. The scene is important because it demonstrates the emotional capacity of the Lukan Jesus, while simultaneously legitimizing the woman's response to the death of her son. In view of the woman's tearful, emotional state, Jesus' compassionate response tacitly affirms the woman's rightful expression of emotion. Rather than rebuking the woman for her sorrow and grief, the Lukan Jesus affirms the active expression of emotion in light of hardship, specifically death. Other expressions of emotion in the narrative include Jesus' amazement (θαυμάζω, 7:9) at the faith of a centurion whose slave is near the point of death, as well as his "great joy" (ἀγαλλιάω, 10:21) at the return of the seventy (-two).

This expression of emotion, however, seems to escalate during the travel narrative. As Jesus begins the long and fateful journey to Jerusalem, he laments the "baptism" that awaits him, even declaring πῶς συνέχομαι (12:50) or "how great is my distress."[55] Though there is some discussion about the interpretation of this difficult phrase, and the controlling verb (συνέχω) has been translated "constrained," "strained," or "hard pressed,"[56]

---

53. Sterling, "Mors Philosophi," 383–402.

54. For a critique of these perspectives, see Green, *Gospel of Luke*, 747.

55. BDAG, 971, s.v. συνέχω.

56. On the various issues surrounding the translation of the verb, see Voorwinde, *Jesus' Emotions in the Gospels*, 132–36.

Luke often uses the term in reference to oppressive forces or circumstances, including the adverse effects of sickness (4:38; Acts 28:8) or the response to fear (8:37). Despite the questions that remain around the interpretation of this Lukan phrase, "it is difficult to divest [t]his statement of emotional content."[57]

The distress that Jesus experiences at the outset of the journey reaches a crescendo during the triumphal entry when, as Jesus is received with joyful celebration, he begins to weep at the sight of the city (19:41). This latter detail is particularly important, for although the entrance to Jerusalem is included in each of the canonical Gospels, only Luke states that Jesus wept (κλαίω, 19:41). The reaction may be triggered by the unbelief of the city, but in view of the emotional scene at the beginning of the journey (12:50), it is difficult to detangle the possible rationales for Jesus' affective response— whether it is prompted by a concern for the city or his impending death. As Jesus' response in vv. 42–44 suggests, however, the fate of Jesus and the unbelief of the city are closely intertwined, and the depiction likely reflects the broad personal and corporate concerns of the Lukan Jesus. Though there may be questions about the motivation for Jesus' affective reaction, there is little doubt that the shedding of tears reflects the narrator's attempt to underscore the emotional depth of Jesus.

It would seem, therefore, that Luke has deliberately framed the travel narrative with explicit emotional signposts.[58] That Jesus is "distressed"

---

57. Ibid., 133.

58 The assumption among many scholars is that Luke minimizes the emotions of Jesus because they are not befitting of the divine. Fitzmyer (*Gospel according to Luke,* 1:95) offers a representative view: "the description of Jesus moved by human emotions in the Marcan Gospel is normally eliminated in the Lucan story, even if they are expressions of love, compassion, or tenderness. The Marcan episodes depict Jesus in a more human way, perhaps too human for the nobility of a character that Luke sought to depict." While this is not to suggest that Luke completely ignores the humanity of Jesus, as O'Toole argues, the third evangelist has redacted Mark to "reflect on the supernatural and divine aspects of Jesus" (*Luke's Presentation of Jesus,* 27). This interpretation may provide an explanation for certain features in the story, but it fails to account for the totality of the narrative. In particular, Luke portrays God in precisely the ways that, according to Fitzmyer and others, the evangelist attempts to avoid in the characterization of Jesus. For example, in the parable of the Vineyard (20:9–18), the landowner—who is widely acknowledged as representing God—responds to the tenants' mistreatment of the servants and son by coming to "destroy" (ἀπόλλυμι; 20:16) the vine-growers. Although the landowner exhibits a modicum of patience, there are discernable limits to his longsuffering, and he ultimately lashes out in violence. Exactly how this is to be interpreted is a matter of debate, but it is hard to escape the seemingly harsh depiction of the divine. In contrast to this vengeful portrayal of God, Luke 15:11–32 presents a different emotional picture. In the parable of the Prodigal Son, which marks the culminating episode in the tripartite sequence of lost items (15:1–7, 8–10), it is the father's

as he moves toward the Holy City (12:50) and weeps upon his entrance (19:41) suggests that the evangelist was not hesitant to depict Jesus with, as Voorwinde observes, "a kaleidoscope of emotional colour."[59] Since neither of these scenes is derived from Mark, it is difficult to conclude that Luke intended to blot out these "diseases or disorders of the soul" from across the Gospel.[60] Rather, when viewed collectively, these scenes appear to validate the emotional expression that many assume is rejected in Luke's passion.

Given this conclusion, it may seem surprising to affirm that, although these interpretations lack the explanatory power to account for the complexity of the Lukan narrative, the underlying observation of these approaches *is not entirely wrong*. Although the Lukan Jesus exemplifies emotional capacity elsewhere in the Gospel, the evangelist appears to downplay Jesus' emotion *within the passion, particularly as it relates to the suffering of Jesus*. In contrast to portrayls in Matthew and Mark, as the Lukan Jesus makes his way to the cross, he petitions those following "to stop weeping" for him (Luke 23:28–31)—an injunction that seemingly contradicts his own demeanor in the near narrative (19:41), as well as his response to the distraught woman in Nain (7:12–17). Even Jesus' final words from the cross make a radical

---

love that dictates the response to the wayward son. Though these scenes do not provide an exhaustive survey, they depict God in ways that are unbecoming of the divine, at least according to many interpreters. If Luke is intent on redacting the emotional portrayal of Jesus, why does the characterization of God still encompass these features? Such an issue is all the more problematic given Luke's christological agenda, which, as Kavin Rowe has persuasively argued, is to narrate the "embodied revelation of κύριος ὁ θεός" in the person of Jesus of Nazareth (*Early Narrative Christology*, 218).

59. Voorwinde, *Jesus' Emotions in the Gospels*, 120.

60. Neyrey, "Absence of Jesus' Emotions," 155. It might be objected that Luke's "marked absence of emotion" is best appreciated within the broader context of the Synoptics. By way of comparison, Mark includes sixteen explicit references to Jesus' emotions, Matthew ten, and Luke five. For a helpful summary of the emotional data in the Gospels, see Voorwinde, *Jesus' Emotions in the Fourth Gospel*, 284–98. Although the statistics are interesting, they require interpretation and may be parsed in different ways. It may be that Luke records fewer statements that describe Jesus' emotions, but it *does not necessarily follow* that Luke's Gospel is less emotional. Though Luke contains fewer references to the emotions of Jesus, the Third Gospel includes significantly more references to the emotions of others (86), as compared to Matthew (47) and Mark (51). In addition, correlating the emotional impact of Luke's narrative requires more than statistical assessment. Standard treatments of the subject are invariably dependent upon redactional analysis and rarely consider the impact of orality upon the audience's perception of the narrative. The traditional approach tacitly assumes that an audience had recourse to Matthew and Mark and was simultaneously able to make the appropriate intertextual comparisons within the unmitigated flow of performance. Given the dynamics of performance, a simple comparison between the Gospels may be intriguing, but it may inadvertently distort the analysis. Despite their statistical differences, all three passion accounts may evoke a strong emotional reaction in their own particular ways.

departure from the Synoptic counterparts. Whereas the Matthean and Markan Jesus dies in utter abandonment—uttering the famous cry of dereliction—"My God, my God, why have you forsaken me? (Matt 27:46; Mark 15:34)—the Lukan Jesus offers a solemn prayer of commitment: "Father, into you hands I commit my spirit" (Luke 23:46).[61]

In view of these disparate characterizations, the question is why Luke deploys a potentially conflicting portrait, particularly when the evangelist intentionally interjects emotional content into the drama as the narrative advances towards Jerusalem? If the literary parallels do not fully account for the dilemma, how is the issue to be explained?

Uses of Emotion in Luke's Passion

Over the years, various scholars have suggested that the Third Gospel evidences characteristics reminiscent of a Greek tragedy.[62] This is not to imply that the totality of the Gospel is modeled after the Greek tragedy, but that certain features within the narrative display tragic elements. Despite these comparisons, there has been little, if any, reflection upon how these elements function within the contours of performance or how the *hic et nunc* of the oral arena shapes the passion scene.

Aristotle's definition of tragedy provides a starting point for discussion. According to Aristotle, a tragedy is

> the imitation of an action that is serious and also, as having magnitude, complete in itself, in language with pleasurable accessories, each kind brought in separately in the parts of the work; in a dramatic, not in a narrative form; with incidents arousing pity and fear . . . [in order] to accomplish its catharsis of such emotions. (*Poet.* 1449b.24–28)[63]

There is much that might be unpacked in this dense summary, but it is important to note that audience participation and the evoking of emotion is not an ancillary consideration. For Aristotle, the affective response is a

---

61. Matthew and Mark both make use of Ps 22:1 in Jesus' final words. Luke, on the other hand, utilizes Ps 31:5. While Psalm 22 concludes on a more hopeful perspective, and some have argued that the broader context of the psalm should frame the interpretive discussion, the varying words of Jesus in the accounts seem to offer a notably different perspective.

62. See, for example, Tiede, *Prophecy and History in Luke-Acts*, 114–17; Tyson, *Death of Jesus in Luke-Acts*, 15. On the potentially even broader influence of Greek tragedy upon Luke, see MacDonald, "Classical Greek Poetry and the Acts of the Apostles," 463–96; Tannehill, "Israel in Luke-Acts," 69–85.

63. All translations come from *The Complete Works of Aristotle*.

defining characteristic of tragedy. Even more specifically, Aristotle suggests that through the development of the tragic plot, performance entices the audience to experience pity and fear, or other "such emotions." With this last phrase, many scholars have suggested that Aristotle is here referring to the category of "distressing emotions," such as grief, hatred, or anger to name but a few.[64]

That Jesus is arrested only after being betrayed by one from his inner circle is congruent with the kind of "horrible" incidents that, according to Aristotle, makes for effective tragedy (*Poet.* 1453b.14). The natural response to the demise of the hero via the machinations of a friend induces audience sympathy or pity, which Aristotle observes is a feeling excited by the sight of some evil, "which befalls one who does not deserve it" (*Rhet.* 1385b.13–14). The feelings aroused by Judas's betrayal (Luke 22:48), the unjust trial, and the "underserved misfortune" (cf. *Poet.* 1453a.4) of the crucifixion are magnified by Luke's emphasis on the innocence of Jesus. Besides Herod's judicial finding (23:15), Pilate three times declares that there are no grounds for bringing legal action against Jesus (23:4, 14–15, 22), and he twice attempts to have him released, but to no avail (23:16, 22). The consistent juxtaposition of Jesus' innocence over and against the injustice of the cross arouses audience sympathy for the character of Jesus. In the present tense of performance, what is individually experienced in the silent reading process is collectively received in oral discourse, triggering an increased emotional intensity through the power of group dynamics.[65]

In conjunction with the temporal dynamics of the performance, it is the limited emotion of Jesus that ironically heightens audience response. Though the idea is somewhat counterintuitive, theatre critics have long observed that restraint and control may accentuate the significance of an event. In fact, at times it is more impactful to downplay a character's emotions, as audience response is driven by the movement and dramatization of the story more than by the passionate display of the affections. The great paradox of the stage is that "in order to have the greatest emotional effect on the spectator, the actor has to be in complete control of his acting behavior."[66] "Just as a bridle on a horse makes its reactions stronger and more immediate, so the theatre, which deals in powerful emotions, needs discipline" for the

---

64. Heath, *Poetics of Greek Tragedy*, 16; Janko, "From Catharsis to the Aristotelian Mean," 350.

65. Pfister, *Theory and Analysis of Drama*, 37.

66. Konijn, "What's On between the Actor and His Audience?," 59. See also Konijn, *Acting Emotions*, 22–23. On the classic statement regarding this relationship between the actor and audience, see Diderot, *Paradox of Acting*.

purpose of directing audience response.[67] In this respect, actors have often been instructed to learn the art of underplaying a role since "with restraint and control, the actions of a character . . . gain immeasurably in significance, beauty and effect."[68] These observations are crucial for understanding Luke's characterization of Jesus. Although Tinsley and others have argued that the passion does not "appeal primarily to our feelings, and certainly does not exploit them," the stylization of the narrative suggests just the opposite.[69] Indeed, what might be misconstrued as unemotional from a literary perspective, in performance has an amplifying effect that exacerbates the emotional response of the audience. Though often overlooked, within the domain of performance, the constrained depiction of Jesus reverberates against the tragic unfolding of the drama and intensifies audience sympathy and pity.[70]

But these emotions are not the only response animated by the passion. Aristotle also suggests that a derivative of the tragic performance is the audience's emotional response for themselves. More specifically, in the effective tragedy an audience is stimulated to experience fear and/or anger as a result of the hero's sufferings. According to Aristotle, anger is "an impulse, accompanied by pain, to a conspicuous revenge for a conspicuous slight directed without justification towards what concerns oneself or towards what concerns one's friends" (*Rhet.* 1378a.31–33). For Luke, although the "conspicuous slight" is undoubtedly the crucifixion, the stimulus for the scene is set in motion long before the passion. The ongoing conflict and animosity between Jesus and the religious leaders lays the emotional seedbed

---

67. Harrop, *Acting*, 45.

68. Pia, *Acting the Truth*, 141. For a discussion of the issue in the cognitive sciences, see Zunshine, *Getting Inside Your Head*, 79–102.

69. Tinsley, *Gospel according to Luke*, 11.

70. While it is true that the Lukan Jesus redirects the women's emotional response on the way to the cross by instructing them to "stop weeping" (23:28), nowhere does he repudiate their expression of grief and pity. For the audience experiencing the scene in the context of performance, Jesus' response to the mourners, besides underscoring the fate of the city, has the effect of legitimizing the audience's emotional reaction to the tragedy of the crucifixion scene. Although Jesus instructs the women to "stop weeping" for him, he subtly justifies the appropriate expression of emotion (i.e., "weep for yourselves," 23:28). This paves the way for an altogether different audience response. Despite Jesus' insistence to the contrary, the validation of emotion has a paradoxical effect upon the audience. In the context of the oral event and the heightened audience participation generated through the *hic et nunc* of performance, Jesus' words encourage a response in direct contrast to their stated intent. Rather than assuaging audience passions, Jesus' words underscore his humility and the tragic nature of the unfolding events. They do not, however, deflect emotional intensity away from the scene of the crucifixion. Instead Jesus' words further incite audience pity and anger at the injustice of the scene in a manner tantamount to Aristotle's understanding of the tragic event.

that intensifies in the passion. Although the Lukan Jesus endures physical suffering in the passion, more prolific throughout the entirety of the Gospel is the response that Jesus receives from his interlocutors. Whether it is the threat of physical violence against Jesus (4:28–30) or the repeated verbal rejection of his words and deeds (e.g., 5:21, 30; 6:2; 7:39; 11:15–16, 53–54; 13:14; 19:47–48; 20:20–22), similar to what Aristotle describes, the hostile exchanges throughout the narrative encourage an audience-inspired anger that simmers throughout the drama and reaches a crescendo at the cross.

The antagonism that an audience experiences as a result of these interactions is not unlike the scene in Luke 11:37–45. The narrative begins with Jesus being invited to partake of a meal with an anonymous Pharisee, but the episode quickly devolves when Jesus offends his host by failing to purify himself. After Jesus rebukes the Pharisees, the account rapidly shifts. An expert in the law, who presumably is a bystander to the unfolding events and is upset by Jesus' response to the Pharisees, interjects: "Teacher when you say this, you insult us too" (11:45). The response is striking in that Jesus' initial answer to the Pharisees is interpreted as a denunciation of the man's own community, even though neither he nor his constituency is addressed. Within the narrative, the assumption is that the lawyer has overheard the rebuke of the Pharisees and has internalized the message, thus evoking a response that evidences a mixture of hurt and anger.

In many respects, the scene exemplifies the kind of audience-participatory offense to which Aristotle refers—the feeling of insult and anger that may be incited when an individual perceives that an ally has been slighted. Of course, these exchanges take place within the story world of the narrative, but they nonetheless illustrate the dynamics that transpire in the performance arena. The audience, situated within the spatio-temporal presence of the narrator, experiences the performance from a vantage point that is not unlike the legal expert. As the performance unfolds and the conflict between Jesus and the religious establishment escalates, the audience becomes increasingly sensitive to the harsh, condemnatory words spoken against Jesus. Similar to the lawyer, the audience perceives the remarks as an attack against their own faith, becoming increasingly agitated as the condemnation escalates. The false accusations (23:2, 10) and persistent mockery by the soldiers (23:11, 36) and religious officials (22:64–65; 23:35), as well as by the individual condemned alongside Jesus (23:39), combine to arouse audience anger. In the end, as the Lukan Jesus hangs from the cross, anger and pity are excited among the community of participants. Although the literary artifact may downplay the emotion of Jesus, contrary to the claims of Stanton and Dibelius, the intent is not to create an account that is "less 'interesting'" and "less likely to 'arouse emotions.'"[71] Instead, through performance the restrained characterization of Jesus has the strategic effect of transferring the expected emotion to the audience.

This expression of audience emotion is justified by the tragic nature of the plot, the affections displayed by the character of Jesus, and the temporal mechanics of live performance. But why? Why does Luke deliberately incite the audience? For what purpose are the emotions provoked? We return to the discussion of tragedy. Aristotle suggests that tragedy entices audience passion, but mere provocation is not the ultimate objective. According to Aristotle, the stirring of emotion is for the purpose of "catharsis" (*Poet.* 1449b.24–28). Although there is considerable debate around this concept,[72] many scholars have suggested that catharsis denotes the clarification and enrichment of the emotions. Through the tragic performance the emotions are stimulated so as to educate and refine one's passions. As David Wiles suggests, "the experience of emotions in the mimetic environment of the theatre helps us to purify and clarify them so they can arise in the right real-life situations."[73] In this respect, "catharsis is *not* the end of tragedy, but one means among others for modeling human character. The function of this modeling, in turn, is not some sort of emotional purgation, as if a tragedy is successful just when its spectators leave the theatre depleted and ready for bed. On the contrary, tragedy leads to understanding, and understanding to right action."[74]

If we consider Aristotle's understanding of catharsis as the aim of tragedy, several features of the Lukan passion dovetail nicely. In particular, unlike in Matthew or Mark, as the Lukan Jesus hangs from the cross, the scene is punctuated by two statements—both of which are clustered around the concept of forgiveness (23:34, 43). In the first, Jesus prays for the forgiveness of those responsible for his demise.[75] The prayer that Jesus offers—"forgive them, for they do not know what they are doing" (23:34)—is almost immediately re-enacted in a second Lukan tradition. In response to the anonymous

---

71. Stanton, *Jesus of Nazareth*, 39. In this respect, Stanton approvingly follows Dibelius, *Gospel Criticism*, 62.

72. For a concise summary of the discussion, see Halliwell, *Aristotle's Poetics*, 350–56.

73. Wiles, "Aristotle's *Poetics* and Ancient Dramatic Theory," 99–100. See also Lear, "Catharsis," 193–217; Winston, *Drama, Narrative and Moral Education*, 53–56; Nussbaum, *Fragility of Goodness*, 288–91; House, *Aristotle's Poetics*, 104–11.

74. Shields, *Aristotle*, 391 (italics original).

75. The Greek text is somewhat ambiguous about the identity of "them" in Jesus' prayer (πάτερ, ἄφες αὐτοῖς, 23:34). The context seems to hold both the Jews and Romans culpable for the crucifixion. See Green, *Gospel of Luke*, 819–20.

but discerning criminal who rebukes his fellow compatriot from the cross, Jesus promises that "today you will be with me in paradise" (23:43).

Although these texts raise numerous historical, exegetical, and theological questions, at issue is the performative impact upon the audience's experience of the story. For the believing audience aligned with the Lukan Jesus, the *hic et nunc* of performance, coupled with the opposition that culminates in the repeated mockery and crucifixion of Jesus, sets off a complex range of audience emotion. The inevitable pity that is felt for Jesus is rivaled only by the similar, if not greater, sense of anger directed at those responsible for Jesus' sufferings. But it is precisely at this point, when audience anger reaches a crescendo, that Luke exploits the theme of forgiveness in order to curtail possible misunderstandings and to purify misguided emotions.[76] As theatre critics have historically observed, if left unchecked, the affections generated through performance may erupt in a "dangerous electricity."[77] Some have even suggested that performances may be "highly infectious"[78] and tantamount to the unleashing of "the plague."[79] Recognizing the powerful synergy between audience and performer, and the potential for misconstrual, Luke shapes the passion in order to exploit audience emotion for a greater theological purpose. Contrary to Matthew and Mark, and perhaps recognizing the potential for misunderstanding, Luke uses the tragic elements of Jesus' death for educational purposes. The evangelist capitalizes on the heightened sense of emotion in order to bring the audience to a greater awareness of how the emotions are to be handled within the context of anger, oppression, and persecution. Luke crafts the scene so that the spirit of nonviolence and forgiveness that characterizes the passion might also characterize the audience's real-life experiences beyond the confines of the performance.

Conclusion

Among biblical scholars, the subject of time has rarely been a topic of scrutiny. When it has, the agenda has typically been set by chirographic perspectives. However, unlike the literary artifact, which is governed by an inherent distance between the reader and events, performance collapses multiple dimensions of time into a unified, experiential context. What scholars have

---

76. The theme of forgiveness is an undercurrent throughout the narrative (e.g., 1:77; 3:3; 5:17–26; 7:40–50; 11:4; 17:3–4).

77. Brook, *Empty Space*, 99.

78. Fischer-Lichte, *Transformative Power of Performance*, 94.

79. Artaud, *Theatre and Its Double*, 15–32.

termed the *hic et nunc* of performance is an ontological feature of the media type that, as Green suggests, functions as a "tunnel to primal emotion."[80] "Performance embodies knowledge" in a unique and heightened fashion "that binds the audience and performer together," and unleashes the "rhetorical power to change attitudes and alter events."[81]

This present tense of performance is strikingly illustrated in a scene that has often been regarded as devoid of emotional depth. Through the dynamic *hic et nunc* of performance, the absence of emotion in Luke's passion is subtly shifted from the character of Jesus to the audience. In this paradoxical exchange, the evangelist creatively amplifies audience emotion and simultaneously arouses feelings of pity and anger. Luke entices the audience so as to transform would-be-disciples through the experience of the passion. While the framework that enlivens this scenario is the Greek tragedy, the foundation for this emotional transaction is the immediacy of the oral event. If Luke's passion is any indication, though *t-i-m-e* has often been shunned as a four-letter word, appreciating the temporal mechanics of the Gospels are crucial to understanding the performative experience and theological agenda of the evangelists.

Bibliography

Aristotle. *The Complete Works of Aristotle: The Revised Oxford Translation.* Edited by Jonathan Barnes. 2 vols. Bollinger Series 71–72. Princeton: Princeton University Press, 1984.

Artaud, Antonin. *The Theatre and Its Double.* Translated by Mary Caroline Richards. Evergreen Original. New York: Grove, 1958.

Augustine, Saint. *Confessions.* Translated by William Watts. 2 vols. LCL. Cambridge: Harvard University Press, 1977–1988.

Aveni, Anthony F. *Empires of Time: Calendars, Clocks, and Cultures.* London: Tauris Parke, 2000.

Bar-Ilan, Meir. "Illiteracy in the Land of Israel in the First Centuries CE." In *Essays in the Social Scientific Study of Judaism and Jewish Society*, edited by Simcha Fishbane et al., 2:46–61 Hoboken, NJ: Ktav, 1990–1992.

Barr, James. *Biblical Words for Time.* Studies in Biblical Theology 1/33. London: SCM, 1962.

Barranger, Milly S. *Theatre: A Way of Seeing.* 6th ed. Belmont, CA: Thomson Wadsworth, 2006.

Beer, Gillian. "Storytime and Its Futures." In *Time*, edited by Katinka Ridderbos, 126–42. Darwin College Lectures. Cambridge: Cambridge University Press, 2002.

Benjamin, Walter. *Illuminations: Essays and Reflections.* Translated by Harry Zohn. New York: Schocken, 1968.

---

80. Green, *Revisionist Stage*, 42.

81. Fine, *Folklore Text*, 64.

Best, Ernest. *Following Jesus: Discipleship in the Gospel of Mark.* JSNTSup 4. Sheffield: JSOT Press, 1981.

Brin, Gershon. *The Concept of Time in the Bible and the Dead Sea Scrolls.* Studies on the Texts of the Desert of Judah 39. Leiden: Brill, 2001.

Brook, Peter. *The Empty Space: A Book about the Theatre: Deadly, Holy, Rough, Immediate.* New York: Atheneum, 1968.

Brown, Raymond E. *The Death of the Messiah: From Gethsemane to the Grave: A Commentary on the Passion Narratives in the Four Gospels.* 2 vols. ABRL. New York: Doubleday, 1994.

Canestri, Jorge, and Leticia Glocer Fiorini, eds. *The Experience of Time: Psychoanalytic Perspectives.* Controversies in Psychoanalysis Series. London: Karnac, 2009.

Cullmann, Oscar. *Christ and Time: The Primitive Christian Concept of Time and History.* Translated by Floyd V. Filson. Philadelphia: Westminster, 1950.

Culpepper, R. Alan. *Anatomy of the Fourth Gospel: A Study in Literary Design.* Foundations and Facets: New Testament. Philadelphia: Fortress, 1983.

De Vries, Simon J. *Yesterday, Today, and Tomorrow: Time and History in the Old Testament.* Grand Rapids: Eerdmans, 1975.

Deterding, Paul E. "The New Testament View of Time and History." *Concordia Journal* 21 (1995) 385–99.

Dibelius, Martin. *Gospel Criticism and Christology.* London: Nicholson & Watson, 1935.

Diderot, Denis. *The Paradox of Acting.* Translated by Walter H. Pollock. New York: Hill & Wang, 1957.

Doble, Peter. *The Paradox of Salvation: Luke's Theology of the Cross.* SNTSMS 87. Cambridge: Cambridge University Press, 1996.

Dolan, Jill. *Utopia in Performance: Finding Hope at the Theater.* Ann Arbor: University of Michigan Press, 2005.

Downs, William Missouri, et al. *The Art of Theatre: A Concise Introduction.* 3rd ed. Boston: Wadsworth, 2013.

Ehrman, Bart D., and Mark A. Plunkett. "The Angel and the Agony: The Textual Problem of Luke 22:43–44." *CBQ* 45 (1983) 401–16.

Esslin, Martin. *An Anatomy of Drama.* New York: Hill & Wang, 1976.

Estes, Douglas. *The Temporal Mechanics of the Fourth Gospel: A Theory of Hermeneutical Relativity in the Gospel of John.* Biblical Interpretation Series 92. Leiden: Brill, 2008.

Fine, Elizabeth C. *The Folklore Text: From Performance to Print.* Bloomington: Indiana University Press, 1984.

Fischer-Lichte, Erika. *Theatre, Sacrifice, Ritual: Exploring Forms of Political Theatre.* London: Routledge, 2004.

———. *The Transformative Power of Performance: A New Aesthetics.* London: Routledge, 2008.

Fitzmyer, Joseph A. *The Gospel according to Luke.* Vol. 1, *Luke I–IX.* AB 28. 2 vols. Garden City, NY: Doubleday, 1981.

Gell, Alfred. *The Anthropology of Time: Cultural Constructions of Temporal Maps and Images.* Explorations in Anthropology. Oxford: Berg, 1992.

Genette, Gérard. *Narrative Discourse: An Essay in Method.* Translated by Jane E. Lewin. Ithaca, NY: Cornell University Press, 1980.

Green, Amy S. *The Revisionist Stage: American Directors Reinvent the Classics.* Cambridge Studies in American Theatre and Drama 3. Cambridge: Cambridge University Press, 2006.

Green, Joel B. *The Gospel of Luke*. NICNT. Grand Rapids: Eerdmans, 1997.

Greene, Brian. *The Fabric of the Cosmos: Space, Time, and the Texture of Reality*. New York: Vintage, 2005.

Halliwell, Stephen. *Aristotle's Poetics*. Chicago: University of Chicago Press, 1998.

Harris, William. *Ancient Literacy*. Cambridge: Harvard University Press, 1989.

Harrop, John. *Acting*. Theatre Concepts Series. London: Routledge, 1992.

Heath, Malcolm. *The Poetics of Greek Tragedy*. Stanford: Stanford University Press, 1987.

Hezser, Catherine. *Jewish Literacy in Roman Palestine*. TSAJ 81. Tübingen: Mohr/ Siebeck, 2001.

Hickox, Rex. *Time: Friend or Foe?* 2nd ed. Bentonville, AR: Rex, 2006.

House, Humphrey. *Aristotle's Poetics*. London: Hart-Davis, 1956.

Janko, Richard. "From Catharsis to the Aristotelian Mean." in *Essays on Aristotle's Poetics*, edited by Amélie Okensberg Rorty, 341–58. Princeton: Princeton University Press, 1992.

Konijn, Elly A. *Acting Emotions: Shaping Emotions on Stage*. Amsterdam: Amsterdam University Press, 2000.

————. "What's On between the Actor and His Audience? Empirical Analysis of Emotion Processes in the Theatre." In *Psychology and Performing Arts*, edited by Glenn D. Wilson, 59–74. Amsterdam: Swets & Zeitlinger, 1991.

Lavender, Andy. "Mise En Scène: Hypermediacy and the Sensorium." In *Intermediality in Theatre and Performance*, edited by Freda Chapple and Chiel Kattenbelt, 55–66. Themes in Theatre: Collective Approaches to Theatre and Performance 2. New York: Rodopi, 2006.

Lear, Jonathan. "Catharsis." In *A Companion to the Philosophy of Literature*, edited by Garry L. Hagberg and Walter Jost, 193–217. Blackwell Companions to Philosophy 44. Chichester, UK: Wiley-Blackwell, 2010.

MacDonald, Dennis R. "Classical Greek Poetry and the Acts of the Apostles: Imitations of Euripides' *Bacchae*." In *Christian Origins and Greco-Roman Culture: Social and Literary Contexts for the New Testament*, edited by Stanley E. Porter and Andrew W. Pitts, 463–96. Text and Editions for New Testament Study 9. Leiden: Brill, 2012.

Millard, Alan. *Reading and Writing in the Time of Jesus*. New York: New York University Press, 2000.

Moloney, Francis J. "Mark 6:6b–30: Mission, the Baptist, and Failure." *CBQ* 63 (2001) 647–63.

Moltmann, Jürgen. "What Is Time? And How Do We Experience It?" *Dialog* 39.1 (2000) 27–34.

Momigliano, Arnaldo. "Time in Ancient Historiography." *History and Theory* 6 (1966) 1–23.

Muilenburg, James. "The Biblical View of Time." *HTR* 54 (1961) 225–52.

Neyrey, Jerome H. "The Absence of Jesus' Emotions: The Lukan Redaction of Lk 22:39–46." *Bib* 61 (1980) 153–71.

Nussbaum, Martha C. *The Fragility of Goodness: Luck and Ethics in Greek Tragedy and Philosophy*. Cambridge: Cambridge University Press, 2001.

O'Toole, Robert F. *Luke's Presentation of Jesus: A Christology*. SubBi 25. Rome: Biblical Institute Press, 2004.

Palu, Ma'afu. *Jesus and Time: An Interpretation of Mark 1.15*. T. & T. Clark Library of Biblical Studies. LNTS 468. London: T. & T. Clark, 2012.

Pavis, Patrice. *Dictionary of the Theatre: Terms, Concepts, and Analysis*. Translated by Christine Shantz. Toronto: University of Toronto Press, 1998.

Pfister, Manfred. *The Theory and Analysis of Drama*. Translated by John Halliday. European Studies in English Literature. Cambridge: Cambridge University Press, 1988.

Phelan, Peggy. *Unmarked: The Politics of Performance*. London: Routledge, 1993.

Pia, Albert. *Acting the Truth: The Acting Principles of Constantin Stanislavski and Exercises: A Handbook for Actors, Directors, and Instructors of Theatre*. Bloomington, IN: AuthorHouse, 2006.

Powell, Mark Allan. *Fortress Introduction to the Gospels*. Minneapolis: Fortress, 1998.

———. *What Is Narrative Criticism?* GBS. Minneapolis: Fortress, 1990.

Power, Cormac. *Presence in Play: A Critique of Theories of Presence in the Theatre*. Consciousness Literature & the Arts 12. New York: Rodopi, 2008.

Resseguie, James L. *Narrative Criticism of the New Testament: An Introduction*. Grand Rapids: Baker Academic, 2005.

Rhoads, David. "Biblical Performance Criticism: Performance as Research." *Oral Tradition* 25 (2010) 157–98.

Ridderbos, Katinka. *Time*. Darwin College Lectures. Cambridge: Cambridge University Press, 2002.

Rowe, C. Kavin. *Early Narrative Christology: The Lord in the Gospel of Luke*. BZNW 139. Berlin: de Gruyter, 2006.

Schildgen, Brenda Deen. *Crisis and Continuity: Time in the Gospel of Mark*. JSNTSup 159. Sheffield: Sheffield Academic, 1998.

Senior, Donald. *The Passion of Jesus in the Gospel of Luke*. Passion Series 3. Collegeville, MN: Liturgical, 1992.

Shellard, Barbara. *New Light on Luke: Its Purpose, Sources and Literary Context*. JSNTSup 215. London: T. & T. Clark, 2004.

Shields, Christopher. *Aristotle*. 2nd ed. Routledge Philosophers. London: Routledge, 2013.

Stanton, Graham N. *Jesus of Nazareth in New Testament Preaching*. SNTSMS 27. Cambridge: Cambridge University Press, 2004.

Sterling, Gregory E. "*Mors Philosophi*: The Death of Jesus in Luke." *HTR* 94 (2001) 383–402.

Tannehill, Robert C. "Israel in Luke-Acts: A Tragic Story." *JBL* 104 (1985) 69–85.

———. *The Narrative Unity of Luke-Acts: A Literary Interpretation*. 2 vols. Foundations and Facets. Philadelphia: Fortress, 1986–1990.

Tiede, David L. *Prophecy and History in Luke-Acts*. Philadelphia: Fortress, 1980.

Tinsley, E. J. *The Gospel according to Luke*. CBC. Cambridge: Cambridge University Press, 1965.

Toro, Fernando de. *Theatre Semiotics: Text and Staging in Modern Theatre*. Translated by John Lewis. Revised and edited by Carole Hubbard. Toronto Studies in Semiotics. Toronto: University of Toronto Press, 1995.

Tyson, Joseph B. *The Death of Jesus in Luke-Acts*. Columbia: University of South Carolina Press, 1986.

Voorwinde, Stephen. *Jesus' Emotions in the Fourth Gospel: Human or Divine?* LNTS 284. London: T. & T. Clark, 2005.

———. *Jesus' Emotions in the Gospels*. London: T. & T. Clark, 2011.

Wagner, Michael F. *The Enigmatic Reality of Time: Aristotle, Plotinus, and Today*. Ancient Mediterranean and Medieval Texts and Contexts. Leiden: Brill, 2008.

Wilch, John R. *Time and Event: An Exegetical Study of the Use of 'ēth in the Old Testament in Comparison to Other Temporal Expressions in Clarification of the Concept of Time*. Leiden: Brill, 1969.

Wilder, Thornton. "Some Thougths on Playwriting." In *Playwrights on Playwriting: The Meaning and Making of Modern Drama from Ibsen to Ionesco*, edited by Toby Cole, 106–15. New York: Hill & Wang, 1960.

Wiles, David. "Aristotle's *Poetics* and Ancient Dramatic Theory." In *The Cambridge Companion to Greek and Roman Theatre*, edited by Marianne McDonald and J. Michael Walton, 92–107. Cambridge Companions to Literature. Cambridge: Cambridge University Press, 2007.

Winfree, Arthur T. *The Geometry of Biological Time*. 2nd ed. New York: Springer, 2001.

Winston, Joe. *Drama, Narrative and Moral Education*. London: Falmer, 1998.

Zunshine, Lisa. *Getting Inside Your Head: What Cognitive Science Can Tell Us about Popular Culture*. Baltimore: Johns Hopkins University Press, 2012.

7

FROM PERFORMANCE
TO TEXT TO PERFORMANCE

The New Testament's Use
of the Hebrew Bible in
a Rhetorical Culture

Kathy Maxwell

THE RECENT (AND RENEWED) INTEREST IN PERFORMANCE-
critical studies of the biblical text has led to insightful and invigorating
encounters with Christian Scripture. The topics of memory and orality have
encouraged many—in studies, classrooms, and churches—to think of the
Bible in terms of sound and rhythm, instead of font and formatting. The field
of performance criticism should, however, not only challenge our notions
of the nature of the text and its delivery but should also affect our understanding of hermeneutics. The central role of orality and performance in the
transmission of Hebrew Bible (HB) and New Testament (NT) material in
the rhetorical culture of the ancient world should lead twenty-first-century
interpreters to adjust both the understanding of ancient hermeneutics and
the modern practice of hermeneutics. A plethora of studies would prove
useful in illuminating this topic, but only one aspect is addressed here. Of
benefit are brief reflections on assumptions made by print and rhetorical

cultures, and a comparison of the two. In the intertwining of oral and written texts, we find the cooperation of narrative and performance-critical insights. As a case study, this project reviews Mark's citation of prophetic material in 1:2–3, citations in an oral composition that are prefaced with the formula, "It is written."

This chapter aims to continue the conversations started, for example, by Vernon Robbins, Holly Hearon and Philip Ruge-Jones, Jonathan Draper, Richard Horsley, John Miles Foley, and others, which in turn are often based on Walter Ong's *Orality and Literacy*, George Kennedy's *New Testament Interpretation through Rhetorical Criticism*, and Werner Kelber's *Oral and Written Gospel*, among others.[1] In other words, as is appropriate in an oral or rhetorical culture, this project is based on the evolving collaboration of scholars past and present.

Definition of Terms

In light of the multiple and competing jargons that have developed in the course of rhetorical, oral, performance, narrative, and audience-critical studies, defining terms will be useful for this discussion. For the purposes of this paper, we will assume Vernon Robbins's terms "rhetorical culture" on the one hand and "print culture" on the other. Robbins observes that often ancient cultures that are designated oral cultures have some sort of written component and written language. A true oral culture makes no use of writing and in fact does not possess a system of writing.[2] Thus, the first-century Mediterranean world, while certainly a more oral culture than the twenty-first-century United States, was not a purely oral culture. A system of writing, and the use of that system, had been an integral part of the Mediterranean culture for thousands of years, even though the vast majority of people within the culture did not have access to the education necessary to join the ranks of the literate.

A "rhetorical culture," according to Robbins's definition, reflects a "lively interaction between oral and written composition."[3] In light of this discussion, for instance, first-century Gospel writers would have learned the HB

---

1. See, for instance, Hearon and Ruge-Jones, ed., *Bible in Ancient and Modern Media*; Horsley et al., eds., *Performing the Gospel*; Kelber, *Oral and the Written Gospel*; Kennedy, *New Testament Interpretation through Rhetorical Criticism*; Ong, *Orality and Literacy*; Robbins, *Exploring the Texture of Texts*.

2. Robbins, "Progymnastic Rhetorical Composition," 114.

3. Ibid., 116. See also Achtemeier's discussion in "*Omne verbum sonat*," 7; and Carr, *Writing on the Tablet of the Heart*, 7–8.

through a combination of oral and written transmission.[4] Based on insights from the instruction in Theon's *Progymnasmata*, first-century authors following a similar practice would have felt free to expand and elaborate upon not only texts from the HB but upon oral and written traditions circulating about Jesus' life and ministry.[5]

The term "print culture" will refer broadly to a modern, Western culture in which mass produced, verbatim, printed literature is commonplace.[6] This culture assumes literacy, ease of access to printed texts, and primacy of place for the printed word. The differences between rhetorical and print cultures, and the assumptions of these cultures' members, play an important role in the discussion of hermeneutics, not only helping answer questions, but also clarifying which questions should be asked.

A bit of clarity regarding the word *text* is helpful as well. One of the differences highlighted by comparing rhetorical and print cultures is the presumed equivalence of the words *written* and *text*. While we are not used to this connotation, in even modern linguistic studies, the word *text* can refer to material both oral and graphic/written. We will adopt this definition here, distinguishing as needed between oral texts and written texts.

Likewise, the word *written* is not very precise. As Wulf Oesterricher points out, there exist written written texts, written oral texts, oral written texts, and oral oral texts.[7] In our print culture, however, *written* generally carries the connotation of something that is set in stone, so to speak, or something that does not change. The fact that both rhetorical and print cultures make use of written texts has led to applying modern conceptions of the text to the ancient rhetorical culture.[8] For this study, we must broaden our understanding of what is written to include the possibility that a written text may be in flux.

Modern usage of quotation marks and indentation, common in modern English, is rightly included in current English translations of the Bible. The quotation marks and indentations in the New Testament that set off words quoted from the HB imply that the words included therein must be a word-for-word recitation. In a print culture, such an implication is expected.

---

4. Robbins suggests that it is not until the late second century that a "polarity" developed between oral and scribal cultures. To assume that this polarity existed at the time of the gospel writing is "a fundamental error" (Robbins, "Progymnastic Rhetorical Composition," 116).

5. See Theon, "Exercises of Aelius Theon," 6–9, 12–14.

6. Robbins, "Oral, Rhetorical, and Literary Cultures," 78.

7. Oesterricher, "Types of Orality in Text," 192.

8. See Achtemeier, "*Omne verbum sonat,*" 3.

After all, this is how students are taught to cite research. Direct quotes must be enclosed within quotation marks. Direct quotes longer than four lines (or so) should be set off and indented as a block quote. Failing to do so is to commit academic dishonesty. What is written by one person cannot be claimed (or changed) by another. The understandable use of quotation marks and indentations may, however, imply characteristics not intended in the context of a rhetorical culture.

If we, as members of a print culture, want to remember something, we write it down. When we want to preserve something just as it is, when something is important, we write it down. This print-culture mindset affects the way we view the biblical text and should, at least to some extent, be set aside in favor of the hermeneutic of a rhetorical culture. We will find that in a rhetorical culture, accurate communication is important; but word-for-word repetition is not necessarily important.

Caveats for This Study

As any project is, this one is subject to limitations, and limitations are best acknowledged up front. First, I am writing from my own subculture within the print culture (specifically from a middle-class, college-educated, moderate-evangelical position). As I describe assumptions made by members of a twenty-first-century print culture about the ancient biblical text, I include my own observations as well as observations of recent scholars, though it is inevitable that each reader may find observations contrary to their own experience, and that important contributions by some pastors and scholars will not, in the end, be included.

Second, I do my best to describe the hermeneutic of this subculture, and while I argue that we would be well served to temper our hermeneutic with greater awareness of that of an ancient rhetorical culture, I do not intend to pass judgment on our hermeneutic. I am a part of this culture and subculture, for better or for worse; however, it is important to consider how an awareness of the rhetorical culture's hermeneutic can benefit our understanding of the biblical text.

Interpretive Assumptions of a Print Culture

In the field of biblical interpretation, a number of assumptions are made that are based on our contemporary print culture. These assumptions work quite well in the modern context, and many of them serve to undergird implicit and explicit hermeneutical practices. Setting a number of these assumptions

to paper will help clarify the tendencies of print culture and highlight differences from the rhetorical culture of the first-century Mediterranean world.

One Static, Authoritative Copy of a Text

First, members of a print culture assume that there is one authoritative
copy of a text. Important information is written down for the purpose of
preservation as well as future reference and transmission. As a result of the
emphasis put on Enlightenment developments like the rise of reason and
the scientific method, many in the Western world today assume that there
is one correct and objective way to describe an event, regardless of how
inadequately that one way may be conveyed. If a text claims to describe
an event, it provides an objective description of what really happened.
That written record should not be altered; to alter it would be considered
dishonest tampering.

To use an oft-cited example, a car accident occurs according to the
rules of physics. There is only one way the accident occurred. It is impossible for the red car to accelerate into the blue car in one scenario, and for
the blue car to accelerate into the red car in another scenario. Either the
red car hit the blue car, or it didn't. A police report is written, often based
on oral testimony, and the report is meant to describe what actually happened. All else being equal, after the author of the report has evaluated
the various oral testimonies and has summarized the actual events, the
objective written report carries more weight than a subjective oral report.
Oral reports may change over time as emotions and memory change. Written reports, however, are often deemed more trustworthy, as they are set
indelibly onto paper.

Indeed we have the expectation that so-called good reporting should
be unbiased. When reporting, even oral reporting as is found on television
news stations, is perceived as subjective, we are frustrated: this is not good
reporting! Whether one gets news from CNN, MSN, Fox, BBC, or *The Daily
Show*, a common complaint among viewers is that the great news anchors
are no more. Instead, we read and hear subjective commentary on events,
often colored by the social and political leanings of the news organization.
We are frustrated by a perceived lack of journalistic integrity, because we
want to hear "just the facts" and "what actually happened."

We carry this expectation of being able to know what actually happened, and the expectation that a printed report is more reliable than oral
testimony, over into our experience with the biblical text. Scholars debate
text-critical questions of which manuscript is most original. At what point

does a document become the original? Are Paul's original ideas contained in his notebooks? Or in the finished letter sent to a church? This question remains theoretical, since archeological efforts have yet to uncover either document, but the question does point to an assumption made by a member of twenty-first-century print culture: we assume that there is an original text, and if we could only find it, we would have the authoritative word of Paul to the Galatians. According to this assumption, any manuscript that differed from the original would be wrong.

It almost goes without saying that a print culture considers the written word to be static. Once written, a text does not change; if it does change, the changed copy is thought to be either less original or incorrect. Changes to a fixed text may improve upon it, as in the case of an updated encyclopedia, but the 2009 edition of *Encyclopedia Britannica*, for example, is different from the first edition, published in the eighteenth century. We appreciate the newer editions, but we would never call it the same text as the document published in 1768. The 1768 version of the encyclopedia is fixed, static. It does not change.

In addition, reading a text in a print culture tends to be a static activity. A book is a fixed object that sits on a solid shelf or desk. It does not move on its own, and it does not change. Words sit still today, in black and white, on a static page. Even a fluid, multicentered, hypertext culture, which Robert Fowler suggests is the next generation for print-centered culture,[9] is based on words fixed on a screen. For those still steeped in print culture, the fact that these words can be changed so easily if not locked down by permissions or some other means calls the reliability of some electronic content into question.

The Text Belongs to the Author

Second, a print culture assumes that the static copy of a text primarily belongs to the author. Today we talk about intellectual property and copyright laws. We teach our undergraduate students to footnote and compile bibliographies, and we expose the specter of plagiarism for all to see. Numerous interpretive methods, influenced at least somewhat by a modern conception of intellectual-property rights, focus on the author's intended meaning as we analyze the text. Because the text belongs (so to speak) to the author, the author, living or dead, has the final say on the meaning of a

---

9. Fowler, "Secondary Orality of the Electronic Age." Fowler suggests that as a hypertext culture, we may be headed back toward conceiving of texts as an evolving collaboration.

text. Text-oriented and reader/audience-oriented interpretations have their place, but within the confines of the author's original intent. This tendency has, of course, been balanced with a healthy awareness of the "intentional fallacy," yet based on compiled knowledge of the historical and literary contexts, we continue to patch together an educated description and evaluation of the author's intended meaning. The concepts of intellectual property and author-centered meaning cause us to view with suspicion changes to what we perceive to be the most original text. When we consider the oral transmission of a text, we assume that it should be memorized word-for-word. To change the author's text, regardless of whether or not those changes reflect what we consider to be the authorial intent, or to conceive an interpretation that goes against what we consider to be the authorial intent is discouraged.

In the world of biblical interpretation, this carries an even more serious consequence—not only are we, the modern interpreters, presuming to change the ancient author's words, but we are daring to change the inspired word of God. Divine inspiration enters the picture, making the landscape more complex.[10] Because the Bible exists for us in written form, we assume that the critical text, as it stands, is the product of divine inspiration. A theory of inspiration by super-intendency implies that God's inspiration continued from the original oral tradition to the later written record to the even later text-critical completion of BHS and the Greek New Testament. The process of canonization defines the boundaries of the inspired texts, and changes to the canon are anathema. Thus, the idea of a static text, which is controlled not only by the original author, but also by God's inspired intent, pervades the evangelical print-culture's hermeneutic.

Widely Available and Accessible Authoritative Text

Third, a print culture assumes that the authoritative copy of the text is widely available and that most people have the ability to cross-reference and refer back to static forms of the text.[11] When we begin to write a scholarly essay, we reference books on our shelves, go to the library, make use of interlibrary-loan services, download journal articles, and generally expect to put our hands on anything we need for the project. Responsible research involves checking the context of each source, understanding its arguments, and synthesizing information as a platform for composing a new piece. The idea that books and other written artifacts would no longer be available for

10. This concept is, of course, not unique to a print-culture perspective. See, for example, Schaper, "Orality/Literacy Problem," 324–42.

11. See Robbins, "Oral, Rhetorical, and Literary Cultures," 78.

wide reference seems almost inconceivable, and indeed is the plot for dystopian stories like *The Book of Eli*.

The assumptions that one authoritative version of the written text exists, that the majority of people have access to that text, and that responsible research involves accurately representing that static text color a print culture's understanding of how historical texts should be written. A survey of the history of the Anabaptists, for instance, would likely be based on the written accounts of Anabaptists themselves: George "Bluecoat" Blaurock, Conrad Grebel, Melchior Hoffman, and Menno Simons, as well as others of that time period. The details in these texts may be influenced by a particular point of view, but a modern author would try to assess their witness objectively, to best discern what actually happened with this group in the sixteenth century.

As we work to understand the interactions ancient authors had with texts, it is reasonable to assume that just as members of a print culture use the methods of research that are most familiar, so too the ancient authors used their most familiar methods. For instance, minute and careful comparison of multiple texts is as easy as toggling between windows on a computer screen, switching views on an iPad, or, for the old-school, consulting one of a dozen books lying open on a desk. We can quickly search and compare, translate, and collate; but in the first century, these research skills were, if available at all, accessible to only a select few and only on a limited basis. To assume that Mark physically was able to compare the texts of Malachi, Deutero-Isaiah, and Exodus as he composed the prologue to the Second Gospel borders on the absurd.[12] Yet this sort of access often is assumed by historical and literary critics alike. Access to texts and the ease and speed with which we can manipulate and search those texts is a distinct advantage that scholars enjoy today. That advantage can, however, turn to disadvantage if we assume, even implicitly, that the ancient authors relied on such practices.

Ability to Cross-Reference a Printed Text

Fourth, when Gospel writers cite a passage from the HB, for example, we assume they were referencing a fixed, printed text, or at least were referencing the memory of a printed text. Because of our assumption that printed texts (or the exact memory of them) were readily available to the biblical authors, we expect quotations of older texts to be exact. Granted, different versions of different texts circulated at different times. The evaluation of these differences has led us to conclusions regarding which witness represents the

---

12. See Carr, *Writing on the Tablet of the Heart*, 159.

most original reading. Fruitful research has been done in evaluating the theological concerns behind various witnesses, in service of explaining why any responsible scribe would ever make changes to the author's original and inspired text. Though theological and logical reasoning may be sympathetically understood, even variants made with the most admirable of motivations are dismissed as less original and therefore inferior. We excuse the well-meaning variants, even the intentional ones, but those variants are valued only for the historical insight they provide, or perhaps as a cautionary tale to would-be translators and textual critics.

The evaluation of such variants extends not only to the ancient manuscript families but also to extrabiblical Christian authors from the earliest centuries—references in lectionaries, apologies, and other sources are assumed to point to both extant and lost versions of the biblical text. In texts where quotations are not exact, when we do not have other witnesses of a particular reading, or when the citations of such quotations are inaccurate, we usually chalk it up to faulty memory on the part of the author, or we assume the author was referencing a text no longer extant. Such mistakes are excused in the case of NT authors because, of course, the NT is as inspired as the HB, and thus, misquotations are not necessarily seen as problematic.

A Written and Read Text

Finally, we assume that the biblical texts primarily were read, not heard. This thinking has started to change over the last few decades, but when we study the biblical texts, the majority of us still default to the assumption of a written and read text, rather than an oral and performed text. Great strides have been made to emphasize the oral nature of the biblical text in its original setting. Very few, however, make a practice of hearing the text rather than reading it—that is simply not the way we do things in a print culture. The assumption of a written and read text necessitates widespread literacy to go along with a widely available authoritative copy, and further supports the conclusion that the text should not or cannot be changed in any way.

An interesting consequence of silent reading is that reading a written text silently replaces the author's voice with the reader's. Any narration, commentary, character speech, or the like is subconsciously colored with the modern reader's preunderstandings and presuppositions. This unavoidable change from the original author and context is one that slips by unnoticed, and contributes to entrenched interpretations of the biblical text. When we read silently, we hear the text in our own voice. In a way, this handicaps us, allowing us to hear only our own inflection and tone. What we hear in our own voice has great persuasive power. We are not used to hearing the text, at least as a whole cloth, in the voice of someone else, let alone through a multiplicity of voices. We cannot hear the inflection or emotion or see the physical action contained in the text. As a result, our experience is of idiosyncratic, two-dimensional, static words on a page, which is of great benefit but does not communicate the full meaning.

Interpretive Assumptions of a Rhetorical Culture

When compared to a print culture, a rhetorical culture naturally is more inclined to remember the oral origins of a text, regardless of whether it currently exists in written form. Certainly we know that the biblical text, both the HB and NT, began as oral tradition—an experience that is quite different than ours. Werner Kelber's work *The Oral and Written Gospel* shifted the way scholars thought about the formation of the Gospel texts.[13] While acceptance came slowly, it is now virtually commonplace to say that the stories that make up the Gospels were developed by some combination of oral and written means. While the ancients were adept at shifting nimbly between oral performance and written text, we must grapple with moving, as the title of this volume suggests, between text to performance.

A Written and Oral/Performed Text

In the first-century Mediterranean world, important information was written down—information that people did not want to lose to the passing of time. David Carr writes that when texts were inscribed, they took on "a numinous, semidivine quality in the cultures where they were transmitted."[14] Even in written form, however, the histories and stories that shaped the culture were meant to be passed down orally. In 1990, Paul Achtemeier argued that a written text needed an oral performance to be communicated and understood.[15] While texts were written in the first-century rhetorical culture, it was in a text's spokenness that what was written became animated once again, possessing power, meaning, and usefulness.

13. Kelber, *Oral and Written Gospel.*

14. Carr, *Writing on the Tablet of the Heart,* 290. See also Schaper's discussion of God as scribe and the light shed on the status of written text in Israelite society: Schaper, "Orality/Literacy Problem," 328–29.

15. Achtemeier, "*Omne verbum sonat.*"

Though written texts preserved the stories, it was mistrusted in antiquity;[16] the most hallowed place for a story to be preserved was on the minds and hearts of the people.

Carr suggests several examples from the HB that support this perspective of the biblical text. A few will suffice to demonstrate that written and oral texts comingled in the rhetorical world of ancient Israel and in the first-century Mediterranean world. Proverbs 22:17–21 says, "Incline your ear and hear my words, and set your heard/mind on my knowledge; for it will be pleasant if you keep them within your belly, if all of them are established on your lips . . . Have I not written for you thirty sayings of advice and knowledge, to show you what is right and true, so that you may give a true answer to those who sent you?" Both hearing and memory contribute to oral preservation, but writing is mentioned too. The thirty wise sayings of the sage are written for future reference, but wisdom is not to preserve the written copy; wisdom is to keep the words within one's belly.[17]

In Deut 6:4–9, Moses tells the Israelites to "keep these words which I am commanding you today on your heart." This inarguably pervasive and oral practice of remembering the words of the Lord involved reciting the words to each other, whether young or old, at every point of the day from the time one woke to the time one lay down to sleep. And yet, Moses's words connect this oral practice with writing the words of the Lord (as the passage describes) *on* the hearts of the people. Certainly no physical writing is explicitly mentioned in this part of the Shema, but the idea of memory being "written" on a person's heart enters biblical tradition very early.[18] "It commands a constant process of recitation of the texts during all activities of the waking day . . . [T]his incision of texts on the heart is part of a broader process of *writing* them throughout one's surroundings."[19]

Moses's successor, Joshua, continues to draw this connection between orality and writtenness. In Josh 1:8, Joshua says, "This book of the law shall not depart out of your mouth," meaning that the people should perform a book, suggesting that a printed text be used as a mnemonic aid. Carr points

---

16. Ibid., 10.

17. See Carr, *Writing on the Tablet of the Heart*, 126–27.

18. See Ibid., 135. Frank Polak argues that "the symbiosis of oral and written literature probably antedates the eighth century by far," perhaps as far back as ancient Sumer, Greece, and Egypt ("Book, Scribe, and Bard," 122). Carr believes that writing started to take hold in Israelite society during the early monarchial period (*Writing on the Tablet of the Heart*, 162–63).

19. Carr, *Writing on the Tablet of the Heart*, 135.

out that "here again we see the joining of the text—'scroll of instruction'—with orality: 'from your mouth.'"[20]

Later in the history of the Israelites, the prophet Isaiah faces people who refuse to listen to the words of God's prophet. Because the people would not listen, Isaiah was commanded that the prophecy be written on a tablet and inscribed on a scroll "so that it may be for a later time, a witness forever" (Isa 30:8).[21] The words were not meant to remain only on a scroll, however. The pervasive habit of reading or reciting *aloud* ensured that if, as Isaiah hoped, the hearts of the people once again became receptive, his prophecy would once again leave the storage of the scroll for the hearts and tongues of the people.

The physical nature of the text hindered detailed study and cross-reference. A general lack of regard for paragraphs, sentences, or even words in both punctuation and line breaks made the sustained physical reading of a text cumbersome.[22] And, of course, even with this combination of oral and written preservation, those with physical and intellectual access to the written forms would have been leaders and the culturally elite. Instead, the written documents "were merely the technology and tangible written talisman for a broader process of passing on to the next generation of leaders the values, views, and less tangible qualities of the ancient, revered tradition."[23]

Robbins's "rhetorical culture" captures the intermingling of oral performance and written texts in the ancient world; those threads are not easily untangled, and I am not sure that they can or need to be, completely. But a consistent awareness of this intermingling can help illuminate the question of the NT authors' use of the HB. For instance, Mark 1:2–3 provides us with a clear example of these intermingled spoken and written tendencies. The oral nature of the gospel combines with a recitation of the prophets' words—a recitation that, however, does not necessarily concern itself with a word-for-word reproduction or a precise attribution.[24] This kind of recitation, and this less than precise attribution illuminates the performative nature of the prophetic words.

---

20. Ibid., 139.

21. Ibid., 144–45.

22. See Achtemeier, "*Omne verbum sonat*," 10–11, 17.

23. Carr, *Writing on the Tablet of the Heart*, 160.

24. Robbins identifies six types of recitation: by replicating the exact words, by omitting some words, by rephrasing the words, by adding a saying from the text, by recasting a narrative into one's own words, and by summarizing several episodes into one (Robbins, "Oral, Rhetorical, and Literary Culture," 83–86).

When oral texts were performed, whether as narrative or dialog, each speaker delivered the text in a unique manner. In fact, a word-for-word recitation of a text could not exactly replicate an earlier performance, even if the text were performed by the same person for the same audience. At the recitation of these words, Mark's hearers recall previous events and, I would argue, earlier and varied reperformances of those remembered events—calling to mind the themes of Exodus, in particular, judgment, protection, and restoration.

The first-century audience is far more likely to have heard the canonical Gospels than to have read an actual text. Unfortunately, as Moore points out, "in attempting to play out the roles of the audiences envisioned by the evangelists, exegetes have failed to give due weight to the fact that these audiences were listeners first and foremost."[25]

Literacy was on the rise during the first century, comparatively, but as Tomas Hägg reminds us, "we are still dealing only with a small proportion of the population."[26] Those who could read, often did so aloud for the education and entertainment of others who remained illiterate. Hägg suggests that "the ability to read, and read easily and for pleasure . . . no doubt carried with it the obligation to read aloud to members of the household, to a circle of friends, perhaps even to a wider audience."[27] Hägg's work in the ancient novels revealed, based on evidence such as repetition and "excessive clarity," that this type of literature was meant to be read aloud to audiences.[28]

Ben Witherington applies this conclusion to NT narrative material as well. He writes that "ancient historical works [such as the Gospels and Acts] were meant to be *heard* primarily and read only secondarily."[29] Burridge's research led him to the conclusion that "reading aloud was one of the main ways of 'publication' in the ancient world, often as entertainment after dinner."[30] The aural nature of the evangelists' audiences would have influenced how they wrote narratives, because "considerable attention had to be given to the aural impression a work would leave on the audience."[31]

---

25. Moore, *Literary Criticism and the Gospels*, 86. Note that even if one was reading to oneself, one was probably reading aloud. Aristotle writes, "Generally speaking, that which is written should be easy to read or easy to utter, which is the same thing" (*Rhet.* 3.5.6).

26. Hägg, *The Novel in Antiquity*, 90.

27. Ibid., 93.

28. Ibid.

29. Witherington, "The Historical and Rhetorical Species of Acts," 87.

30. Burridge, "About People, by People, for People," 141.

31. Witherington, "The Historical and Rhetorical Species of Acts," 87.

The repetitions and attention to clarity noted by Hägg in the ancient novels support this conclusion.

Intertextuality from Memory

Unlike a print culture, a rhetorical culture contains few written copies of a text, and only a few people read and have access to them. Detailed cross-referencing in print was rarely possible. Instead, cross-referencing was done from memory—from the memory of a text that existed in dynamic form, in flux between oral and written form. A note should be made here that the phrase "from memory" in this case does not necessarily mean a word-for-word replication.[32] If it did, we would immediately have to ask, word-for-word from which text? Even a word-for-word recitation of an oral text does not achieve the kind of exact replication we think of when we use the phrase. Nevertheless, a different kind of cross-referencing occurred in the ancient rhetorical culture. Carr writes that

> it is increasingly clear how much of Israelite literature is likewise "intertextual." But it is not intertextual in the sense that early Israelite authors were constantly engaged in a process of visually consulting, citing, and interpreting separate written texts . . . [F]ully educated literate specialists in those other cultures also demonstrably added to that curriculum at key points [at times] authoring new works that often echo those works in which the scribal author was trained.[33]

Carr proposes that "successive generations of master Israelite scribes revised and augmented this education-enculturation curriculum as conditions changed . . . Ancient authors could copy texts, but they did not require the ancient texts to be before them. Instead, they had already ingested such texts in the process of their education-enculturation."[34] Polak proposes that "a synthesis along these lines" is more powerful if "in particular the oral performance is accorded its due place in culture and society."[35]

---

32. I do not mean to dismiss the possibility of word-for-word recitation. Certainly the New Testament alone contains numerous examples of verbatim quotations from either another Gospel or the LXX (Matt 21:13, 42; 22:32, etc.).

33. Carr, *Writing on the Tablet of the Heart*, 159.

34. Ibid.

35. Polak, "Book, Scribe and Bard," 132.

Multivalent Texts Belong to the Community

The text may be reappropriated for various contexts and audiences. Robbins writes that "our challenge is to understand the kind of scribal activity that does not refrain from progymnastic rhetorical composition, that is, the level of rhetorical composition that re-performs written and oral sources and traditions in the manner we see in the *Progymnasmata*."[36] Theon's handbook reveals that paraphrase and elaboration were exercises undertaken by advanced students of rhetoric.[37] According to Theon, paraphrase "consists of changing the form of expression while keeping the thoughts."[38] Rhetors may paraphrase texts by syntactical paraphrase ("keep the same words but transpose the parts"); paraphrase by addition ("keep the original words and add to them"); paraphrase by subtraction ("drop many of the elements of the original"); and paraphrase by substitution ("replace the original word with another").[39] Theon considered the ability to paraphrase an entire speech "the result of perfected ability."[40] Elaboration involves "language that adds what is lacking in thought and expression."[41] Among other motivations, elaboration may serve to say things "more appropriately, or more opportunely,"[42] implying that rhetors may elaborate in order to make a text more appropriate for a particular audience or, perhaps, a different context. Thus, a performer may make personal interpretation, as appropriate. Holly Hearon suggests that "in the retelling the text would be modified and adapted as the occasion and audience demanded. Thus, while an oral text may have gained circulation (or re-circulation) through a written text, once in circulation it could take on a life of its own."[43]

Hellenistic rhetorical practice undoubtedly influenced the Gospel writers, but the habit of reappropriating texts for a new audience or context came not only from Greco-Roman practice but also from Jewish culture. Carr posits that ancient Israelite education "necessarily built on alphabetic education but moved far beyond it in involving the reading, performance, and ingestion of cultural texts."[44] Use of traditional material in fresh composition was common in ancient Israel, and, in Carr's opinion, this habit

36. Robbins, "Progymnastic Rhetorical Composition", 118.

37. Theon, *Exercises*, 13.

38. Ibid., 70.

39. Ibid.

40. Ibid., 71.

41. Ibid.

42. Ibid.

43. Hearon, "Implications of Orality for Studies of the Biblical Text," 9.

44. Carr, *Writing on the Tablet of the Heart*, 126.

left clear marks that led to discussion of the various sources involved in the Documentary Hypothesis. These sources, however, are not necessarily written texts, and indeed most likely were not physical documents available to the ancient Israelite scribes, but were oral traditions that had been ingested and then repurposed in service of a new composition.[45] In addition, as times, audiences, and contexts changed in ancient Israel, texts (oral and written) were "revised and augmented,"[46] in order to preserve their effectiveness or, perhaps, to render the written text more conducive to memorization. For example, the relationship between law codes in Exodus and Deuteronomy likely involves some revision based on the developing Israelite society, though debate continues over the details of this relationship.[47] Indeed, whereas in a print culture, texts belong to their authors, in a rhetorical culture, texts were property of communities, open for revision, paraphrase, or elaboration as the needs of the community dictated.[48]

Robbins lists three characteristics of progymnastic rhetorical composition, but for this paper the second is most pertinent. Theon encourages his students not just to copy a rhetorical piece or reproduce it word-for-word but instead to reformulate the piece—to expand or contract, to shift the cases of words, to rephrase. "The requirement is clarity, not verbatim repetition. This exercise exhibits an approach to tradition that is different from a 'copying' environment. When writers have learned this exercise, they move their eyes and ears freely away from a 'source' as they 'compose the tradition anew' with as much or as little verbatim replication as they wish."[49] This is how, for instance, Robbins explains the wording differences in the Gospels.[50]

Thus, in a rhetorical culture, there are multiple, authoritative versions of a text. It was not crucial for quotations to be exact; in fact, older traditions could be used to make new points. The audience was required to make the conceptual connection when the speaker offered an echo or allusion, but the details need not be the same. In fact, what use would it be if the details *were* the same?

---

45. Ibid., 159.

46. Ibid.

47. See ibid., 137 n. 105.

48. With that said, I would argue that the text is still best understood from the author's rhetorical horizon. A study more concerned with the evolution of a text in a print (or hypertext) culture may be less preoccupied with the author's ancient horizon. The goal of this project, however, is to better understand the way the biblical text came to be. Thus consideration of a rhetorical-culture mindset is necessary.

49. Robbins, "Progymnastic Rhetorical Composition," 120.

50. See also Robbins, "Oral, Rhetorical, and Literary Cultures," 81.

Applying a Rhetorical Culture Hermeneutic

The comparison of print and rhetorical cultures helps bring clarity to examining NT authors' use of the HB, revealing differences in basic ways of thinking about a text. For instance, as a member of a print culture, I am predisposed to ask what went wrong when the formula "It is written" introduces a reading that does not line up with the citation from the HB. Did the NT authors have access to manuscripts lost to us through time? Did they have faulty memories? Was it not important to get a quotation right?

If, as recent scholarship has claimed, both the HB and the NT originated as oral texts, and if we have hopes of better understanding the biblical text through the lens of performance and oral delivery, why is it that NT authors introduced quotations from the HB with the words, "It is *written*"? Was this introductory formula simply a differently worded form of "As it is said," or did the inclusion of the word *written* carry particular weight? Did the written text carry a greater authority? Was the fact that an idea was written give it special qualities? Were the most important stories, histories, songs, or prophecies written as a mark of their importance, after they were delivered orally for a period of time?

These questions arise from a print culture, but when we consider the nature of a rhetorical culture, our conception of the questions begins to change. I would suggest that these questions originate in a print-culture environment, and may be concerns alien to an ancient rhetorical culture. What is needed is not only an understanding of the text, but an understanding of how the ancients conceived of the text.

Of course today we have a written text that is largely a compilation of "caught" or inscribed performance—we deal with a solidified, written text, and we have the task of imagining what that text would be if we could dissolve it once more into an oral performance. A basic understanding of the ancient rhetorical culture, however, suggests a more complex relationship. For instance, by the time we read the prophetic quotation found in Mark 1:2–3, we are seeing a text that has, both in written and oral form, been performed, reperformed, and inscribed at least four times—it has moved from oral to written to oral and back again. A citation that Mark claims is from Isaiah ("as it is written in Isaiah the prophet") is in fact a conglomeration of Isa 40:3, Exod 23:20, and Mal 3:1.[51] If, as a member of a rhetorical culture,

---

51. That some of the Alexandrian and Western scribes corrected Mark's citation from "Isaiah" to "the prophets" proves interesting in light of this essay. On one hand, we might argue that even early preservers of the Gospel text were concerned with precise citation and corrected Mark's error. On the other hand, however, we might argue that we have here an example of rhetorical scribes—scribes who did not feel compunction

Mark understands his role as recalling and recasting earlier performances of the Exodus story, in particular, this conflation works fine. In fact, Isa 40:3 is already a reperformance of the exodus event, with some of the details changed for the new, exilic context. In turn, Malachi is a reperformance of Exodus and Isaiah—a commentary on Isaiah's commentary.

Operating in a print culture, as members of an active audience, we move through several steps as we read Mark 1:2–3. First, we recognize the identification of a prophetic text from the HB. The introductory formula alerts us, even if the prophecy itself goes unrecognized. Second, upon investigation, we may realize that the citation is not solely from Isaiah, and may even go as far as to recognize the conglomeration with Malachi. Finally, those steeped in the text may identify the exodus as the event that lies behind the prophetic words. All three of these recognitions, however, come to us by way of an experience of Mark 1:2–3 that is shaped by our print-culture context. We can look up the Isaiah passage to verify both the allusion to it and the deviance from it. We check annotations and cross-reference notes to trace the hint of Exodus language. The first-century experience would, I imagine, have been much different.

In a rhetorical culture, the active audience's common memory and experience of the text would come not primarily from a written text but from oral tradition. The result, I suggest, is, not a linear, step-by-step investigation of the source of Mark's citation, but a more organic awareness of not only the postexilic warning of Malachi but also the exilic language of Deutero-Isaiah, and the identity-forming story of the Exodus. Wrapped up in this awareness is not only a historical awareness of the words *back through* time, but an attentiveness to the ongoing exodus event that has *traveled forward*, from the days of Moses, Isaiah, and Malachi, and finally to the evangelist.

Thus, while uncovering the layers of Mark's allusion in 1:2–3 might take a good deal of page flipping for a twenty-first-century reader, a person in the first century, Mark included, would have a shared, societal well of knowledge on which to draw. Experiencing the Exodus story through oral performance, in all its renditions, and synthesizing the Exodus theme through generations of cultural and cultic history, provides the first-century hearer not only with the shared well of knowledge necessary to understand Mark's allusion, but also with the flexibility necessary for appreciating the freedom Mark takes with "Isaiah's" words.

Simply understanding that these are ancient words of prophecy, a modern audience who is at least paying attention allows Mark's story to

---

when altering Mark's text. This scribe's experience provided him with the knowledge that Mark 1:2–3 was not only the words of Isaiah. A change of this sort was minor and matter of fact.

move forward. The words that open the Second Gospel introduce John the Baptizer and foreshadow the already announced coming of the Son of God.

But an active ancient audience (and an active modern audience who is willing to do the legwork) benefits even more from the allusion, uncovering details not available on just a surface level. This audience, though, must do more than simply pay attention. This audience must work with the performer, connecting allusions, making use of a shared well of information. As a result, this coworking, coperforming audience has helped create the texture of the story—an old texture, that reaches back hundreds of years. This story, the "good news of Jesus Christ, the Son of God," is the continuing story of God's presence and deliverance, that was started in Egypt, renewed in exile, warned against in the postexile, and is now coming to fruition in the person of Jesus Christ. Reimagining the performances of the Exodus theme in each of these contexts will help the print-culture reader recapture the complexity of Mark's brief allusion: "the beginning of the good news of Jesus Christ."

Mark's opening citation in 1:2–3 refers to the Exodus story, a central and identity-forming event for the Israelite people. The story of the exodus had been passed on orally for generations (Exod 12:6; 13:8, etc.). After the Shema, Deuteronomy 6 "concludes with a picture of education, this time a dialogue in which the children ask about the meaning of the statutes and commandments that their parent is constantly reciting (Deut. 6:20), and the parent then puts them in the context of God's rescue of Israel from Egypt, gift of the land, and promise of life and righteousness if the people obey them (Deut. 6:21–25)."[52] One form of these words was finally captured in written form, perhaps during the exilic period, destined to become the text we now know as Exodus. Exodus 23:20 alludes to God's constant and guiding presence during the exodus and beyond. God's messenger guides and guards the covenant people. This statement is given in the midst of law, following the giving of the Ten Commandments in chapter 20. In the middle of the listing of law, God declares, "I am going to send an angel in front of you, to guard you on the way and to bring you to the place that I have prepared." The people are to "be attentive to him and listen to his voice." They are to "not rebel against him" (v. 21).

That text, oral or written, is picked up in the prologue of Deutero-Isaiah (Isa 40:3). The context is different now. No longer are God's people enslaved in Egypt, no longer are they awaiting the fulfillment of the Abrahamic promise of the land. Those events are in their past, and God's people are in exile, disciplined for their faithlessness and forgetfulness, once again in a strange land, but this time by their own hands. The prophet proclaims the

---

52. Carr, *Writing on the Tablet of the Heart*, 135.

hope of a new exodus—a greater one—in which God will deliver the people and restore the relationship broken by years of covenant breaking.

Just as the historical contexts of Exodus and Deutero-Isaiah differed, so some have suggested that the composition and compilation process for Deutero-Isaiah was quite different from that of Exodus. Carr believes that "prophets like Isaiah mark the emergence of oral-written prophetic education that could serve as the context for transmission of a given instruction to later generations."[53] Rhetorical culture's hybrid of written and oral texts, however, is still in view. Having ingested (so to speak) older material,[54] Deutero-Isaiah composes a new word based on the template provided by the older material (in this case, at least in part, from the account in Exodus 23).[55] While Deutero-Isaiah contains markers of being a planned, written document, even written texts were composed for oral delivery, thus making Deutero-Isaiah a combination of written and oral literature.[56] The words of the prophet, in this combination of media, are performed, likely multiple times in multiple forms, even after they have been inscribed. Finally, though, during the exilic or postexilic period, one form of this performance is preserved in written form in the collection of oracles we now know as Isaiah.

Later, after the exiles return, the story from Exodus and from Isaiah is adopted by the prophet Malachi (Mal 3:1). Malachi knows the story of the Exodus, and he knows that Isaiah repurposed that story for the exilic context. Indeed, God promised a new exodus through the exilic prophet. But that grand exodus was not to be, as Malachi now knows. So Malachi uses this same story, dissolves it into another context, and adopts it for another purpose. He makes a play on his own name—"my messenger"—as he adjusts the themes from both Exodus and Isaiah for his postexilic audience. According to Watts, Malachi is responding to the "failed" Exodus of Isaiah.[57] The new exodus was delayed—or it failed—because God's people failed to recognize the new deliverer, Cyrus. As Watts puts it, Israel failed to "accept Yahweh's methods or Cyrus his agent."[58] For this blindness, Malachi warns of impending judgment. Yahweh is coming in a new exodus, and woe to those who are unprepared. In the postexilic period, Malachi's prophecy was

---

53. Ibid., 145.

54. Theon's *Exercises* recommend that the very beginning of education should involve students learning "good examples from ancient prose works . . . by heart" (Theon, *Exercises*, 9).

55. Carr, *Writing on the Tablet of the Heart*, 159.

56. Gitay, "Deutero-Isaiah: Oral or Written?," 185–97.

57. Watts, "Mark," 116.

58. Ibid., 115.

composed, delivered, composed, repeated, and, once again, finally inscribed in written form, in the book we now know as Malachi.

Finally we arrive at the first-century text of Mark. Cultural memory was key to the Gospels—not only the cultural memory of Jesus and his words and deeds[59] but also older memories of the exile, the prophets, and that defining event of the exodus. Joanna Dewey writes that "memory continually structures and adapts tradition to support community identity and needs in the present."[60] This applies to the Exodus reperformances as well. Mark picks up the thread that runs from Exodus through Isaiah and on through Malachi, recalling, perhaps even subconsciously, each one. But Mark has a new setting, audience, and message.

Mark is telling the good news of Jesus, Son of God—the one who is the ultimate Deliverer out of the ultimate Captivity. This exodus in Mark's mind is an exodus like no one has ever seen. When Mark cites Isaiah, he recalls for his audience multiple performances of this most well-known story: the exodus from Egypt that was effective for a time, and the Exodus from Babylon that was not fully realized and that has threatening consequences for the unprepared. Mark claims that the former exodus events are coming to fruition in the person of Jesus, Son of God. God's people are still in need of a deliverer (though not from Egypt or Babylon), God still raised up a deliverer (though not Moses or Cyrus), and a messenger (though not Malachi) announces that there is still a threat of judgment for those who fail to recognize "Yahweh's methods or . . . his agent."[61] Mark uses parallels and echoes "so that what is new is framed in terms of what is already known."[62] The introduction to Mark's narrative, however it was formulated, was written and performed over and again, in different contexts and renditions, but eventually, like the exodus event, and the prophecies of Isaiah and Malachi, the oral tradition was inscribed with ink, and we know these beginning words to the Gospel of Jesus, Son of God, as Mark 1:2–3.

Similar words from Exodus, Isaiah, and/or Malachi are used by Matthew and Luke to describe John the Baptist (Matt 3:1–6; Luke 3:1–6). Each Gospel writer uses the references to earlier material in different ways.[63] The similarity, however, is that, even among themselves, the evangelists felt free

---

59. Dewey, "The Gospel of Mark as Oral Hermeneutic," 72.

60. Ibid.

61. Cf. Watts, "Mark," 115.

62. Dewey, "Oral Methods of Structuring Narrative in Mark," 40.

63. See Robbins, "Interfaces of Orality and Literature," 129–35, for further discussion.

to reframe and repurpose earlier authors' words in ways more appropriate to their text and audience.

Conclusion

Interpreters of the Bible who find themselves members of print culture (or perhaps soon hypertext culture) benefit from recognizing the differences between habits and assumptions of print and rhetorical cultures. Often the mere activity of naming assumptions allows us, not necessarily to change our own horizon (for who can successfully do so?), but to compensate for applying our own tendencies to the ancient text. The process of producing a text, oral or written, is decidedly different as we move between the ancient world and our own.

Recognizing these differences frees ancient writers, including the Gospel authors, from some expectations of modern hermeneutics. The Gospel writers, for instance, do not labor under the responsibility of precise citation based on printed texts (though this practice does exist in the ancient world), or the obligation to acknowledge the original author in complete and correct assignations. The ancient author is also relieved of the task of carefully cross-referencing printed texts. This contemporary obligation is a particular hardship, given the physical nature of texts and the limited availability of manuscripts. Finally, ancient authors are released from the requirement of identifying and restraining an earlier text to the original context. I am not suggesting that modern interpreters adopt this ancient hermeneutic, at least not wholesale. As we compose texts as participants in our own culture, citation is important, as is intellectual property, and historical and literary contextual study. If, however, our goal is to understand the process by which *ancient* texts came to be, we are well served by studying that process on their terms, rather than our own.

Awareness of the differences between print and rhetorical culture also allows space for a different kind of study of textual variants. As Carr suggests, rather than consider variants "a distraction from reconstructing an ur-exemplar," we might do well to understand them instead as "crucial access points to a process of textual mastery and performance not always measured by central reference copies."[64] The opening monologue to a short film called *The Last Bookshop* begins,

> There have always been stories, ever since the earliest days. I suppose in the beginning rather than autographic colors and noise, stories were more like dreams spoken aloud. They were

64. Carr, *Writing on the Tablet of the Heart*, 291.

bison on cave walls and campfire myths on how the world was born. Those verbal stories—that's where it must all have begun. They were magic. They were alive. But being alive, they also had to die. They vanished with the breath of the storyteller, to be reincarnated, evolving, mutating with each retelling, until eventually the original stories were lost forever.[65]

I would argue instead that, like a phoenix, these stories are not lost, but that they live forever, taken up and given new life by storytellers and scribes in each successive generation. In a small way, textual variants of the biblical texts allow us glimpses into the cycles of an evolving text. Considering the rather circuitous path (in our opinion) of a text's formation in a rhetorical culture allows us to understand the more organic and collaborative process of the production of ancient texts. We are able to appreciate the rhetorical culture in which the biblical texts grew, recognizing the give-and-take of both oral and written development, through the media of both text and performance.

Bibliography

Achtemeier, Paul J. "*Omne verbum sonat*: The New Testament and the Oral Environment of Late Western Antiquity." *JBL* 109 (1990) 3–27.

Aristotle. *The Art of Rhetoric*. Translated by John H. Freese. LCL. Cambridge: Harvard University Press, 1926.

Burridge, Richard. "About People, by People, for People: Gospel Genre and Audiences." In *The Gospel for all Christians: Rethinking the Gospel Audiences*, edited by Richard Bauckham, 113–45. Grand Rapids: Eerdmans, 1998.

Carr, David M. *Writing on the Tablet of the Heart: Origins of Scripture and Literature*. Oxford: Oxford University Press, 2005.

Dewey, Joanna. "The Gospel of Mark as Oral Hermeneutic." In *Jesus, the Voice, and the Text: Beyond "The Oral and the Written Gospel,"* edited by Tom Thatcher, 71–88. Waco, TX: Baylor University Press, 2008.

———. "Oral Methods of Structuring Narrative in Mark." *Int* 43 (1989) 32–44.

Fowler, Robert M. "How the Secondary Orality of the Electronic Age Can Awaken Us to the Primary Orality of Antiquity or What Hypertext Can Teach Us About the Bible with Reflections on the Ethical and Political Issues of the Electronic Frontier." http://homepages.bw.edu/~rfowler/pubs/secondoral/index.html#anchor45421/.

Gitay, Yehoshua. "Deutero-Isaiah: Oral or Written?" *JBL* 99 (1980) 185–97.

Hägg, Tomas. *The Novel in Antiquity*. Revised by the author. Berkeley: University of California Press, 1983.

Hearon, Holly E. "The Implications of Orality for Studies of the Biblical Text." In *Performing the Gospel: Orality, Memory, and Mark*, edited by Richard A. Horsley et al., 3–20. Minneapolis: Fortress, 2006.

---

65. Dadd and Fryer, *The Last Bookshop*.

Hearon, Holly E., and Philip Ruge-Jones, eds. *The Bible in Ancient and Modern Media: Story and Performance.* BPCS 1. Eugene, OR: Cascade Books, 2009.

Horsley, Richard A., et al., eds. *Performing the Gospel: Orality, Memory, and Mark.* Minneapolis: Fortress, 2006.

Kelber, Werner H. *The Oral and the Written Gospel: Hermeneutics of Speaking and Writing in the Synoptic Tradition, Mark, Paul and Q.* 1983. Voices in Performance and Text. Bloomington: Indiana University Press, 1997.

Kennedy, George A. *New Testament Interpretation through Rhetorical Criticism.* Chapel Hill: University of North Carolina Press, 1984.

Moore, Stephen D. *Literary Criticism and the Gospels: The Theoretical Challenge.* New Haven: Yale University Press, 1989.

Oesterreicher, Wulf. "Types of Orality in Text." In *Written Voices, Spoken Signs: Tradition, Performance, and the Epic Text,* edited by Egbert Bakker and Ahuvia Kahane, 190–214. Center for Hellenic Studies Colloquia. Cambridge: Harvard University Press, 1997.

Ong, Walter. *Orality and Literacy: The Technologizing of the Word.* New Accents. London: Methuen, 1982.

Polak, Frank H. "Book, Scribe, and Bard: Oral Discourse and Written Text in Recent Biblical Scholarship." *Prooftexts* 31 (2011) 118–40.

Robbins, Vernon K. *Exploring the Texture of Texts: A Guide to Socio-Rhetorical Interpretations.* Valley Forge, PA: Trinity, 1996.

———. "Interfaces of Orality and Literature in the Gospel of Mark." In *Performing the Gospel: Orality, Memory, and Mark,* edited by Richard Horsley et al., 125–46. Minneapolis: Fortress, 2006.

———. "Oral, Rhetorical, and Literary Cultures: A Response." *Semeia* 65 (1994) 75–91.

———. "Progymnastic Rhetorical Composition and Pre-Gospel Traditions—A New Approach." In *The Synoptic Gospels: Source Criticism and the New Literary Criticism,* edited by Camille Focant, 111–48. BETL 10. Leuven: Peeters, 1993.

Schaper, Joachim. "Exilic and Post-Exilic Prophecy and the Orality/Literacy Problem." *VT* 55 (2005) 324–42.

Theon, Aelius. "The Exercises of Aelius Theon." In *Progymnasmata: Greek Textbooks of Prose Composition and Rhetoric,* translated by George A. Kennedy, 3–72. Writings from the Greco-Roman World 10. Atlanta: Society of Biblical Literature, 2003.

Watts, Rikk E. "Mark." In *Commentary on the New Testament Use of the Old Testament,* edited by G. K. Beale and D. A. Carson, 111–250. Grand Rapids: Baker Academic, 2007.

Witherington, Ben III. "Finding Its Niche: The Historical and Rhetorical Species of Acts." In *SBLSP* 35 (1996) 67–97. Atlanta: Scholars, 1996.

8

"THIS IS MY . . ."

Toward a Thick Performance of the Gospel of Mark

Richard W. Swanson

WHEN YOU READ A SCENE OUT OF THE GOSPEL OF MARK, WHAT are you reading? This is a question I have had to ask and answer frequently in my years of working with the actors who make up the Provoking the Gospel Storytelling Project. Together we have created performances of biblical texts from both Testaments, in a wide variety of settings, for many different kinds of audiences. It seems a simple question, but it is not. You are reading the Bible, but only if you are Christian. Jews, of course, have a Bible, but it (of course) does not include the Gospel of Mark, though the Gospel of Mark includes a good bit of material from the Jewish Bible. You are reading Scripture, which is subject to the same territory-marking activity as is the Bible, but with more participants, since many groups name their core texts Scripture.

These are the easy complications.

A Text Thick with Complications

When you read a scene out of the Gospel of Mark, you are reading a passage that presents itself as (in some sense) historically and geographically referential. It brings with it two millennia of "having-been-read," and shows the effects of having been seen by all of those eyes, with all of their varying presuppositions and judgments and conclusions. It has been translated and carried from place to place, century to century. It has been interpreted, and though it was late in growing its own first-written commentary, it has (beginning especially in the later twentieth century) grown an entire forest of commentaries, with leaves[1] devoted to every page, every word, every verb tense and image, every plot structure. It has been read over, read into, read around, and written out.

And of course the process of writing out has its own complications. With such a long history of being studied in written form, it was natural that interpreters imagined that the text had a textual beginning. Synoptic hypothesizers supposed that the Gospel being read was laid out on a library table along with Q (and Special Matthew and Special Luke, if the interpreter hypothesizing happened to be B. H. Streeter) in order to accomplish the composition of the other canonical, measured Gospels. These orderly compositions were imagined to be the written work of writers with written sources.

Of course, back behind it all was the "Oral Tradition," which apparently was atomized, being ordered only according to taxonomy: Dominical Sayings were grouped with Dominical Sayings, and so forth.

And then things became more complicated still.

The Complication of Having-Been-Spoken

With more serious consideration of the phenomenon of orality came a new appreciation for the reality of oral composition. In an ancient world with low literacy rates (and in which the skill to read and write was understood to be the sort of trick you could train a slave to do), the stories that were finally inscribed had to have lived as oral performances long before anyone wrote them down. But the complications do not end there. Oral performance and inscription do not exist in rigidly separated worlds. When Papias evinces a

---

1. To steal an image from Moore (*Mark and Luke in Poststructuralist Perspectives,* xiii): "Leaf through this book, recently a tree. Penned to its trunk are two readings. One is of Mark, 'The Gospel of the Mark,' the other is of Luke, 'The Gospel of the Look' . . . Between them, Jesus hangs suspended. He may or may not have escaped decomposition, but how could he escape deconstruction?"

preference for the "living word" over inscription, it is clear that both forms of what would become Scripture were living options in the community. And, as Lourens de Vries[2] points out so carefully, oral performance and inscription do not mean the same thing, or imply the same patterns of interaction, in every culture that possesses and tells living stories.

So, when you read the Gospel of Mark, what are you reading? A historical process, a discrete text, a fossil of an ancient performance, Scripture, history: you are reading all this and much more. Any responsible interpretive practice will aim to read the Gospel as it is embraced by the "much more," and this creates real complications.

A New Methodology and Its Critics

Into this complex situation enters performance criticism, a new methodology hailed as uniquely enlightening and useful, sometimes even touted as the harbinger of a paradigm shift in biblical studies. Audiences of all sorts speak of the incredible emotional impact of seeing and hearing the stories that they have usually known only through silent reading. Performance-critical work has drawn considerable interest from substantial scholars: David Rhoads, Joanna Dewey, Margaret Lee, Brandon Scott, and Tom Boomershine, to name only a few. Performance-critical analysis has also worked its way into an increasing number of presentations at the Society of Biblical Literature's annual meeting.

But in the midst of this increased interest and activity one also hears dismissive critiques. If the accumulated interpretive methods that have grown out of textual and historical analysis may be said (with only slight apologies due to Clifford Geertz)[3] to generate "thick readings" of biblical texts, then the dismissive critiques may be characterized as focusing on the alleged "thinness" of performance analysis. Geertz notes that an ethnographer who would aim to be responsible and provide an adequate reading of a culture is faced with "a multiplicity of complex conceptual structures, many of them superimposed upon or knotted into one another, which are at once strange, irregular, and inexplicit."[4] The Bible is surely characterized by the presence of "complex conceptual structures . . . knotted into one another," and thus the history of text-based interpretation of the Bible, in a similar effort to create responsible and adequate readings, has produced its own "thick descriptions," detailed and nuanced readings of biblical texts and the

2. See especially De Vries, "Local Oral-Written Interfaces," 68–98.

3. See Geertz, *Interpretation of Cultures*.

4. Ibid., 9–10.

worlds out of which they come and within which they have been read. In-deed, next to a multivolume textual and historical analysis of the Gospel of Mark, for instance, testimonials to the emotional impact of a performance might very well sound thin. There are no footnotes in a performance, and there is no scholarly dithering out of competing interpretive lines, but no one really expected that there would be. Still, questions are asked about thinness, both in the hallways and in scholarly articles, and the issue must be addressed.

Indeed, there is thinness to be found in some performances of biblical texts. Perhaps the performer aims to reconstitute ancient performance prac-tice. Perhaps she aims to embody the informal performance history behind the formalized existing text. Perhaps she aims to enact Scripture with all its claims on truth and audience. Each of these aims, by itself, is a thin slice of the whole interpretive enterprise. Performance requires the making of choices, the accepting of limitations even in the midst of the "much more." Some of the current dissatisfaction surrounding performance-critical work is lodged in uneasiness about this limited and limiting focus.

Further, some scholars are nervous that the methodology will yield uncritical proselytism. This same nervousness attended the early develop-ment of literary-critical interpretation of biblical texts, and before even that, it was directed at practitioners of canonical criticism. Thick interpretive practice developed, in significant part, as a check on theological ideology that simply needed the biblical text as a pretext for exercising its own pre-existing agenda. It must be noted that the nervousness was more than occa-sionally warranted. Some readers of the canonical story did indeed operate with an all-determining *Vorverständnis* that was applied uncritically to ev-ery text that was interpreted. Some books written advocating performance as a mode of biblical interpretation explicitly expect that it will prove a good tool for evangelism. While it would be odd to expect that all students of biblical narrative swear off all interest in the mission of the church, or that they interpret Scripture with no interest in how it affects people, still one must expect more than simple instrumental use of Scripture out of scholars who interpret the Bible.

Other scholars note that the richness of history is lost in contempo-rary performance. Even when the interpreter-performer applies a careful and thorough theological critique to her work, still the performance that results takes place in the contemporary world and takes advantage of con-temporary performance idioms. Of course, this is always the case with any interpretation or translation. The task is always to carry the old text across the "broad, ugly ditch" into a very different language and world, and such activity always results in gains and losses.[5] Translations may be boring or biting or breezy, but they always are contemporary. Interpretations, however conventional, are always the result of reading old texts in new contexts, and some new contexts may indeed require a radical rereading that takes account of radical changes.[6] But even such rereadings establish themselves in the face of older readings. Rereading is therefore always symbiotic with reading[7] and must be seen and heard as it stands in harmony and dissonance with previous practice.

Others charge that the richness of the text is overshadowed by historicistic performing that aims only to repristinate ancient practice. John Miles Foley tells of viewing a scholarly performance of traditional tales.[8] The performance aimed and claimed to reproduce historical practice, as determined by scholarly research. This aim and claim was even buttressed, says Foley, by having the performers wear academic robes for the entire televised fiasco. Foley also joined the audience for a performance of old tales by traditional storytellers. One could argue that such performers were, in fact, more traditional, more historically accurate, than the televised academic droning—but that is not exactly Foley's point. He argues, rather, that what is traditional about the popular storytellers is precisely their contemporaneity. They engage the audience. They improvise (within traditional bounds) on old stories. They reproduce the historical process of carrying forward the tradition; they do not act as curators of museum-quality artifacts. John D. Niles argues that old traditions actually require (not just tolerate) the activity of what he calls "strong tradition bearers," who vigorously rework old stories as they tell them in new settings.[9]

Other critiques of performance-critical analysis have noted the expectation, common among some practitioners, that performance will stabilize and establish readings of texts by reducing the multiple potential meanings generated in the history of interpretation. Whether one expects such simplification to be possible (or salutary) depends on a great many

---

5. Lessing wrote: "I live in the 18th century, in which miracles no longer happen" (from "On the Proof of the Spirit and of Power," in Chadwick, *Lessing's Theological Writings*, 52). It is that particular sense of absence that created the necessity of carrying the truths of religion, embedded in biblical stories, across the trench that yawned between then and now.

6. For instance, consider Fackenheim's *The Jewish Bible after the Holocaust*. Fackenheim argues that interpretive traditions can be ruptured by extraordinary catastrophes, and that any subsequent reading must (and in fact does) take this into account.

7. Some would even say that it is parasitic.

8. See Foley, *How to Read an Oral Poem*, 84ff.

9. Niles, *Homo Narrans*, 179ff.

factors, including (particularly) one's view of the state of textual stability in a poststructuralist interpretive world, but pragmatists must still grant that sometimes it works. And sometimes it does not.

An Attempt at Thick Reading in Performance-Critical Analysis

However it is done, performance raises, and with particular urgency, the issue of the "much more" that must shape the interpretation of a biblical text. Performers, at least in the theater, have always had to negotiate this difficulty.[10] Musicians playing instruments that did not exist when Bach wrote his music have known this as well.[11] Literary analysts have had to learn it.[12] Biblical interpreters have dealt with it fitfully. Now it is our turn to take this seriously.

In this essay, I will develop a thick reading of the three identifications of Jesus as "son of God" in the Gospel of Mark, beginning in the first chapter with God's words spoken through the torn heavens: "You are my son, the beloved" (1:11). This thick reading will explore the complications created by the text's history of having been read, having been spoken, and having been reflected upon theologically. For each of these three texts, I will present suggestions for what might become a thick performance of this significant thematic and structural element in Mark's story. These suggestions will build upon each other and will culminate in an exploration of my work with composer Christopher Stanichar and poet Patrick Hicks in creating a performance of the *St. Mark Passion*, and of its potential as a thick performance of this scene, one that benefits from and embodies the results of a thick literary and historical reading of the text.

10. For a particularly challenging discussion, see Feinberg (*Embodied Memory: The Theatre of George Tabori*), especially the discussion of Tabori's staging of plays based on the Holocaust in late twentieth-century Germany. See especially the analysis of Tabori's play *The Merchant of Venice as Performed in Theresienstadt*. See also the performance, *Defiant Requiem*, created by conductor Murry Sidlin to honor and remember the Jews who created a performance of Verdi's *Requiem* inside the walls of Theresienstadt. The 1943 performance was an embodiment of both compliance and resistance, having been commanded by the Nazis as part of the project of *Verschönerung*, and simultaneously providing an opportunity to "sing to [the Nazis] what we could never say to them," to quote the conductor of the first performance, Rafael Schächter.

11. See Taruskin, *Text and Act*. See especially his essay, "The Pastness of the Present and the Presence of the Past" (ibid., 90–154).

12. Here see Booth's discussion (*The Company We Keep*, 421–82) of the ethics of reading *The Adventures of Huckleberry Finn* in a world that has had a century to think about race-based slavery and its effects on a culture.

A Thick Reading of Mark 1

Though we are reading the words of the voice from the split sky that calls Jesus "son," we must notice the storytelling context in which the voice speaks. Before these words cut into the story, the storyteller has already established the story world as a world layered deep with remembrance. By focusing on acts of remembrance, I mean to argue that Mark's story is layered deep not simply with historical detail and biblical quotation or allusion but with memories from decisive moments in the life of the Jewish people, preserved memories that function as constitutive acts that create a "people prepared,"[13] not specifically for the coming of Jesus, or even for the advent of a messiah in general, but prepared to understand its life (as a distinctively Jewish life) as an act of resistance to Roman domination.[14] The superscription quiets the room and makes it clear that the story about to be told has depth and soaring heights: it is a story about a character named Ἰησοῦς, whose name calls the memory of Joshua into the room, Joshua the rescuer, the leader, the victor. This is a person named by a family that knows Jewish story. This character, Ἰησοῦς, has the title, Χριστός, tied to him. While it is clear that this title does not have a single, focused meaning, the meanings that it does have are all powerful and significant. He is anointed: that makes him a priest or a king. The rest of the story will make it clear that Χριστός mostly means "king," at least for this storyteller (and for the bulk of other uses of the term in other contemporaneous Jewish texts), but at this early point in the story, it is only clear that this character calls into the story the depths of Jewish memory.

The manuscript tradition argues with itself over whether this character is also called υἱοῦ θεοῦ, another identification with considerable weight. The interpretive tradition has likewise argued about this identification, with the dogmatic and sermonic branches finding in this textual variant warrant for the claim that Jesus is divine and human, no matter how difficult this might prove to explain, even to Christians. Even in the more analytic streams of the interpretive tradition there is a willingness to hear in this identification some sort of exaltation of the historical person, Jesus, to divine (or quasi-divine) status, regardless of whether Mark's storyteller had such an understanding or intention.

As Donald Juel argued, carefully and persuasively, the title υἱοῦ θεοῦ refers primarily to the king of Israel by way of Psalm 2 and its coronation

---

13. To borrow a notion from Luke 1:17.

14. Here see the discussion of the "arts of resistance" in Scott's *Domination and the Arts of Resistance*. See also the discussion of the function of storytelling in Jackson, *Politics of Storytelling*.

language.[15] The term is used with that referent at Qumran, so it will not do to dismiss it as a Christian innovation that crept in when Christian Gentiles imported notions of divinized humans from pagan mythology.[16]

Once the superscription is finished, the story proper begins. And again the storyteller wades into remembrance. If, as seems likely, Mark's story emerges out of the oral composing of skilled storytellers who could not read or write, then the opening phrase, καθὼς γέγραπται, testifies again to the complexity of the story in front of us. Perhaps the phrase enters the story at a late date, when the story is being written down, and with inscription comes consultation of Scripture. Perhaps Mark's storyteller is one of those few who could read and write, so the story is inscribed from the beginning.[17] More likely, it seems to me, Mark's storyteller gives evidence of the complicated kind of world described by Lourens de Vries.[18] Orality and inscription coexisted, with each bearing witness to the importance of the other. Traditional society, particularly a Jewish traditional society, honored the already-written Torah and Prophets, even if the individual honoring tradition could not read that tradition.[19] Writing may well have been in the control of the elites, but the tradition belonged to the people; the stories were the remembrance of the whole people. This was not merely a matter of piety. It was a matter of identity maintenance, which becomes especially important under Roman domination. Being Jewish meant many things, but one thing it seems to have meant was knowing the stories that offered a different construal of the world from that imposed by the Romans.[20]

The storyteller says γέγραπται (the Greek perfect tense nicely rendered by Martin Luther as *es steht geschrieben*, "it stands written"), and the storyteller means it. It does stand written, surely in the Torah scroll, and just as surely on the hearts of the Jewish community. Isaiah seems to have been important, and not only to the emerging Christian movement. Isaiah and Lamentations (and Job) dance together in Jewish interpretation throughout

15. See Juel, *Messianic Exegesis*, 77ff.

16. See Hurtado's argument in *How on Earth Did Jesus Become a God?* See also Segal, *Two Powers in Heaven*.

17. Such a supposition would, however, require us to figure out whether the storyteller was an elite, or the slave of an elite. It would matter. If the story is told by one with power, the narrative aim, at some point, will be to justify and preserve that power. And if the story is told by a slave, the situation is, potentially, rather different.

18. See de Vries, "Local Oral-Written Interfaces," 68–98.

19. See Carr's detailed discussion of this matter in Carr, *Writing on the Tablet of the Heart*; and Carr, *The Formation of the Hebrew Bible*.

20. See Horsley, *Hearing the Whole Story*; Portier-Young, *Apocalypse against Empire*.

the postexilic period, offering brave hope and critical analysis to faithful people in a world dominated by brutal foreign powers.

Once the matter of inscription is brought into the story, the storyteller complicates this by bringing also a voice, identified as coming from Isaiah and describing John the Baptist. This choice by the storyteller is worth a short pause. This story, now long inscribed on a page and long studied there, is a story brought into motion by a voice that is narrated from within the story. This voice does not speak, does not sing or whisper: it bellows like an animal. What the voice bellows comes also from deep remembrance, from old hopes inscribed in Torah. This voice is followed immediately by another voice, this one acting as a herald. This is, again, not simple speech, not casual communication. John's voice sounds like a trumpet, and the whole Jewish population hears it, shares the remembrance, and responds. It would appear that these memories do indeed stand written on the hearts of a faithful and durable Jewish community.

When the Jewish population swirls out to the Jordan in its response, they meet the body out of which the voice comes, itself an embodiment of old memories. Jewish faith has met such a striking character before, and Jews meet this character repeatedly when stories are told about Elijah, when stories are told about preparing for the messianic age, and when stories of the hearing of the *bat qol*, that echo of the voice of God ringing in a world where God has gone silent.[21] It should be noted also that this means that the storyteller herself is translating, carrying old memories and hopes across the same old "broad, ugly ditch" that Lessing had to cross, and under very similar circumstances.

The storyteller has thus created in the audience an expectation that the coming story requires of them remembrance and informed listening. Would the members of the audience have been able to read Isaiah to check the accuracy of the citation? No, of course not.[22] But that does not mean that they would not (at least many of them) have had the hopes exemplified in the hashed quotations and hybrid remembrances written on the tablets of their hearts. That inscription told Mark's audience who they were in a complicated world, and told them how to listen to this story full of old memories that had grown into hopes.

What about the Gentiles in the audience? Would they have been shut out of the story by the Jewish remembrance with which the story begins? Perhaps. Surely those complete outsiders who happened upon this story by

---

21. Note that Elijah is one of the diagnostic signs of an active encounter with the *bat qol*.

22. And if they could, they would have found the same thing that shows up in the margins of the Nestle-Aland edition of the Mark's Gospel: it is a composite quotation.

chance would catch none of the echoes. But perhaps this underestimates them. If the Jewish audience is a community surrounded by crowds of "god-fearers" that we know about from ancient texts, perhaps these apprentices to Torah knew enough of the tradition to hear the story productively. If Daniel Boyarin is correct when he argues that Christianity does not "emerge" from the larger Jewish community (linguistically, theologically, or even sociologically) at least until the fourth century,[23] and if Mark's story is properly told in such a setting, then there is a potential audience that might know the old stories and traditions very well indeed[24]—not so well, perhaps, as a deeply observant Jewish audience with Torah written on its heart; but apprentices to this ancient faith might still hear and remember rather a lot.

It is also possible to perform a story loaded with references that not all the audience can catch. In fact, this is the norm for any sort of performance. Audience competence is never universal and uniform, no matter what is being performed. At any orchestra concert, some in the audience have played the Brahms Second Symphony, some have heard it a few times live, some have several recordings at home (and some prefer the Claudio Abbado, Berliner Philharmoniker recording, while still admitting the attractiveness of the old Bruno Walter rendition), and some know as much about Brahms as can be learned from listening to his lullaby on a windup toy for babies. Good art opens the door to mixed audiences. Even a fully public audience, with few Jews in attendance, will feel the significance of the depth of remembrance as the story begins. And any audience that is moved by the story will feel the need to find a guide to help them explore the depths that they do not yet understand.

But the story is underway, and the audience, though in part confounded, is engaged in listening and remembering, and in learning to listen and in learning to remember.

---

23. See Boyarin, "Semantic Differences: or 'Judaism' / 'Christianity,'" 65–86.

24. Note, however, that the complications reach into the stratosphere if we imagine such an audience. Is the story told as part of an argument for Jesus? Is the story told as a Jewish story of hope under Roman domination, with Jesus as the proper candidate for Messiah? (Everyone in Boyarin's mixed community lives under Roman domination, but not everyone in the community would accept Jesus as Messiah.) Or in its telling the crucifixion of the Messiah in the person of Jesus, is the story told as a story of the attempt to crush Jewish hope at the time of Pontius Pilate and at the time of the First Jewish Revolt? If so, the scene in which Pilate identifies Jesus as "king of the Jews" even as he tortures him to death becomes powerfully significant.

Jesus and Change:
A Consequence of His Thick Identity

And then Jesus enters the scene. He comes from Nazareth, from Galilee, from a place not yet imagined in the telling of this story, and he comes because he is drawn into the swirl around John and around the remembrance stirred by his activity at the Jordan, that old point of entry into the promises of God. He flows into the story that he will subsequently dominate, and he flows in the way all characters have entered it: he is drawn to John's act of re-membrance, and he is purified in the Jordan for the enactments that are still to come. Jesus, like the whole Jewish world, is prepared for decisive change. Jesus comes up out of the water; and he sees the barrier of the sky being split apart, ruptured so that change can enter the story. A voice is heard, speaking through the rip in the universe, and the voice enacts the change for which the characters and the story world itself have been waiting.

Before we consider what the voice says, and why it makes such a dif-ference, note that the telling of the story itself changes exactly at this point. It is perhaps a small change, but it is a real one. The storyteller has been narrating, as is customary in Greek as in English, in secondary tenses (aor-ists and imperfects, in various voices). Once the voice speaks, the narra-tion changes and the pneuma casts Jesus (ἐκβάλλω, present tense) out into the wilderness. The word leaps out of the past and expresses a present act with a vividness a performer ought not ignore. In the midst of a narrated world, already past and gone, an action emerges and is narrated before it is completed. Past-tense narration lends a sense of stability and survivability to storytelling; after all, if the story is being told in the present, someone lived through whatever happened, even if only to be able to say with the messengers in the book of Job, "And I, even only I, escaped to tell the tale" (1:15). When a story is narrated in the present tense, the audience cannot yet know if anyone will live to tell the tale later. It is fitting that the pneuma, entering through the crack in the stable universe, acts in the uncontrollable present tense, and it is fitting that this acting follows immediately upon the speaking of God.

The content of God's short speech certainly possesses the motive force to effect such a decisive change. Σὺ εἶ ὁ υἱός μου, says the voice, thus link-ing Jesus with a distinguished set of remembered characters who also are called "son": the anointed king of Israel, the son of Abraham, and the son of Isaac, to name three decisive characters. In Psalm 2, at the coronation, God refers to the king as "son." In Genesis 22, God refers to Isaac as Abraham's well-loved son. And in Isaiah 42, God refers to Jacob (and thus all Israel) as a beloved son, supported and cherished. When the voice applies the same words to Jesus, all this deep remembrance is wound around him, and because naming is determinative in Jewish story, this deep remembrance becomes his nature.[25] This means that the storyteller has composited Jesus out of the memories and hopes of Jewish faith: as son of Abraham, he is the long-delayed hope of an abundant future, brought to the altar for slaughter. As son of Isaac, he is the embodiment of the renewed people of God's promise, born out of the silence that existed between Abraham and his well-loved son after the Akedah. As son of God and anointed king, he is the promise of the return of Jewish rule, and not just to Judah but also to the universe.[26] These words establish a thick identity for Jesus in this narrative world. He, a character who wanders in from Galilee with a name (Jesus = Joshua) out of another strand of deep remembrance,[27] leaves the scene embodying old stories and old hopes and old memories, all of which establish the Jewish community in the midst of a dangerous, abusive world.

The thickness of this story is really quite remarkable. There is scarcely a line that is not wrapped with deep memory and old hope. This thickness calls for, and has created a long, thick history of having-been-read, text upon text. This cannot be set aside and must be honored by any responsible mode of interpretation. If performance criticism cannot do this, it will only provide another, perhaps even crucial, thin layer in the larger enterprise of thick reading. And since ancient performance for ancient audiences would have had access to (at least many of) the thick elements simply as a result of the story's having been performed, then if performance criticism cannot generate thick performance, it will have to be acknowledged as weakening the interpretive project.

First Thoughts about Thick Performance

So how does a performer embody this thickness in a performance?

Some of this is handled by the tacit agreement established between the performer and the audience, at least when the story was first told. The story cues the audience to expect the story to be wrapped in and formed by old

25. In Genesis 2, whatever the newly formed mud-creature (Adam) calls to newly formed creatures, that is their name and identity.

26. This, of course, is the symbol of all that is good and safe and wholesome for a Jewish storyteller and a Jewish audience. It would be unreasonable to expect any faith or any people to anticipate hope and wholesomeness to speak a language other than their own.

27. The stories of Joshua are troubling stories, and they are stories of crossing the Jordan into the land of promise. To miss either the violence or the hope is to miss everything essential about the Joshua stories.

stories, hopes, and memories, and then turns the audience loose to feel the deep remembrance below the surface of the new story.

Some of this is handled by the text itself. Some lines are explicitly identified as a speaking of the inscribed tradition. Once the storyteller says, "It stands written," the audience knows that old memories are entering the scene. But, as has been pointed out, there is much more memory in this scene than appears in the isolated lines of explicit quotation.

But what does a performer do when the audience lives in a world distant and separate from the world out of which the story comes to us? Jesus comes to the Jordan from far away, but we come to the story from a much greater distance, a distance made greater by our millennia-long encounter with the story as a vehicle for Christian theology, as a part of a Christian lectionary, all in service of Christian dogmatics and apologetics. We could decide that the story *is* what the story has *become*, but that defeats the key strategy deployed by the ancient storyteller, who wrapped every bit of the performance in deep, ancient memory. Programmatic forgetfulness will prove a poor storytelling strategy for such a narrative.

While the larger question of how thick performance might be staged is on the table, we might do better to ask a smaller, more focused question: how might we perform the voice that speaks from the sky?

To start simply, what does the voice of God sound like? A student in one of my classes noticed that many performers resorted to a style she called "Biblical Ponderous" any time the ancient storyteller called old memories into service. The sonorous, usually baritone, intonations (probably owed in the main to Charlton Heston's encounter with the burning bush in *The Ten Commandments*)[28] set those old echoes apart from the rest of the story, but they caused more problems than they solved. In the end, most of Mark's story is wrapped in old hopes, in citations and allusions to old Scripture, and that leaves very little that isn't performed in ringing, remote tones. That makes for poor storytelling. Beyond that, this way of signaling the presence of a voice from the distant past functions, in my student's estimation (and mine), to exclude members of the audience who do not already recognize the citations and allusions. It sounds far too much like stereotypical bad preaching to ever work as a tool to engage an audience, which is always what a storyteller must do before doing anything else.

Perhaps the voice of God sounds like it did in the animated *Prince of Egypt*, where the voice was assembled out of the whispers of the entire cast overlaid with Val Kilmer speaking the lines clearly. This is another kind of

---

28. The voice belonged to Donald Hayne, according to IMDB.com. Hayne had a voice even deeper than Heston's.

Biblical Ponderous, I suppose, but at least it incorporated alto and soprano voices in the background, and at least it doesn't (yet) sound like stereotypical bad preaching. But the question begging to be asked is, how does this sonic trick embody the specific thickness of the text? It creates an interesting sound, but that sound only signals that this voice is somehow different from the other voices that have been heard to this point in the story. That is a significant advance, but it does not carry, by itself, any greater meaning.

Whatever it sounds like, given the way memory and hope are wrapped around the words spoken, the voice embodies remembrance. Perhaps the voice could speak as if recollecting the words from old memories, old hopes.

A Thick Reading of Mark 9

The question is intensified when the voice next speaks in Mark's story. The whole flowing narrative context is relevant to our reading of that voice, but a thick reading of that entire context is too complicated to include in this brief study. I will focus on the ascent of the mountain and the hearing of the voice at the top.

The mountain, as interpreters have long noted, is an appropriate place for a theophany, and Jewish Scripture provides many theophany stories that Jewish audiences may well have known (given how pervasive quotations of those stories are in biblical, extrabiblical, and rabbinic texts). When Jesus and the selected disciples go up on the high mountain, they are alone enough to encounter God. When they see Jesus arrayed in shining clothes, white beyond earthly possibility, theophany seems certain. The appearance of Moses and Elijah seals it. Both encountered the voice of God on a mountain. Both are characters from among the remembrances inscribed on the Jewish heart; even more, they are paradigmatic representations of the Torah and the Nevi'im. That links them with the earlier scene with its reference to inscription (γέγραπται). That further links them to the act of remembrance that the story embodies.

But with the scene on the mountain in the company of Moses and Elijah comes a new issue: when the voice speaks, despite all the new elements to the scene that mark an elevation over the first scene, the voice (nearly) repeats itself. Such repetition is a regular feature in biblical stories. For instance, the telling of the Akedah (Gen 22) is punctuated by repetitions. Whenever Abraham is addressed, by God or by Isaac, he responds, "Here I am." And when the address comes from Isaac (identified in the LXX as the ἀγαπητός [Gen 22:2] just as Jesus is in Mark 1:11), Abraham responds, with elaborate clarity, "Here I am, my son." Whenever a scene of the story is completed, the storyteller concludes it by telling the audience, "they went, the two of them, together." These repetitions pace and punctuate the story. They also intensify the quality of the characters and of their relationship, which act together to sharpen the bite of the story.

The same thing happens in Mark's Gospel. The scene on the mountain incorporates repetition not only of the words spoken by the voice; Elijah, too, is a repetition. The sky, as well, is apparently still split, and this recalling of the first scene functions as a kind of repetition. And when all this comes together, the words spoken are not simply a repetition; they are a refrain, a reprise, a restatement, a recapitulation, an intensification. Jesus encounters the voice of God on a mountain, and is again addressed as υἱός, as ἀγαπητός, again linked to the memory of Isaac and of Jacob. Once again language appropriate to the anointed king is applied to him.

Further Thoughts about Thick Performance

How might this thickness be incorporated into performance? The scene needs to be played so that the audience will feel the connection to other theophanies, particularly the one experienced by Moses on Mount Sinai and the one experienced by Elijah when he heard the still, small voice on Mount Horeb.[29] Perhaps the ground is littered with items from the older stories: stone tablets, maybe a burning bush, maybe a cave from which Elijah emerges, his face wrapped in his cloak, to meet Jesus and hear the voice from the cloud. Current audiences will not catch all of these quotations from Jewish scriptural memory, but they will note the weight of the images and will (at least) feel the force of the theophany.

The scene will also need to be played so that the explicit links to chapter 1 become clear. Perhaps the scene on the mountain is lit so that it recalls visually the scene at the Jordan. If the lighting changed when the sky was ripped, perhaps that lighting effect could return in this scene.[30] That raises an interpretive issue (perhaps small), however. The storyteller never informs us that the rip in the sky was healed, so it might be appropriate for the lighting to have been altered in *every* scene since chapter 1, though this would, over time, extinguish the dramatic effectiveness of the original change.

---

29. This might be the same place as Mount Sinai. Or not. The old stories are thick, and contradictory, at this point.

30. This would echo and modify something perceived by Rudolf Bultmann. Bultmann (and many others) saw the scene on the mountain as a misplaced resurrection account (*History of the Synoptic Tradition*, 259ff). Perhaps, at least in Mark's story, it is rather a re-placed baptism account.

Perhaps the actor playing Elijah will dress in ways that explicitly echo the costume worn by John the Baptist in chapter 1. This would actually be a reverse echo, since John's clothing recalled Elijah for ancient audiences. Perhaps such a reverse echo would help current audiences make a link that would have been obvious to ancient audiences. Or perhaps you could even use the same actor that played John the Baptist to play the part of Elijah. That would establish the linkage even more tightly. The storyteller, after all, does something very similar to that during the descent from the mountain, after the voice has finished speaking: the storyteller has Jesus hint (quite vigorously) that John is Elijah, and Elijah is John.

As noted above, the performance of the voice from the cloud will be crucial. A solo performer, especially when she is performing as a storyteller without benefit of theatrical accoutrements, has only her own voice with which to work. This is a powerful scene, one that may indeed beg for a voice in the realm of Biblical Ponderous, and a solo performer can do this as well as an ensemble, with or without stage equipment. Even if Biblical Ponderous is rejected as a bad idea whose time has also passed, the scene begs to be performed with a voice more substantial even than the one heard by the Jordan. At the Jordan, only Jesus sees the ripping of the sky, and perhaps only he hears the voice. On the mountain, Peter, James, and John hear the voice, and they hear it in the company of Moses and Elijah. If the scene by the river with the descending dove is a classic *bat qol* scene, with the daughter of a voice drifting in as an echo, perhaps the voice this time is louder, more substantial.

There are many ways to accomplish this. Here an ensemble performing the story has many advantages, particularly when performing onstage. Perhaps the voice, whether in Biblical Ponderous mode or not, comes into the scene disembodied, from somewhere up in the flyspace. The use of such a theatrical convention contributes its own element of thickness, drawing the audience's memory back to generations of biblical movies. This is not the same act of remembrance performed by Mark's ancient storyteller and audience, but it may be somewhat similar. Or not. The performer will have to decide. There are too many bad biblical movies in existence for this choice to be made heedlessly, but there are also many audiences that really like those bad biblical movies. The quotation might help, or hinder, or it might do both. The performer will have to decide.

The presence of an ensemble cast affords other possibilities as well. Perhaps the cast as a whole could speak the lines,[31] thus embodying the

---

31. As in *The Prince of Egypt*, a rather good movie that many audiences will have seen and enjoyed.

fact that in the ancient world out of which the story comes, the words of the act of remembrance were written on the hearts of the faithful people. In this case, the history of having-been-read may prove a significant help in developing a thick playing of the scene.

If the repetition of the words first heard in chapter 1 is understood as an intensification of those words, then the voice heard in chapter 9 must be an echo "with advantages,"[32] one that develops and solidifies what was heard the first time. As is clear from a thick reading of the two scenes in which God speaks, there is a great deal to develop and solidify. Though current audiences may well hear little of this, ancient audiences will (at least in the aggregate) have heard much of it as an act of memory and hope. If this scene intensifies this memory and hope, a performer has to find a way to let the audience feel it.

When composer Christopher Stanichar, poet Patrick Hicks, and I collaborated to create our *St. Mark Passion* for choir and actors, we had to address this question. The performance began with the choir singing and establishing the textual and prophetic background for the story Mark tells. For the opening movement, I wove together bits from Mark's citation of Isaiah, from Lamentations, and from Isaiah, all of which stand behind the way the ancient storyteller began the story. (In the libretto, as may be seen in the first movement, quoted below, I used an atypical transliteration of the Hebrew original in order to help choirs familiar with neither Hebrew nor with standard phonetic alphabets to pronounce the words correctly.)

A Voice cries:
In the wordless wilderness
clear a road for Mercy,
raise a road for Justice

A Voice cries:
Eh-kha!? [= How can it be!?]
She sits abandoned
the city great with people is now a widow
Sarah is forced to slave

---

32. The notion of "with advantages" is borrowed from the Agincourt scene in Shakespeare's *Henry V*. See the interesting discussion of theatrical memory by Warren-Heys, "Creating Memory in Shakespeare's Henry V." The entire issue is devoted to memory and is available online: http://www.northernrenaissance.org/remember-with-advantages-creating-memory-in-shakespeares-henry-v/.

A Voice cries:
Eh-lee Zee-ohn! [= Wail, O Zion!]
>Wail like a woman exhausted in her labor
>Wail like a bride wearing sackcloth
>>Mourning the husband of her youth

A Voice cries:
>This is our God
>>We have waited,
>>>Tense like a twisted string
pulled taut,
>>We have waited for Justice:
>>>Waited for Mercy
>>>>We have waited.

A Voice cries:
In the wordless wilderness
clear a road for Mercy
>raise a road for Justice
>*Eh-lee Zee-ohn!*

The actors entered during the choir's singing of this opening movement. I created a character called the Poet, a woman of mature years who speaks for old memories and traditions and speaks with the authority granted by deep faithfulness and with the courage earned through the experience of a life both strong and long, and she begins the scene by speaking the first stanza of a poem written by Patrick Hicks. The poem links the cry of dereliction at the end of Mark's story to the similar cries heard in every human generation.[33] A stanza of the poem begins every new scene, and the entire poem is repeated and interwoven in the final scene played by the actors. After this initial speaking, the beginning of Mark's story was played straight through from the superscription through the testing of Jesus in the wilderness.

---

33. For instance, this is the second stanza of Hicks's poem that introduces the second act of our *St. Mark Passion*: "The betrayal of our own bodies,/ car crashes that rob us of family,/ hearts that stop beating,/ blown out blood vessels,/ children that are miscarried,/ drownings on a perfect summer day— / the unloving dark swallows us all./ *Eloi eloi lema sabachthani,* / *Eloi eloi lema sabachthani.*" Subsequent stanzas forge connections also to the slaughter of the First and Second World Wars. These lines are used with permission of the poet.

I left the first scene at the Jordan in the hands of the actors alone, dividing the lines between two powerful characters, the Poet and Jesus.[34] The Poet, as the voice of deep tradition, caught Jesus coming up out of the water and spoke the words from the sky: You are my son, the beloved, with you I am well-pleased. The scene, set in the context of old hopes and new poetry, is powerful and tender. The Poet welcomes and recognizes Jesus with the tender pride of a parent and the words of old memory.

When we came to the scene on the mountain, the actors again played it, with the Poet and Jesus playing central roles in the telling of the story. As soon as the voice spoke out of the cloud (again, the Poet spoke the words), however, the scene froze and the choir sang an exploration of the depths of what had been spoken.

A Voice cries:
You are my son,
the beloved.
With you I am well-pleased.

This is my son,
the beloved,
hear him.

Look:
Jacob
My servant
whom I support,

Israel
my chosen
with whom my soul is well-pleased.

This is my son,
hear him.

I have been silent and still,
I have been deaf to your cries;
Now like a woman in labor I will groan.

34. The Poet is the character who speaks in our Saint Mark Passion when an authoritative voice is needed. Thus she is the voice of prophecy and faithful Jewish observance. Jesus (portrayed by a woman in our production) is played as young, vigorous, and promising, though still in need of nurturance and mentoring by the Poet.

Now I will pant
Now I will gasp.
A voice cries:
hear him.

Israel was despised; abandoned, alone;
A man of dismaying pain, a man who knows weakness.
Surely our weakness and our wounds he has carried
  Surely our shock is his, now, too.

This is my son,
hear him.

In this choral movement, the words from the cloud are interwoven with the passages from Isaiah that they echo, using my own translation of those passages. In addition to interweaving the specific echo about Jacob and Israel, I also wove in other bits from Isaiah that are thematically related to the waiting with which Mark's whole story begins and to the suffering of God's servant—both the Jewish people and the Jewish Messiah—that Mark uses to undergird his story of the Messiah whom Rome would crucify. Though audiences may well not know to look for these passages in Isaiah, the description of the Suffering Servant is likely written on their hearts and inscribed in their memories, and the theme of desperate waiting connects to the lived experience of almost everyone. This alone marks a development and an advance beyond the simple hearing of the voice from the split sky in chapter 1, and both scenes are enriched as a result. The fact that these words are sung is also significant. Spoken words are powerful, but words that have melody, harmony, and rhythm are even more powerful. Throughout the *St. Mark Passion*, the depths of the story, the memories and prophecies that make it larger than simple life, are always sung by the choir. In this particular movement, Stanichar incorporated melodies from the Russian Orthodox liturgy appropriate to the theme of apotheosis. Though only a few in the audience will have caught the explicit liturgical and theological quotation, all will have felt the effect of ascending into the heavenly spheres of deeper meaning, rising with the music to new heights.

When Jesus goes back down the mountain after the choir sings, he has been linked to key hopes and memories (from both Jewish and Christian history), and the story about him has become itself an act of remembrance, for current audiences as it was for ancient audiences. This is one kind of thick performance, and it benefits from the ability of music, and perhaps particularly of choral music, to sound the greater dimensions and deeper memories that shape Mark's story. This is a larger act of translation, properly called intersemiotic translation,[35] that brings to a current audience something of the act of remembrance that would have been part of the experience of the performance of the text for an ancient audience. Remembrance has been escalated by the recapitulation on the mountain in the presence of Moses and Elijah, the Torah and the Nevi'im, the sacred memory written on faithful hearts.

A Thick Reading of Mark 15

Once again, in service of the brevity of this study, we leap over great expanses of Mark's story and arrive at the crucifixion scene in chapter 15. Here, in the presence of Jesus, who has died in agony, and in the presence of the Roman murderers and the Jewish watchers, the centurion who had watched over the torture that killed Jesus looks at the corpse on the cross and says, ἀληθῶς οὗτος ὁ ἄνθρωπος υἱὸς θεοῦ ἦν.

Interpreters have argued long and well over what he might have meant. Recent interpretive work seems generally to grant that the words are somehow ironic from the point of view of the audience. In the Gospel of Luke the centurion only says that the dead man was innocent. No irony is needed to interpret such a telling of the story: innocent people are murdered every day. But Mark's storyteller has the Roman soldier call Jesus "son of God," by which he could mean that Jesus was somehow associated with divinity, whether in terms of the quality of his life or in terms of some sort of heavenly biology. The Jewish audience for the story would have heard those possibilities and would have heard also a title properly applied to the Messiah, the king of Israel. The audience would also have heard that same title applied to Jesus at the very beginning of Mark's story.

This could be a miraculous confession on the part of a Roman soldier who had, up to that miraculous moment, functioned as overseer of the torture, as murderer.[36] If that is the case, the centurion is in on the irony along with the Jewish audience.

As Donald Juel and others (myself included) have suggested,[37] the centurion's words could also be a taunt delivered to a naked, dead guy hanging

---

35. The term is Jakobson's ("On Linguistic Aspects of Translation," 232–39). For the application of this notion to biblical translation, see the essays collected in Maxey and Wendland's *Translating Scripture for Sound and Performance*.

36. See especially the essay by Iverson, "A Centurion's 'Confession,'" 329–50.

37. See, for instance, Juel's discussion in his inaugural lecture at Princeton Theological Seminary, "'Your Word is Truth,'" 13–32. See also my discussion in Swanson, *Provoking the Gospel of Mark*.

on a Roman cross under a title that calls him the king of the Jews. In that case the audience members, who know that "king of the Jews" and "son of God" are functionally equivalent titles (on the basis of the coronation psalm, Psalm 2), still get the irony: the murderer himself makes an unwitting confession of the identity of Jesus, established since the superscription. In this case, however, the audience also gets a surprise. There is a twist in Mark's story. This decisive identification of Jesus as son and Messiah comes out of the most unlikely mouth, and only after Jesus has died an agonizing death without the anesthetic benefits of a martyr's ending. Martyrs die at peace with confessions of faith on their lips. Jesus dies, screaming out his life, after accusing God of abandoning him. It fits with Mark's storytelling strategy for the decisive moment of identification to be somewhat surprising.[38] The first believing confession of Jesus as Messiah earns Peter a sharp rebuke, and the act of anointing Jesus as Messiah is performed by a woman who is rebuked by the surrounding crowd. But the insistent association of Χριστός with a death by torture carries a shock that current Christian audiences will likely miss. Messiahs ought not die at the hands of Roman torturers. This twist in the properly expected story is crucial to Mark's story.

In order to read this scene properly, we need to step back and note its structural connection to the other two scenes in which Jesus is identified as "son of God," in chapters 1 and 9. But before we look closely at that connection, I would like to look first at another structural element that holds the death scene in place. Before the centurion calls Jesus the son of God (15:39), Pilate calls him king of the Jews (15:2), and before that the chief priest calls him the Messiah, the son of the Blessed (14:61). Once again, all of these titles are functionally equivalent. Each is spoken by an opponent of Jesus involved in his eventual death at the hands of the Romans. Even the chief priest, though Jewish, is forced to be part of the Roman control system and functions as an assistant in the Roman project to dominate its empire. Literary-critical interpreters often see these scenes as linked in being ironic identifications of Jesus by opponents.

These scenes succeed each other on the way to the death that the storyteller has held in front of the audience since chapter 2. Of course, the audience already knew that Jesus would be crucified and raised in the course of the story, but we often retell ourselves stories that we know very well indeed. These stories are similar to each but not identical. As noted, they involve equivalent, but not identical, titles. The scenes feature two Roman officials and a Jewish official, though all are held in the grip of Rome.

---

38. See especially the essay by Rindge, "Reconfiguring the Akedah and Recasting God," 755–74.

In the first two scenes, though they are ironic identifications, the speaker is presented as asking a question, not as making a statement. Pilate does indeed ask, though it is clear that his question is a taunt, not an interrogation. He can have no interest in Jesus' royal or religious identity. He is simply playing a game with a prisoner who will soon be crucified. Jesus has been brought to him as a troublemaker. Pilate routinely punished such people publicly in order to make clear to the dominated population the cost of opposing Rome. The chief priest also asks Jesus whether he is the Messiah, though it should be noted that his so-called question is twisted by the storyteller, twisted in ways not always noted by translators.[39] In 14:61 the chief priest is presented as questioning Jesus, and the substance of that questioning consists in his saying (λέγει) to Jesus, "You are the Messiah, the son of the Blessed" (14:61). Of course, it could still be a question, but it is worth noting that, though Greek can and frequently does identify questions by inverting subject and verb as does English, this sentence does not invert the order. This is true for Pilate's words as well. Again the sentence is spoken so that, even if it is introduced as a question, it is a positive statement, an ironic identification.

In the case of the words of the centurion, Jesus is dead and done being questioned. The statement is clearly a statement, though (as noted) there is a vigorous argument about whether it is a miraculous confession or a malicious taunt. For now, what matters is that his words mean the same thing as those spoken by the chief priest and by Pilate.

What also matters is that the two three-part structures are linked at the death scene. In chapter 1 and chapter 9, God speaks and claims Jesus as son, thus linking him with other characters of sacred memory. In chapters 14 and 15, the chief priest and Pilate speak and identify Jesus as son of God, Messiah, and king. In chapter 15, the centurion brings these two story structures together. The scene can be read productively either as miraculous or malicious. In either case the audience hears a truth that contradicts the surface appearance of the text. In either case there is a surprise, a twist. Either the opponents of Jesus are portrayed as surprised by the miraculous change in the centurion, or the audience is surprised by the stark silence of God (when the established pattern requires speech) and by the sheer victory of Rome over the Messiah and messianic hope.

---

39. This twist is better represented in the old King James Version than in the New Revised Standard Version, which conflates the chief priest's asking and saying into a single translated verb.

A Thicker, Closer Reading of
the Death of the Messiah

When Jesus dies in chapter 15, he dies in a scene that explicitly echoes the baptism and the transfiguration. These very different stories share common elements, easily seen, easily noted by an audience. Elijah is impossible to miss in chapters 1 and 9, and chapter 15 goes to even greater lengths to draw the audience's ears to the name of Elijah. The ripping of the heavens or of the curtain is likewise striking. Only God could have done this. The voice that speaks is, in each case, the focus of the scene. All things build toward it, and the story changes immediately upon the completion of the speech.

In the death scene, each of these elements comes with a twist. Elijah is present at the end only because characters in the story who do not understand Aramaic (that is to say, Romans) misunderstand an embedded remembering of Psalm 22. But it is not simply a misunderstanding: it is twisted into a taunt. People who cannot speak Aramaic are presented (impossibly, it would seem) as understanding a great deal about Elijah and his significance as a forerunner for release and restoration. The bystanders hear Jesus' cry of agony, and the storyteller has them twist it into a demonstration of the failure of the hope of the faithful.

The rip is also complex. It is destructive; the word itself makes this clear. The Gospel of Luke has the heavens opened, which implies that they can again be closed. In Mark's story, the heavens and the curtain are ripped, and any repair (if one were possible) would leave a scar, a visible seam marking the attempt at mending. In Mark, the ripping is done from above, by God, and the purpose is not clear. Despite centuries of Christian assertion that the ripping removes a Jewish barrier erected between God and people, this simply doesn't ring true. God has access to creation in Jewish Scripture and in rabbinic story. And people have access to God, both in prayer and in study in all of Jewish tradition. Both the sky and the curtain are indeed barriers, but they function to maintain stability and to allow the safe functioning of the ordinary world. Why destroy such a barrier? What is the outcome? The storyteller leaves the audience to wonder.

The voice, to be consistent, should also contain a twist and should even, perhaps, somehow destroy a stabilizing structure. In order for this death scene to parallel the baptism and transfiguration scenes, God should speak. But God does not. Instead, a deadly enemy speaks Perhaps this is a theological twist, an odd sort of twisted incarnation of the voice of God under the form of an enemy: a centurion. There surely are other characters in Mark's story, the legion of demons particularly, who have identified Jesus insightfully despite being enemies. But even granting this, it should still be

God's voice at this point in the story. The structured patterns make that clear. God has only spoken twice, and he has always said the same thing. Never has another voice intruded when God's was expected.

The death scene also echoes the scenes played in the presence of the chief priest and of Pilate. The shared element is chiefly the functionally equivalent identification of Jesus by an opponent controlled by Rome. There is a progression to this series of scenes. The chief priest could be somewhat neutral, or, more likely (both in narrative and historical terms), he is acting as a distant early warning system for Pilate, having been charged with stopping troublemakers before they can get anything started. Pilate is the tipping point in this series. The chief priest delivers the troublemaker, as required. Pilate now delivers Jesus to the Roman torturers and to a Roman death, as he did for so many other Jews during those years.

The centurion could be a reversal of the developing pattern. If so, the point is that even Pilate is finally ineffective in his attempt to ridicule and suppress Jewish hope and memory, despite Roman power and brutality. This could work, but it seems to me a poor fit in the story patterns that have been developing.

The centurion's words could also be a confirmation of the developing patterns. If so, the point could be that Roman force was finally deadly and effective, despite durable Jewish remembrance. This fits well with Pilate's act of nailing his taunt to the cross. It fits also with what we know of Pilate's character from history, and with what I find to be the most persuasive reading of the pattern seen in chapters 1, 9, and 15.

A Thick Performance of the Death of the Messiah

But what might performance suggest about this scene?

In the thinnest possible performance of the scene, it would be impossible for the audience to make a link to the baptism and transfiguration. But that supposes an ignorant audience incapable of engaging in the act of remembrance that the rest of the story assumes (from the very beginning with its citations of prophetic memory and references to both Joshua and the Messiah). It also supposes a particularly inattentive audience, who somehow misses the focus on Elijah's name in this scene. This scenario seems unlikely, and irresponsibly thin. The text itself is thick, and a proper performance must find a way to translate not only the bare words but also the thickness of the text.

In the *St. Mark Passion* that Stanichar, Hicks, and I created, the centurion's words are spoken by a single voice, a Roman voice, and I chose to play them as a clear taunt delivered by a character who noted that God was incapable of speech, and unable to stop Roman violence. I chose this, not because it is the only possible playing of the text, and not because the text could allow it (texts can allow almost anything), but because the twist in the pattern seems to me to demand it. Where God should speak, it is only a murderer who talks, and he speaks in the silence of the crushing of memory and hope.

This same twist is seen at the very end of Mark's story. When the only messengers given word of the resurrection should speak, they flee and are forever silent. That particular twist seems to be part of the DNA of Mark's entire story, so much so that my colleague, composer Christopher Stanichar, labored to find a way to express this same twist in the music with which our *St. Mark Passion* concludes. The actors have finished their work and they have left in silence. The choir has sung its final piece, a piece that pulls together the themes of mourning and memory, waiting and hoping, that have undergirded Mark's whole story, quoting again Isaiah and Lamentations as they did in the opening movement of the *St. Mark Passion*. Their last words are also the last words of Mark's story, a translation of ἐφοβοῦντο γάρ. The instrumentalists have brought the whole composition to its close, recapitulating themes and climbing through chords that echo Russian Orthodox liturgical enactments of the resurrection. The music progresses to its final chord, a beautifully settled E-flat major chord, itself an expression of the resurrection. And then, into this chord comes the cello playing an F-flat, a minor second in the closing chord, creating tension just when the audience had every reason to expect resolution.

For a sense of this painful tension, play for yourself the resulting tone cluster. An E-flat major chord (E-flat, G, B-flat) expresses, even embodies, the full completion of Mark's narrative arc. This has indeed been the story of Jesus, Messiah, son of God. Mark set out to tell that story, and Mark has succeeded. Old hopes have been recalled and brought into the present. But then add the F-flat (which is also an E-natural) to the chord. This is not simply an extra note, a supplement that enriches the sound. It is a note that does not belong to the musical scale established by the E-flat major chord. Every note in the key of F-flat (or E-natural) stands one half step apart from every note in the key of E-flat. None of the chords is shared; none of the steps on the scale creates the suggestion of a natural resolution to the tension,[40] though

---

40. The way, for instance, adding the seventh note of the scale to the chord based on the fifth note of the scale (the "V chord") begs for a return to the tonic chord and musical completion.

such natural resolutions are common throughout Western music. The two musical structures simply exclude each other.

This painful refusal of resolution aptly embodies the painful refusal that makes Mark's narrative what it is. Perhaps more important, it performs that refusal in a way that catches an audience and holds it. This is, indeed, a thick performance, fully as thick as any heavily footnoted academic text: fully as thick, but much more evocative. This "much more" is what responsible interpreters have always been seeking. This thick performance realizes something essential in the Gospel of Mark: it is the story of a crucified Messiah, of hope enacted and deferred. It is an act of remembrance of the way God's promises have been fulfilled and blocked throughout Jewish history.

Some Last Thoughts (for Now) on Thick Performance

Thick performance is not only possible; it is necessary. The question of how to read the words of the centurion by the cross remains complicated, but this work toward a thick performance of the scene clearly yields a possible and coherent playing of the scene. More important, a thick performance brings into the scene the interpretive thickness, the weight of memory and hope that would have been part of the experience of the most likely ancient audience. The kind of thick performance represented by our *St. Mark Passion*, with an ensemble of actors and a choir of singers, surely does not replicate ancient practice, but it does arguably reproduce ancient audience competence and experience. Performance-critical work, it should be clear, need not be in bondage to proselytism or any other ideology. It does not simply repristinate ancient practice, though it can work in that idiom, at least so long as it attends to the necessary task of translating the whole experience of the text, not just the words. Neither does performance-critical work eliminate the polyvalence of texts; it does not end the problem posed by the reality of multiple meanings. Performance definitely requires the performer to make decisions, but real performers make real decisions that preserve some of the generative tension within a text, the tension that vibrates between possible readings, potential playings.

All this amounts to intersemiotic translation: the practice of translating whole sign systems, not just thin words. In the case of Mark's story, and particularly the words spoken from the sky, "You are my son," what must be translated is the act of remembrance embodied in the ancient text. Ancient audiences had the memories from Isaiah written on the tablets of their hearts. Most current audiences do not. Ancient Jewish audiences knew those old memories and hopes as they had danced with a painful history, from the destruction of the first temple to the destruction of the second, and beyond. They knew how memories from Isaiah cut through memories from Lamentations, and from more recent catastrophes that had also required lamentation. The thick translation we attempted in our creation of the *St. Mark Passion* is one way to translate all of this remembrance for a current audience that lacks a memory. It is not the only way to do this, but it is necessary to do it.

Bibliography

Booth, Wayne C. *The Company We Keep: An Ethics of Fiction*. Berkeley: University of California Press, 1988.

Boyarin, Daniel. "Semantic Differences: or 'Judaism' / 'Christianity.'" In *The Ways that Never Parted: Jews and Christians in Late Antiquity and the Early Middle Ages*, edited by Adam H. Becker and Annette Yoshiko Reed, 65–86. Minneapolis: Fortress, 2007.

Bultmann, Rudolf. *History of the Synoptic Tradition*. Translated by John Marsh. New York: Harper & Row, 1963.

Carr, David M. *The Formation of the Hebrew Bible*. New York: Oxford University Press, 2011.

———. *Writing on the Tablet of the Heart: Origins of Scripture and Literature*. Oxford: Oxford University Press, 2005.

Chadwick, Henry, ed. *Lessing's Theological Writings*. A Library of Modern Religious Thought. Stanford: Stanford University Press, 1956.

De Vries, Lourens. "Local Oral–Written Interfaces and the Nature, Transmission, Performance, and Translation of Biblical Texts." In *Translating Scripture for Sound and Performance: New Directions in Biblical Studies*, edited by James A. Maxey and Ernst R. Wendland, 68–98, BPCS 6. Eugene, OR: Cascade Books, 2012.

Fackenheim, Emil. *The Jewish Bible after the Holocaust: A Re-Reading*. Manchester: Manchester University Press, 1990.

Feinberg, Anat. *Embodied Memory: The Theatre of George Tabori*. Iowa City: University of Iowa Press, 1999.

Foley, John Miles. *How to Read an Oral Poem*. Urbana: University of Illinois Press, 2002.

Geertz, Clifford. *The Interpretation of Cultures: Selected Essays*. New York: Basic Books, 1973.

Horsley, Richard. *Hearing the Whole Story: The Politics of Plot in Mark's Gospel*. Louisville: Westminster John Knox, 2001.

Hurtado, Larry W. *How on Earth Did Jesus Become a God? Historical Questions about Earliest Devotion to Jesus*. Grand Rapids: Eerdmans, 2005.

Iverson, Kelly R. "A Centurion's 'Confession': A Performance-Critical Analysis of Mark 15:39." *JBL* 130 (2011) 329–50.

Jackson, Michael. *The Politics of Storytelling: Violence, Transgression, and Intersubjectivity*. Critical Anthropology 3. Copenhagen: Museum Tusculanum Press, 2002.

Jakobson, Roman. "On Linguistic Aspects of Translation." In *On Translation*, edited by Reuben Brower, 232–39. Harvard Studies in Comparative Literature 23. Cambridge: Harvard University Press, 1959.

Juel, Donald. *Messianic Exegesis: Christological Interpretation of the Old Testament in Early Christianity*. Philadelphia: Fortress, 1988.

———. "'Your Word is Truth': Some Reflections on a Hard Saying." In *Shaping the Scriptural Imagination: Truth, Meaning, and the Theological Interpretation of the Bible*, by Donald Juel, 13–32. Edited by Shane Berg and Matthew L. Skinner. Waco, TX: Baylor University Press, 2011.

Maxey, James A., and Ernst R. Wendland, eds. *Translating Scripture for Sound and Performance: New Directions in Biblical Studies*. BPCS 6. Eugene, OR: Cascade Books, 2012.

Moore, Stephen D. *Mark and Luke in Poststructuralist Perspectives: Jesus Begins to Write*. New Haven: Yale University Press, 1992.

Niles, John D. *Homo Narrans: The Poetics and Anthropology of Oral Literature*. Philadelphia: University of Pennsylvania Press, 1999.

Portier-Young, Anathea E. *Apocalypse against Empire: Theologies of Resistance in Early Judaism*. Grand Rapids: Eerdmans, 2011.

Rindge, Matthew S. "Reconfiguring the Akedah and Recasting God: Lament and Divine Abandonment in Mark." *JBL* 131 (2012) 755–74.

Scott, James C. *Domination and the Arts of Resistance: Hidden Transcripts*. New Haven: Yale University Press, 1992.

Segal, Alan F. *Two Powers in Heaven: Early Rabbinic Reports about Christianity and Gnosticism*. Studies in Judaism in Late Antiquity 25. Leiden: Brill, 1977.

Stanichar, Christopher, et al. *St. Mark Passion: A Cantata Based on the Suffering of the Messiah according to the Gospel of Mark*. http://christopherstanichar.com/catalogue.html/.

Swanson, Richard W. *Provoking the Gospel of Mark: A Storyteller's Commentary*. Cleveland: Pilgrim, 2005.

Taruskin, Richard. *Text and Act: Essays on Music and Performance*. New York: Oxford University Press, 1995.

Warren-Heys, Rebecca. "'[R]emember, with advantages': Creating Memory in Shakespeare's Henry V." *Journal of the Northern Renaissance* 2 (2010). http://www.northernrenaissance.org/remember-with-advantages-creating-memory-in-shakespeares-henry-v/.

BIBLIOGRAPHY

Achtemeier, Paul. "*Omne verbum sonat*: The New Testament and the Oral Environment of Late Western Antiquity." *JBL* 109 (1990) 3–27.

Aristotle. *The Art of Rhetoric*. Translated by John H. Freese. LCL. Cambridge: Harvard University Press, 1926.

———. *The Complete Works of Aristotle: The Revised Oxford Translation*. Edited by Jonathan Barnes. 2 vols. Bollinger Series 71–72. Princeton: Princeton University Press, 1984.

Artaud, Antonin. *The Theatre and Its Double*. Translated by Mary Caroline Richards. Evergreen Original. New York: Grove Press, 1958.

Augustine, Saint. *Confessions*. Translated by William Watts. 2 vols. LCL. Cambridge: Harvard University Press. 1977–1988.

Aveni, Anthony F. *Empires of Time: Calendars, Clocks, and Cultures*. London: Tauris Parke, 2000.

Balogh, Josef. "Voces Paginarum." *Philologus* 82 (1926) 84–109, 202–40.

Bar-Ilan, Meir. "Illiteracy in the Land of Israel in the First Centuries CE." In *Essays in the Social Scientific Study of Judaism and Jewish Society*, edited by Simcha Fishbane et al., 2:46–61. 2 vols. Hoboken, NJ: Ktav, 1990–1992.

Barr, James. *Biblical Words for Time*. Studies in Biblical Theology 33. London: SCM, 1962.

Barranger, Milly S. *Theatre: A Way of Seeing*. 6th ed. Belmont, CA: Wadsworth, 2006.

Bassler, Jouette M. "The Galileans: A Neglected Factor in Johannine Community Research." *CBQ* 43 (1981) 243–57.

———. "Mixed Signals: Nicodemus in the Fourth Gospel." *JBL* 108 (1989) 635–46.

Bauckham, Richard. "For Whom Were Gospels Written?" In *The Gospels for All Christians: Rethinking the Gospel Audiences*, edited by Richard Bauckham, 9–48. Grand Rapids: Eerdmans, 1998.

———. *Jesus and the Eyewitnesses: The Gospels as Eyewitness Testimony*. Grand Rapids: Eerdmans, 2006.

Bauer, David R. *The Structure of Matthew's Gospel: A Study in Literary Design*. JSNTSup 31. Sheffield: Almond, 1988.

Beer, Gillian. "Storytime and Its Futures." In *Time*, edited by Katinka Ridderbos, 126–42. Darwin College Lectures. Cambridge: Cambridge University Press, 2002.

Benjamin, Walter. *Illuminations: Essays and Reflections*. Translated by Harry Zohn. New York: Schocken, 1968.

Best, Ernest. *Following Jesus: Discipleship in the Gospel of Mark*. JSNTSup 4. Sheffield: JSOT Press, 1981.

Betz, Hans Dieter. *The Sermon on the Mount*. Hermeneia. Minneapolis: Fortress, 1995.

Boomershine, Thomas E. "Audience Address and Purpose in the Performance of Mark." In *Mark as Story: Retrospect and Prospect*, edited by Kelly R. Iverson and Christopher W. Skinner, 115–42. SBLRBS 65. Atlanta: Society of Biblical Literature, 2011.

Booth, Wayne C. *The Company We Keep: An Ethics of Fiction*. Berkeley: University of California Press, 1988.

———. *The Rhetoric of Fiction*. Chicago: University of Chicago Press, 1961.

Botha, Pieter J. J. *Orality and Literacy in Early Christianity*. BPCS 5. Eugene, OR: Cascade Books, 2012.

Boyarin, Daniel. "Semantic Differences: or 'Judaism' / 'Christianity.'" In *The Ways That Never Parted: Jews and Christians in Late Antiquity and the Middle Ages*, edited by Adam H. Becker and Annette Yoshiko Reed, 65–86. Minneapolis: Fortress, 2007.

Brant, Jo-Ann A. *Dialogue and Drama: Elements of Greek Tragedy in the Fourth Gospel*. Peabody, MA: Hendrickson, 2004.

Brin, Gershon. *The Concept of Time in the Bible and the Dead Sea Scrolls*. Studies on the Texts of the Desert of Judah 39. Leiden: Brill, 2001.

Brook, Peter. *The Empty Space: A Book about the Theatre: Deadly, Holy, Rough, Immediate*. New York: Atheneum, 1968.

Brown, Raymond E. *The Birth of the Messiah: A Commentary on the Infancy Narratives in Matthew and Luke*. Garden City, NY: Doubleday, 1977.

———. *The Death of the Messiah: From Gethsemane to the Grave: A Commentary on the Passion Narratives in the Four Gospels*. 2 vols. ABRL. New York: Doubleday, 1994.

———. *The Gospel according to John*. 2 vols. AB 29–29a. New York: Doubleday, 1966.

———. *Introduction to the New Testament*. ABRL. New York: Doubleday, 1997.

Bultmann, Rudolf. *History of the Synoptic Tradition*. New York: Harper & Row, 1963.

Burnett, Fred W. "Characterization and Reader Construction of Characters in the Gospels." *Semeia* 63 (1993) 1–28.

Burridge, Richard. "About People, by People, for People: Gospel Genre and Audiences." In *The Gospels for all Christians: Rethinking the Gospel Audiences*, edited by Richard Bauckham, 113–45. Grand Rapids: Eerdmans, 1998.

Canestri, Jorge, and Leticia Glocer Fiorini, eds. *The Experience of Time: Psychoanalytic Perspectives*. Controversies in Psychoanalysis Series. London: Karnac, 2009.

Carr, David M. *The Formation of the Hebrew Bible*. New York: Oxford University Press, 2011.

———. *Writing on the Tablet of the Heart: Origins of Scripture and Literature*. Oxford: Oxford University Press, 2005.

Carter, Warren. *John: Storyteller, Interpreter, Evangelist*. Peabody, MA: Hendrickson, 2006.

———. *Matthew and the Margins: A Sociopolitical and Religious Reading*. Bible and Liberation Series. Maryknoll, NY: Orbis, 2000.

Chadwick, Henry, ed. *Lessing's Theological Writings*. A Library of Modern Religious Thought. Stanford: Stanford University Press, 1956.

Chatman, Seymour. *Story and Discourse: Narrative Structure in Fiction and Film*. Ithaca, NY: Cornell University Press, 1978.

Collins, Adela Yarbro. *Mark: A Commentary on the Gospel of Mark*. Hermeneia. Minneapolis: Fortress, 2007.

Conway, Colleen M. *Men and Women in the Fourth Gospel: Gender and Johannine Characterization*. SBLDS 167. Atlanta: Society of Biblical Literature, 1999.

Cullmann, Oscar. *Christ and Time: The Primitive Christian Concept of Time and History*. Translated by Floyd V. Filson. Philadelphia: Westminster, 1950.

Culpepper, R. Alan. *Anatomy of the Fourth Gospel: A Study in Literary Design*. Foundations and Facets: New Testament. Philadelphia: Fortress, 1983.

Dadd, Richard, and Dan Fryer. *The Last Bookshop*. http://webakestuff.co.uk/2013/04/the-last-bookshop-2/.

Davies, W. D., and D. C. Allison. *A Critical and Exegetical Commentary on the Gospel according to Saint Matthew*. 3 vols. ICC. Edinburgh: T. & T. Clark, 1988.

Dean, Margaret E. "The Grammar of Sound in Greek Texts: Toward a Method of Mapping the Echoes of Speech in Writing." *ABR* 44 (1996) 53–70.

Deterding, Paul E. "The New Testament View of Time and History." *Concordia Journal* 21 (1995) 385–99.

De Vries, Lourens. "Local Oral-Written Interfaces and the Nature, Transmission, Performance, and Translation of Biblical Texts." In *Translating Scripture for Sound and Performance: New Directions in Biblical Studies*, edited by James A. Maxey and Ernst R. Wendland, 68–98. BPCS 6. Eugene, OR: Cascade Books, 2012.

De Vries, Simon J. *Yesterday, Today, and Tomorrow: Time and History in the Old Testament*. Grand Rapids: Eerdmans, 1975.

Dewey, Joanna. "The Gospel of Mark as Oral Hermeneutic." In *Jesus, the Voice, and the Text: Beyond "The Oral and the Written Gospel,"* edited by Tom Thatcher, 71–88. Waco: Baylor University Press, 2008.

———. *The Oral Ethos of the Early Church: Speaking, Writing, and the Gospel of Mark*. Biblical Performance Criticism 8. Eugene, OR: Cascade Books, 2013.

———. "Oral Methods of Structuring Narrative in Mark." *Int* 43 (1989) 32–44.

Dibelius, Martin. *Gospel Criticism and Christology*. London: Nicholson & Watson, 1935.

Diderot, Denis. *The Paradox of Acting*. Translated by Walter H. Pollock. New York: Hill and Wang, 1957.

Doan, William, and Terry Giles. *Prophets, Performance, and Power: Performance Criticism of the Hebrew Bible*. New York: T. & T. Clark, 2005.

Doble, Peter. *The Paradox of Salvation: Luke's Theology of the Cross*. SNTSMS 87. Cambridge: Cambridge University Press, 1996.

Dolan, Jill. *Utopia in Performance: Finding Hope at the Theater*. Ann Arbor: University of Michigan Press, 2005.

Downs, William Missouri, et al. *The Art of Theatre: A Concise Introduction*. 3rd ed. Boston: Wadsworth, 2013.

Duke, Paul D. *Irony in the Fourth Gospel*. Atlanta: John Knox, 1985.

Ehrman, Bart D., and Mark A. Plunkett. "The Angel and the Agony: The Textual Problem of Luke 22:43–44." *CBQ* 45 (1983) 401–16.

Esslin, Martin. *An Anatomy of Drama*. New York: Hill & Wang, 1976.

Estes, Douglas. *The Temporal Mechanics of the Fourth Gospel: A Theory of Hermeneutical Relativity in the Gospel of John*. Biblical Interpretation Series 92. Leiden: Brill, 2008.

Fackenheim, Emil L. *The Jewish Bible after the Holocaust: A Re-Reading*. Manchester, UK: Manchester University Press, 1990.

Farmer, William R., ed. *Anti-Judaism and the Gospels*. Harrisburg, PA: Trinity, 1999.

Feinberg, Anat. *Embodied Memory: The Theatre of George Tabori*. Studies in Theatre History and Culture. Iowa City: University of Iowa Press, 1999.

Fine, Elizabeth C. *The Folklore Text: From Performance to Print.* Bloomington: Indiana University Press, 1984.

Fischer-Lichte, Erika. *Theatre, Sacrifice, Ritual: Exploring Forms of Political Theatre.* London: Routledge, 2004.

———. *The Transformative Power of Performance: A New Aesthetics.* London: Routledge, 2008.

Fitzmyer, Joseph A. *The Gospel according to Luke.* Vol. 1, *Luke I–IX.* AB 28. Garden City, NY: Doubleday, 1981.

Foley, John Miles. *How to Read an Oral Poem.* Urbana: University of Illinois Press, 2002.

Fowler, Robert M. "How the Secondary Orality of the Electronic Age Can Awaken Us to the Primary Orality of Antiquity or What Hypertext Can Teach Us about the Bible with Reflections on the Ethical and Political Issues of the Electronic Frontier." http://homepages.bw.edu/~rfowler/pubs/secondoral/index.html#anchor45421/.

———. *Let the Reader Understand: Reader-Response Criticism and the Gospel of Mark.* Minneapolis: Fortress, 1991.

Frei, Hans W. *The Eclipse of Biblical Narrative: A Study in Eighteenth and Nineteenth Century Hermeneutics.* New Haven: Yale University Press, 1974.

Geertz, Clifford. *The Interpretation of Cultures: Selected Essays.* New York: Basic Books, 1973.

Gell, Alfred. *The Anthropology of Time: Cultural Constructions of Temporal Maps and Images.* Explorations in Anthropology. Oxford: Berg, 1992.

Genette, Gérard. *Narrative Discourse: An Essay in Method.* Ithaca: Cornell University Press, 1980. *Novel in Antiquity*

Gitay, Yehoshua. "Deutero-Isaiah: Oral or Written?" *JBL* 99 (1980) 185–97.

Green, Amy S. *The Revisionist Stage: American Directors Reinvent the Classics.* Cambridge Studies in American Theatre and Drama 3. Cambridge: Cambridge University Press, 2006.

Green, Joel B. *The Gospel of Luke.* NICNT. Grand Rapids: Eerdmans, 1997.

Greene, Brian. *The Fabric of the Cosmos: Space, Time, and the Texture of Reality.* New York: Vintage, 2005.

Hadas, Moses. *Ancilla to Classical Reading.* Columbia Bicentennial Editions and Studies. New York: Columbia University Press, 1954.

Haenchen, Ernst. *John: A Commentary on the Gospel of John.* Vol. 1, *Chapters 1–6.* 2 vols. Translated by Robert W. Funk. Hermeneia. Philadelphia: Fortress, 1984.

Hägg, Tomas. *The Novel in Antiquity.* Revised by the author. Berkeley: University of California Press, 1983.

Hakola, Raimo. "The Burden of Ambiguity: Nicodemus and the Social Identity of the Johannine Christians." *NTS* 55 (2009) 438–55.

Halliwell, Stephen. *Aristotle's Poetics.* Chicago: University of Chicago Press, 1998.

Harris, William V. *Ancient Literacy.* Cambridge: Harvard University Press, 1989.

Harrop, John. *Acting.* Theatre Concepts Series. London: Routledge, 1992.

Hearon, Holly E. "The Implications of Orality for Studies of the Biblical Text." In *Performing the Gospel: Orality, Memory, and Mark,* edited by Richard A. Horsley et al., 3–20. Minneapolis: Fortress, 2006.

Hearon, Holly E., and Philip Ruge-Jones, eds. *The Bible in Ancient and Modern Media: Story and Performance.* Biblical Performance Criticism 1. Eugene, OR: Cascade Books, 2009.

Heath, Malcolm. *The Poetics of Greek Tragedy*. Stanford: Stanford University Press, 1987.

Hezser, Catherine. *Jewish Literacy in Roman Palestine*. TSAJ 81. Tübingen: Mohr/ Siebeck, 2001.

Hickox, Rex. *Time: Friend or Foe?* 2nd ed. Bentonville, AR: Rex, 2006.

Horsley, Richard A. *Hearing the Whole Story: The Politics of Plot in Mark's Gospel*. Louisville: Westminster John Knox, 2001.

Horsley, Richard A., et al., eds. *Performing the Gospel: Orality, Memory, and Mark*. Minneapolis: Fortress, 2006.

House, Humphrey. *Aristotle's Poetics*. London: Hart-Davis, 1956.

Howard-Brook, Wes. *Becoming Children of God: John's Gospel and Radical Discipleship*. 1994. Reprinted, Eugene, OR: Wipf & Stock, 2003.

Hurtado, Larry W. *How on Earth Did Jesus Become a God? Historical Questions about Earliest Devotion to Jesus*. Grand Rapids: Eerdmans, 2005.

Incigneri, Brian J. *The Gospel to the Romans: The Setting and Rhetoric of Mark's Gospel*. Biblical Interpretation Series 65. Leiden: Brill, 2003.

Iverson, Kelly R. "A Centurion's 'Confession': A Performance-Critical Analysis of Mark 15:39." *JBL* 130 (2011) 329–50.

Jackson, Michael. *The Politics of Storytelling: Violence, Transgression, and Intersubjectivity*. Critical Anthropology 3. Copenhagen: Museum Tusculanum Press, 2002.

Jakobson, Roman. "On Linguistic Aspects of Translation." In *On Translation*, edited by Reuben Brower, 232–39. Harvard Studies in Comparative Literature 23. Cambridge: Harvard University Press, 1959.

Janko, Richard. "From Catharsis to the Aristotelian Mean." In *Essays on Aristotle's Poetics*, edited by Amélie Okensberg Rorty, 341–58. Princeton: Princeton University Press, 1992.

Juel, Donald. *Messianic Exegesis: Christological Interpretation of the Old Testament in Early Christianity*. Philadelphia: Fortress, 1988.

———. "'Your Word is Truth': Some Reflections on a Hard Saying." In *Shaping the Scriptural Imagination: Truth, Meaning, and the Theological Interpretation of the Bible*, by Donald H. Juel, 13–32. Edited by Shane Berg and Matthew L. Skinner. Waco: Baylor University Press, 2011.

Keener, Craig S. *Gospel of John: A Commentary*. 2 vols. Peabody, MA: Hendrickson, 2003.

Kelber, Werner H. *The Oral and the Written Gospel: Hermeneutics of Speaking and Writing in the Synoptic Tradition, Mark, Paul and Q*. 1983. Reprinted, Voices in Performance and Text. Bloomington: Indiana University Press, 1997.

Kennedy, George A. *New Testament Interpretation through Rhetorical Criticism*. Studies in Religion. Chapel Hill: University of North Carolina Press, 1984.

Kloppenborg, John S. *Q Parallels: Synopsis, Critical Notes & Concordance*. Foundations and Facets. Reference Series. Sonoma, CA: Polebridge, 1988.

Koester, Craig. *Symbolism in the Fourth Gospel: Meaning, Mystery, Community*. 2nd ed. Minneapolis: Fortress, 2003.

Konijn, Elly A. *Acting Emotions: Shaping Emotions on Stage*. Amsterdam: Amsterdam University Press, 2000.

———. "What's On between the Actor and His Audience? Empirical Analysis of Emotion Processes in the Theatre." In *Psychology and Performing Arts*, edited by Glenn D. Wilson, 59–74. Amsterdam: Swets & Zeitlinger, 1991.

Kuhn, Thomas. *The Structure of Scientific Revolutions*. Chicago: University of Chicago Press, 1962.

Kysar, Robert. *John, the Maverick Gospel*. 3rd ed. Louisville: Westminster John Knox, 2007.

———. "The Making of Metaphor: Another Reading of John 3:1–15." In *What Is John?* Vol. 1, *Readers and Readings of the Fourth Gospel*, 21–41. Edited by Fernando F. Segovia. 2 vols. Atlanta: Scholars, 1996.

Lavender, Andy. "Mise En Scène: Hypermediacy and the Sensorium." In *Intermediality in Theatre and Performance*, edited by Freda Chapple and Chiel Kattenbelt, 55–66. Themes in Theatre: Collective Approaches to Theatre and Performance 2. Amsterdam: Rodopi, 2006.

Lear, Jonathan. "Catharsis." In *A Companion to the Philosophy of Literature*, edited by Garry L. Hagberg and Walter Jost, 193–217. Blackwell Companions to Philosophy 44. Chichester, UK: Wiley-Blackwell, 2010.

Lee, Margaret E. "A Method for Sound Analysis in Hellenistic Greek: The Sermon on the Mount as a Test Case." DTheol diss., Melbourne College of Divinity, 2005.

Lee, Margaret Ellen, and Bernard Brandon Scott. *Sound Mapping the New Testament*. Salem, OR: Polebridge, 2009.

Loubser, J. A. (Bobby). *Oral and Manuscript Culture in the Bible: Studies in the Media Texture of the New Testament—Exploratory Hermeneutics*. 2nd ed. BPCS 7. Eugene, OR: Cascade Books, 2013.

Luz, Ulrich. *Matthew 1–7: A Commentary*. Translated by W. C. Linns. Continental Commentaries. Minneapolis: Augsburg, 1989.

MacDonald, Dennis R. "Classical Greek Poetry and the Acts of the Apostles: Imitations of Euripides' *Bacchae*." In *Christian Origins and Greco-Roman Culture: Social and Literary Contexts for the New Testament*, edited by Stanley E. Porter and Andrew W. Pitts, 463–96. Text and Editions for New Testament Study 9. Leiden: Brill, 2012.

Malbon, Elizabeth Struthers. *Mark's Jesus: Characterization as Narrative Christology*. Waco, TX: Baylor University Press, 2009.

Marcus, Joel. *Mark 1–8: A New Translation with Introduction and Commentary* AB 27. New York: Doubleday, 2000.

Martyn, J. Louis. *History and Theology in the Fourth Gospel*. New York: Harper & Row, 1968.

Maxey, James A., and Ernst R. Wendland, eds. *Translating Scripture for Sound and Performance: New Directions in Biblical Studies*. BPCS 6. Eugene, OR: Cascade Books, 2012.

McCracken, David. "Character in the Boundary: Bakhtin's Interdividuality in Biblical Narratives." *Semeia* 63 (1993) 29–42.

McLuhan, Marshall. *Understanding Media: The Extensions of Man*. New York: McGraw-Hill, 1964.

Meeks, Wayne. "The Man from Heaven in Johannine Sectarianism." *JBL* 91 (1972) 44–72.

Michaels, J. Ramsey. *The Gospel of John*. NICNT Grand Rapids: Eerdmans, 2010.

Millard, Alan. *Reading and Writing in the Time of Jesus*. New York: New York University Press, 2000.

Moloney, Francis J. *The Gospel of John*. SP 4. Collegeville, MN: Liturgical, 1998.

———. "Mark 6:6b–30: Mission, the Baptist, and Failure." *CBQ* 63 (2001) 647–63.

Moltmann, Jürgen. "What Is Time? And How Do We Experience It?" *Dialog* 39/1 (2000) 27–34.

Momigliano, Arnaldo. "Time in Ancient Historiography." *History and Theory* 6 (1966) 1–23.

Moore, Stephen D. *Literary Criticism and the Gospels: The Theoretical Challenge.* New Haven: Yale University Press, 1989.

—————. *Mark and Luke in Poststructuralist Perspectives: Jesus Begins to Write.* New Haven: Yale University Press, 1992.

Muilenburg, James. "The Biblical View of Time." *HTR* 54 (1961) 225–52.

Munro, Winsome. "The Pharisee and the Samaritan in John: Polar or Parallel?" *CBQ* 57 (1995) 710–28.

Nelson, William. "From 'Listen, Lordings' to 'Dear Reader.'" *University of Toronto Quarterly* 46 (1977) 110–24.

Neyrey, Jerome H. "The Absence of Jesus' Emotions—the Lukan Redaction of Lk 22:39–46." *Bib* 61 (1980) 153–71.

Niles, John D. *Homo Narrans: The Poetics and Anthropology of Oral Literature.* Philadelphia: University of Pennsylvania Press, 1999.

Nussbaum, Martha C. *The Fragility of Goodness: Luck and Ethics in Greek Tragedy and Philosophy.* Cambridge: Cambridge University Press, 2001.

Oesterreicher, Wulf. "Types of Orality in Text." In *Written Voices, Spoken Signs: Tradition, Performance, and the Epic Text,* edited by Egbert Bakker and Ahuvia Kahane, 190–214. Center for Hellenic Studies Colloquia. Cambridge: Harvard University Press, 1997.

Ong, Walter J. *Orality and Literacy: The Technologizing of the Word.* New York: Methuen, 1982.

—————. *The Presence of the Word: Some Prolegomena for Cultural and Religious History.* New Haven: Yale University Press, 1967.

O'Toole, Robert F. *Luke's Presentation of Jesus: A Christology.* SubBi 25. Rome: Biblical Institute Press, 2004.

Palu, Ma'afu. *Jesus and Time: An Interpretation of Mark 1.15.* LNTS 468. London: T. & T. Clark, 2012.

Pavis, Patrice. *Dictionary of the Theatre: Terms, Concepts, and Analysis.* Translated by Christine Shantz. Toronto: University of Toronto Press, 1998.

Pfister, Manfred. *The Theory and Analysis of Drama.* Translated by John Halliday. European Studies in English Literature. Cambridge: Cambridge University Press, 1988.

Phelan, Peggy. *Unmarked: The Politics of Performance.* London: Routledge, 1993.

Pia, Albert. *Acting the Truth: The Acting Principles of Constantin Stanislavski and Exercises: A Handbook for Actors, Directors, and Instructors of Theatre.* Bloomington, IN: AuthorHouse, 2006.

Polak, Frank H. "Book, Scribe, and Bard: Oral Discourse and Written Text in Recent Biblical Scholarship." *Prooftexts* 31 (2011) 118–40.

Portier-Young, Anathea E. *Apocalypse against Empire: Theologies of Resistance in Early Judaism.* Grand Rapids: Eerdmans, 2011.

Powell, Mark Allan. *Fortress Introduction to the Gospels.* Minneapolis: Fortress, 1998.

—————. *What Is Narrative Criticism?* GBS. Minneapolis: Fortress, 1990.

Power, Cormac. *Presence in Play: A Critique of Theories of Presence in the Theatre.* Consciousness, Literature & the Arts 12. Amsterdam: Rodopi, 2008.

Quintilian. *Institutes of Oratory*. Translated by Donald A. Russell. 5 vols. LCL. Cambridge: Harvard University Press, 2002.

Reinhartz, Adele. *Befriending the Beloved Disciple: A Jewish Reading of the Gospel of John*. New York: Continuum, 2001.

———. "The Gospel of John: How the 'Jews' Became Part of the Plot." In *Jesus, Judaism and Christian Anti-Judaism: Reading the New Testament after Holocaust*, edited by Paula Fredriksen and Adele Reinhartz, 99–116. Louisville: Westminster John Knox, 2002.

Rensberger, David. "Anti-Judaism and the Gospel of John." In *Anti-Judaism and the Gospels*, edited by William R. Farmer, 120–57. Harrisburg, PA: Trinity, 1999.

———. *Johannine Faith and Liberating Community*. Philadelphia: Westminster, 1988.

Resseguie, James L. *Narrative Criticism of the New Testament: An Introduction*. Grand Rapids: Baker Academic, 2005.

Rhoads, David. "Biblical Performance Criticism: Performance as Research." *Oral Tradition* 25 (2010) 157–98.

———. "Performance Criticism: An Emerging Methodology in Second Temple Studies—Part I." *BTB* 36 (2006) 118–33.

———. "Performance Criticism: An Emerging Methodology in Second Temple Studies—Part II." *BTB* 36 (2006) 164–84.

Rhoads, David, et al. *Mark as Story: An Introduction to the Narrative of a Gospel*. 3rd ed. Minneapolis: Fortress, 2012.

———. "Reflections." In *Mark as Story: Retrospect and Prospect*, edited by Kelly R. Iverson and Christopher W. Skinner, 261–82. SBLRBS 65. Atlanta: Society of Biblical Literature, 2011.

Ridderbos, Katinka. *Time*. Darwin College Lectures. Cambridge: Cambridge University Press, 2002.

Rindge, Matthew S. "Reconfiguring the Akedah and Recasting God: Lament and Divine Abandonment in Mark." *JBL* 131 (2012) 755–74.

Robbins, Vernon K. *Exploring the Texture of Texts: A Guide to Socio-Rhetorical Interpretations*. Valley Forge, PA: Trinity, 1996.

———. "Interfaces of Orality and Literature in the Gospel of Mark." In *Performing the Gospel: Orality, Memory, and Mark*, edited by Richard Horsley et al., 125–46. Minneapolis: Fortress, 2006.

———. "Oral, Rhetorical, and Literary Cultures: A Response." *Semeia* 65 (1994) 75–91.

———. "Progymnastic Rhetorical Composition and Pre-Gospel Traditions—A New Approach." In *The Synoptic Gospels: Source Criticism and the New Literary Criticism*, edited by Camille Focant, 111–48. BETL 10. Leuven: Peeters, 1993.

Robinson, James M., et al., eds. *The Critical Edition of Q*. Hermeneia Supplements. Minneapolis: Fortress, 2000.

Rowe, C. Kavin. *Early Narrative Christology: The Lord in the Gospel of Luke*. BZNW 139. Berlin: de Gruyter, 2006.

Ruge-Jones, Philip. "Omnipresent, Not Omniscient: How Literary Interpretation Confuses the Storyteller's Narrating." In *Between Author and Audience in Mark: Narration, Characterization, Interpretation*, edited by Elizabeth Struthers Malbon, 29–43. New Testament Monographs 23. Sheffield: Sheffield Phoenix, 2009.

Schaper, Joachim. "Exilic and Post-Exilic Prophecy and the Orality/Literacy Problem." *VT* 55 (2005) 324–42.

Schildgen, Brenda Deen. *Crisis and Continuity: Time in the Gospel of Mark*. JSNTSup 159. Sheffield: Sheffield Academic, 1998.

Schneiders, Sandra M. *Written That You May Believe: Encountering Jesus in the Fourth Gospel*. New York: Crossroad, 1999.

Schweitzer, Albert. *The Quest of the Historical Jesus*. Translated by W. Montgomery et al. Edited by John Bowden. Fortress Classics in Biblical Studies. Minneapolis: Fortress, 2001.

Scott, James C. *Domination and the Arts of Resistance: Hidden Transcripts*. New Haven: Yale University Press, 1992.

Segal, Alan F. *Two Powers in Heaven: Early Rabbinic Reports about Christianity and Gnosticism*. Studies in Judaism in Late Antiquity 25. Leiden: Brill, 1977.

Senior, Donald. *The Passion of Jesus in the Gospel of Luke*. Passion Series 3. Collegeville, MN: Liturgical, 1992.

Shellard, Barbara. *New Light on Luke: Its Purpose, Sources and Literary Context*. JSNTSup 215. London: T. & T. Clark, 2004.

Shields, Christopher. *Aristotle*. 2nd ed. Routledge Philosophers. London: Routledge, 2013.

Shiner, Whitney. *Proclaiming the Gospel: First-Century Performance of Mark*. Harrisburg, PA: Trinity, 2003.

Skinner, Christopher W., ed. *Characters and Characterization in the Gospel of John*. LNTS 461. London: T. & T. Clark, 2013.

Slusser, Michael. "Reading Silently in Antiquity." *JBL* 111 (1992) 499.

Stanichar, Christopher, et al. *St. Mark Passion: A Cantata Based on the Suffering of the Messiah according to the Gospel of Mark*. http://christopherstanichar.com/catalogue.html/.

Stanton, Graham N. *Jesus of Nazareth in New Testament Preaching*. SNTSMS 27. Cambridge: Cambridge University Press, 2004.

Sterling, Greg. "*Mors Philosophi*: The Death of Jesus in Luke." *HTR* 94 (2001) 383–402.

Swanson, Richard W. *Provoking the Gospel: Methods to Embody Biblical Storytelling through Drama*. Cleveland: Pilgrim, 2004.

———. *Provoking the Gospel of Mark: A Storyteller's Commentary*. Cleveland: Pilgrim, 2005.

Tannehill, Robert C. "Israel in Luke-Acts: A Tragic Story." *JBL* 104 (1985) 69–85.

———. *The Narrative Unity of Luke-Acts: A Literary Interpretation*. 2 vols. Foundations and Facets. Philadelphia: Fortress, 1986–1990.

Taruskin, Richard. *Text and Act: Essays on Music and Performance*. New York: Oxford University Press, 1995.

Theon, Aelius. "The Exercises of Aelius Theon." In *Progymnasmata: Greek Textbooks of Prose Composition and Rhetoric*, translated by George A. Kennedy, 3–72. Writings from the Greco-Roman World 10. Atlanta: Society of Biblical Literature, 2003.

Tiede, David L. *Prophecy and History in Luke-Acts*. Philadelphia: Fortress, 1980.

Tinsley, E. J. *The Gospel according to Luke*. CBC 4. Cambridge: Cambridge University Press, 1965.

Tolbert, Mary Ann. *Sowing the Gospel: Mark's World in Literary-Historical Perspective*. Minneapolis: Fortress, 1989.

Toro, Fernando de. *Theatre Semiotics: Text and Staging in Modern Theatre*. Translated by John Lewis. Revised and edited by Carole Hubbard. Toronto Studies in Semiotics. Toronto: University of Toronto Press, 1995.

Tyson, Joseph B. *The Death of Jesus in Luke-Acts*. Columbia: University of South Carolina Press, 1986.

Von Wahlde, Urban C. "The Johannine 'Jews': A Critical Survey." *NTS* 28 (1982) 33–60.

Voorwinde, Stephen. *Jesus' Emotions in the Fourth Gospel: Human or Divine?* LNTS 284. London: T. & T. Clark, 2005.

———. *Jesus' Emotions in the Gospels*. London: T. & T. Clark, 2011.

Wagner, Michael F. *The Enigmatic Reality of Time: Aristotle, Plotinus, and Today*. Ancient Mediterranean and Medieval Texts and Contexts. Leiden: Brill, 2008.

Wallace, Daniel B. *Greek Grammar Beyond the Basics: An Exegetical Syntax of the New Testament*. Grand Rapids: Zondervan, 1996.

Warren-Heys, Rebecca. "'[R]emember, with advantages': Creating Memory in Shakespeare's Henry V." *Journal of the Northern Renaissance* 2 (2010). http://www.northernrenaissance.org/remember-with-advantages-creating-memory-in-shakespeares-henry-v.

Watts, Rikk E. "Mark." In *Commentary on the New Testament Use of the Old Testament*, edited by G. K. Beale and D. A. Carson, 111–250. Grand Rapids: Baker Academic, 2007.

Weeden, Theodore J. *Mark—Traditions in Conflict*. Philadelphia: Fortress, 1971.

Wilch, John R. *Time and Event: An Exegetical Study of the Use of 'ēth in the Old Testament in Comparison to Other Temporal Expressions in Clarification of the Concept of Time*. Leiden: Brill, 1969.

Wilder, Thornton. "Some Thoughts on Playwriting." In *Playwrights on Playwriting: The Meaning and Making of Modern Drama from Ibsen to Ionesco*, edited by Toby Cole, 106–15. New York: Hill & Wang, 1960.

Wiles, David. "Aristotle's *Poetics* and Ancient Dramatic Theory." In *The Cambridge Companion to Greek and Roman Theatre*, edited by Marianne McDonald and J. Michael Walton, 92–107. Cambridge Companions to Literature. Cambridge: Cambridge University Press, 2007.

Winfree, Arthur T. *The Geometry of Biological Time*. 2nd ed. Interdisciplinary Applied Mathematics 12. New York: Springer, 2001.

Winston, Joe. *Drama, Narrative and Moral Education: Exploring Traditional Tales in the Primary Years*. London: Falmer, 1998.

Wire, Antoinette Clark. *The Case for Mark Composed in Performance*. BPCS 3. Eugene, OR: Cascade Books, 2011.

Witherington, Ben, III. "Finding Its Niche: The Historical and Rhetorical Species of Acts." In *SBLSP* 35 (1996) 67–97. Atlanta: Scholars, 1996.

Yamasaki, Gary. *Perspective Criticism: Point of View and Evaluation*. Eugene, OR: Cascade Books, 2012.

Zunshine, Lisa. *Getting Inside Your Head: What Cognitive Science Can Tell Us about Popular Culture*. Baltimore: Johns Hopkins University Press, 2012.

AUTHOR INDEX

Achtemeier, Paul J., 24, 84n9, 96, 159n3, 160n8, 167, 168n16, 169n22, 180, 211
Allison, Dale C., 118n16, 130, 213
Aristotle, 147–51, 153, 156, 170, 180, 211
Artaud, Antonin, 152n79, 153, 211
Augustine, 132n3, 153, 211
Aveni, Anthony F., 131, 132n3, 153, 211

Bacon, B. W., 101
Bakker, Egbert, 181, 217
Balogh, Josef, 84n9, 96, 211
Bar-Ilan, Meir, 138n24, 153, 211
Barnes, Jonathan, 153, 211
Barr, James, 132n5, 153, 211
Barranger, Milly S., 140n34, 153, 211
Bassler, Jouette M., 59, 62–63, 68n55, 77, 211
Bauckham, Richard, 30n4, 51, 81, 82n4, 83, 95, 96, 180, 211, 212
Bauer, David R., 101–2, 130, 211
Beale, G. K., 181, 220
Becker, Adam H., 209, 212
Beer, Gillian, 137n22, 138, 139n26, 140n31, 153, 211
Benjamin, Walter, 141, 153, 211
Berg, Shane, 210
Best, Ernest, 135n12, 154, 211
Betz, Hans Dieter, 126n17, 130, 211
Boomershine, Thomas E., xiii, 2, 19, 24, 80–96, 133, 184, 212
Booth, Wayne C., 87n14, 96, 187n12, 209, 212
Boyarin, Daniel, 191, 209, 212

Brant, Jo-Ann A., 54n1, 55, 69n58, 70n61, 72n66, 77, 212
Brin, Gershon, 132n5, 154, 212
Brook, Peter, 152n77, 154, 212
Brower, Reuben, 210, 215
Brown, Raymond E., 61n27, 62n33, 65n46, 77, 82n5, 83, 96, 105n11, 130, 143–44, 154, 212
Bultmann, Rudolf, 196n30, 209, 212
Burnett, Fred W., 56n9, 58n16, 77, 212
Burridge, Richard, 170, 180, 212

Canestri, Jorge, 132n4, 154, 212
Carr, David M., 24, 84n9, 96, 159n3, 165n12, 167–69, 171–72, 173n45–47, 176n52, 177, 179, 180, 189n19, 209, 212
Carter, Warren, 57n11, 60–61, 65n45, 77, 115n14, 130, 212
Chapple, Freda, 155, 216
Chatman, Seymour, 58n14, 78, 212
Cole, Toby, 157, 220
Collins, Adela Yarbro, 81, 83, 96, 212
Conway, Colleen M., 58n15, 62n34, 69n57, 78, 213
Cullmann, Oscar, 132n5, 154, 213
Culpepper, R. Alan, 57n11, 62n32, 63n37, 78, 133–37, 154, 213

Davies, W. D., 118n16, 130, 213
Dean, Margaret E., 98n1, 130, 213
Deterding, Paul E., 132n5, 154, 213
De Vries, Lourens, 184, 189, 209, 213
De Vries, Simon J., 132n5, 154, 213
Dewey, Joanna, xiii, xv, 1–26, 47, 49, 133, 178, 180, 184, 213

Dibelius, Martin, 150–51, 154, 213
Diderot, Denis, 148n66, 154, 213
Doan, William, 24, 68n52, 70n61,
    77n76, 78, 213
Doble, Peter, 143, 154, 213
Dolan, Jill, 140n35, 154, 213
Downs, William Missouri, 141n42, 154,
    213
Draper, Jonathan, 159
Duke, Paul D., 59n21, 62n32, 63n37,
    78, 213

Ehrman, Bart D., 142n44, 154, 213
Esslin, Martin, 141, 142n43, 154, 213
Estes, Douglas, 132n5, 154, 213

Fackenheim, Emil L., 186n6, 209, 213
Farmer, William R., 60n25, 78, 213
Feinberg, Anat, 187n10, 209, 213
Fielding, Henry, 85–86, 89, 135
Fine, Elizabeth C., 153n81, 154, 214
Fiorini, Leticia Glocer, 132n4, 154, 212
Fischer-Lichte, Erika, 139n28, 141n39,
    141n40, 152n78, 154, 214
Fishbane, Simcha, 153, 211
Fitzmyer, Joseph A., 143, 145n58, 154,
    214
Focant, Camille, 181, 218
Foley, John Miles, 24, 159, 186, 209, 214
Fowler, Robert M., 83, 87–88, 96, 163,
    180, 214
Fredriksen, Paula, 78, 218
Frei, Hans W., 8, 24, 87, 96, 214

Geertz, Clifford, 184, 209, 214
Gell, Alfred, 132n4, 154, 214
Genette, Gérard, 134, 136n18, 154, 214
Giles, Terry, 24, 68n52, 70n61, 77n76,
    78, 213
Gitay, Yehoshua, 177n56, 180, 214
Goodwin, Mark, 60n25
Green, Amy S., 153, 154, 214
Green, Joel B., 144n54, 151n75, 154, 214
Greene, Brian, 132n4, 155, 214

Hadas, Moses, 84n9, 96, 214
Haenchen, Ernst, 65n46, 78, 214
Hagberg, Garry L., 155, 216

Hägg, Tomas, 170–71, 180, 214
Hakola, Raimo, 57n12, 78, 214
Halliwell, Stephen, 151n72, 155, 214
Harris, William V., 12n19, 24, 84n9, 96,
    138n24, 155, 214
Harrop, John, 149n67, 155, 214
Hearon, Holly E., xiii–xv, 19, 24, 53–79,
    159, 172, 180–81, 214
Heath, Malcolm, 148n64, 155, 215
Hezser, Catherine, 24, 138n24, 155, 215
Hickox, Rex, 132n6, 155, 215
Hicks, Patrick, xv, 187, 198–99, 207, 215
Horsley, Richard A., 24, 25, 159, 180,
    181, 189n20, 209, 214, 215, 218
House, Humphrey, 151n73, 155, 215
Howard-Brook, Wes, 65n47, 78, 215
Hubbard, Carole, 156, 219
Hurtado, Larry W., 189n16, 209, 215

Incigneri, Brian J., 83n8, 96, 215
Iverson, Kelly R., ix–x, xiv, 19, 51, 96,
    131–57, 202n36, 209, 212, 215,
    218

Jackson, Michael, 188n14, 209, 215
Jakobson, Roman, 202n35, 210, 215
Janko, Richard, 148n64, 155, 215
Jost, Walter, 155, 216
Juel, Donald, 188, 189n15, 202, 210, 215

Kahane, Ahuvia, 181
Kähler, Martin, 47
Kattenbelt, Chiel, 155, 216
Keener, Craig S., 61n27, 62n34, 63n36,
    65n47, 78, 215
Kelber, Werner H., 2, 25, 159, 167, 181,
    215
Kennedy, George A., 159, 181, 215
Kloppenborg, John S., 110n12, 130, 215
Koester, Craig, 57n11, 78, 215
Konijn, Elly A., 148n66, 155, 215
Kuhn, Thomas, 2–4, 19, 25, 216
Kysar, Robert, 61, 72n64, 78, 216

Lavender, Andy, 140n37, 155, 216
Lea, Thomas, 60n25
Lear, Jonathan, 151n73, 155, 216

Lee, Margaret E., xiv, 97–130, 99n2, 112n13, 116n15, 184, 216
Lessing, Gotthold, 186n5, 190, 209, 212
Luz, Ulrich, 115n14, 126n18, 130, 216

MacDonald, Dennis R., 147n62, 155, 216
Malbon, Elizabeth Struthers, 34, 51, 216
Marcus, Joel, 81–83, 96, 216
Martyn, J. Louis, 82, 96, 216
Maxey, James A., 25, 202n35, 202, 209, 210, 213, 216
Maxwell, Kathy, 158–81
McCracken, David, 58n15, 78, 216
McDonald, Marianne, 157, 220
McLuhan, Marshall, ix, 216
Meeks, Wayne, 57n11, 62n33, 63n37, 65n45, 78, 216
Michaels, J. Ramsey, 59n21, 61n29, 62n33, 63n36, 63n39, 64n40, 65n46, 78, 216
Michie, Donald, xiii, xv, 47, 49
Millard, Alan, 138n24, 155, 216
Moloney, Francis J., 62n33, 64n41, 65n47, 78, 135n12, 155, 216
Moltmann, Jürgen, 131, 155, 217
Momigliano, Arnaldo, 132n4, 155, 217
Moore, Stephen D., 170, 181, 183n1, 210, 217
Muilenburg, James, 132n5, 155, 217
Munro, Winsome, 62n33, 64n42, 65n45, 78, 217

Nelson, William, 85, 96, 217
Neyrey, Jerome H., 143, 144, 146n60, 155, 217
Niles, John D., 186, 210, 217
Nussbaum, Martha C., 151n73, 155, 217

Oesterricher, Wulf, 160
Ong, Walter J., 25, 84n9, 96, 159, 181, 217
O'Toole, Robert F., 143, 145n58, 155, 217

Palu, Ma'afu, 132n5, 155, 217
Pavis, Patrice, 138n25, 139n27, 156, 217
Pennington, John, xv

Pfister, Manfred, 141n42, 148n65, 156, 217
Phelan, Peggy, 140, 156, 217
Pia, Albert, 149n68, 156, 217
Pitts, Andrew W., 155, 216
Plunkett, Mark A., 142n44, 154, 213
Polak, Frank, 168n18, 171, 181, 217
Porter, Stanley E., 155, 216
Portier-Young, Anathea E., 189n20, 210, 217
Powell, Mark Allan, 56n8, 57n13, 58n17, 78, 135n14, 136, 143, 156, 217
Power, Cormac, 140n36, 156, 217

Quintilian, 71, 74–75, 141, 218

Reed, Annette Yoshiko, 212
Reinhartz, Adele, 60n25, 62n34, 78, 218
Rensberger, David, 60n25, 65n45, 78, 218
Resseguie, James L., 56n8, 57n13, 78, 137, 156, 218
Rhoads, David, ix, xiii, xv, 1–26, 25, 31n5, 32n8, 38n12, 47, 49, 51, 55n5, 58n17, 67n49, 68n53, 76n74, 78, 133, 156, 184, 218
Ridderbos, Katinka, 131, 153, 156, 211, 218
Rindge, Matthew S., 203n38, 210, 218
Robbins, Vernon K., 159, 160n4, 160n6, 164n11, 169, 172–73, 178n63, 181, 218
Robinson, James M., 110n12, 130, 218
Rorty, Amélie Okensberg, 155, 215
Rowe, C. Kavin, 146n58, 156, 218
Ruge-Jones, Philip, xv, 19, 24, 27–52, 28n2, 51, 159, 181, 214, 218

Schächter, Rafael, 187n10
Schaper, Joachim, 164n10, 167n14, 181, 218
Schildgen, Brenda Deen, 132n5, 156, 219
Schneiders, Sandra M., 57n11, 61n29, 64n42, 79, 219
Schweitzer, Albert, 4, 5, 25, 219

Scott, Bernard Brandon, xiv, 25, 99n2,
    112n13, 116n15, 130, 184,
    188n14, 216
Scott, James C., 188n14, 210, 219
Segal, Alan F., 189n16, 210, 219
Segovia, Fernando F., 78, 216
Senior, Donald, 142, 156, 219
Shakespeare, William, 53, 198n32
Shellard, Barbara, 143, 156, 219
Shields, Christopher, 151n74, 156, 219
Shiner, Whitney, 26, 32n7, 52, 84n9,
    96, 219
Sidlin, Murry, 187n10
Skinner, Christopher W., 51, 57n12, 79,
    96, 212, 219
Skinner, Matthew L., 210
Slusser, Michael, 84n10, 96, 219
Stanichar, Christopher, xv, 187, 198,
    201, 207, 210, 219
Stanton, Graham N., 150–51, 156, 219
Sterling, Gregory, 144n53, 156, 219
Streeter, B. H., 183
Swanson, Richard W., xv, 19, 36n11, 52,
    182–210, 202n37, 210, 219

Tannehill, Robert C., 143n48, 147n62,
    156, 219
Taruskin, Richard, 187n11, 210, 219
Thatcher, Tom, 25, 26, 180, 213
Theon, Aelius, 160, 172–73, 177, 181,
    219

Tiede, David L., 147n62, 156, 219
Tinsley, E. J., 149, 156, 219
Tolbert, Mary Ann, 95, 96, 219
Toro, Fernando de, 139, 156, 219
Tyson, Joseph B., 147n62, 156, 220

Von Wahlde, Urban, 61n27, 79, 220
Voorwinde, Stephen, 144n56, 146, 156,
    220

Wagner, Michael F., 132n4, 157, 220
Wallace, Daniel B., 54n2, 64n41, 79, 220
Walton, J. Michael, 157, 220
Warren-Heys, Rebecca, 198n32, 210,
    220
Watts, Rikk E., 177, 178n61, 181, 220
Weeden, Theodore J., 82, 96, 220
Wendland, Ernst, 25, 202n35, 209, 210,
    213, 216
Wilch, John R., 132n5, 157, 220
Wilder, Thornton, 140, 157, 220
Wiles, David, 151, 157, 220
Wilson, Glenn D., 155, 215
Winfree, Arthur T., 132n4, 157, 220
Winston, Joe, 151n73, 157, 220
Wire, Antoinette Clark, 28n1, 52, 220
Witherington, Ben, 170, 181, 220

Yamasaki, Gary, 29n3, 52, 220

Zunshine, Lisa, 149n68, 157, 220